Toward Integrative Corporate Citizenship

Toward Integrative Corporate Citizenship

Research Advances in Corporate Social Performance

Marc Orlitzky
Associate Professor of Management, Pennsylvania State University Altoona, USA.

and

Diane L. Swanson
Professor of Management, Kansas State University, USA.

First published 2008 by
PALGRAVE MACMILLAN

Palgrave Macmillan in the UK is an imprint of Macmillan Publishers Limited, registered in England, company number 785998, of Houndmills, Basingstoke, Hampshire RG21 6XS.

Palgrave Macmillan in the US is a division of St Martin's Press LLC, 175 Fifth Avenue, New York, NY 10010.

Palgrave Macmillan is the global academic imprint of the above companies and has companies and representatives throughout the world.

Palgrave® and Macmillan® are registered trademarks in the United States, the United Kingdom, Europe and other countries.

ISBN-13: 978–0–230–20187–3   hardback
ISBN-10: 0–230–20187–3   hardback

This book is printed on paper suitable for recycling and made from fully managed and sustained forest sources. Logging, pulping and manufacturing processes are expected to conform to the environmental regulations of the country of origin.

A catalogue record for this book is available from the British Library.

Library of Congress Cataloging-in-Publication Data
Orlitzky, Marc, 1970–
    Toward integrative corporate citizenship : research advances in
        corporate social performance / Marc Orlitzky and Diane L. Swanson.
            p. cm.
    Includes index.
    ISBN 13: 978–0–230–20187–3 (alk. paper)
        1. Social responsibility of business. I. Swanson, Diane L. II. Title.
    HD60.O75 2008
    658.4'08–dc22

                                                                2008020652

10   9   8   7   6   5   4   3   2   1
17   16   15   14   13   12   11   10   09   08

Printed and bound in Great Britain by
CPI Antony Rowe, Chippenham and Eastbourne

In memoriam
Erika Orlitzky (1920–2000)
and
Charlotte Swanson (1888–1972)

Contents

List of Tables

List of Figures

List of Abbreviations

CSP	Corporate social performance
CC	Corporate citizenship
SRI	Socially responsible investment
G theory	Generalizability theory
CEP	Corporate environmental performance
CFP	Corporate financial performance
CSR	Corporate social responsibility
SIM	Social Issues in Management
ROA	Return On Assets
ROIC	Return on Invested Capital
SD	Standard Deviation
CAPM	Capital Asset Pricing Model
ROE	Return on Equity
EPS	Earnings Per Share
CERES	Coalition for Environmentally Responsible Economies
WHO	World Health Organisation
R&D	Research and Development
IABS	International Association for Business and Society
SBU	Strategic Business Unit
EMBA	Executive MBA
OLS	Ordinary least-squares

Acknowledgments

We have both benefited greatly from collegial relationships formed in the International Association for Business and Society, the Society for Business Ethics and the Social Issues in Management and Organizations and the Natural Environment Divisions of the Academy of Management as well as related professional groups. Along with those we thank individually below, we jointly wish to express our gratitude to the following people in these associations for their inspired work and lasting influence on our thinking: Adele Barsh, Tima Bansal, Melissa Baucus, Ann Buchholtz, Rogene Buchholz, Jerry Calton, Archie Carroll, Phil Cochran, Denis Collins, Peter Dahler-Larsen, Robbin Derry, Tom Donaldson, Craig Dunn, Fred Evans, Steve Feldman, Linda Ferrell, O.C. Ferrell, Robert Frederick, Ed Freeman, Jeff Frooman, Bob Giacalone, Virginia Gerde, Kathy Getz, Dan Gilbert, Amy Hillman, Tom Jones, Margaret Kelso, Bob Kolb, Nancy Kurland, Barrie Litzky, Jeanne Logsdon, Tammy Mac Lean, Mary Mallott, Dick Mason, Roger McHaney, Ian Mitroff, Millie Myers, Richard Nielsen, Mark Pagell, Steve Payne, Joe Petrick, Afzal Rahim, Sue Ravenscroft, Chwen Sheu, Prakash Sethi, Don Siegel, Bill Sodeman, Phil Trocchia, Linda Treviño, Deborah Vidaver-Cohen, Sandra Waddock, Steve Wartick, Jim Weber, Pat Werhane, Duane Windsor, Donna Wood, David Wasieleski, Gary Weaver, Rich Wokutch, and Jiyun Wu.

Additionally, we would like to thank those people who have helped and supported us in our individual efforts, as follows:

Marc Orlitzky: The work presented in this book represents the culmination of several years of work. There are dozens of people to whom I would like to express my gratitude for their help and support – even at the risk of forgetting a few names.

First of all, several professors at the University of Iowa and especially the members of my dissertation committee – Frank Schmidt, chair, Jerry Rose, Jim Price, Barry Markovsky, and my mentor Sara Rynes – helped me clarify my thoughts on a challenging research program, which would go on to win two research awards in 2004. Special thanks belong to the members of the International Association for Business and Society Awards Committee as well as the chairs of the Moskowitz Award Committee, Lloyd Kurtz and Pietra Rivoli.

As an undergraduate student at American University, I was most encouraged to choose an academic career by John Benjamin, professor of Real Estate Finance. I remember my first four years in the USA with great fondness. Many students and professors had more to do with this than they will probably ever know: Ajay Adhikari, Anthony Ahrens, Jessica Bailey, Barbara Bird, James Butts, Peter Chinloy, Davina Friedman, Kathy Getz, Peter Hansen, Arthur Harris, Thomas Husted, David Jacobs, Julia Lane, Richard Linowes, Robert Losey, Jason Martin, Michael Mass, Phillip Scribner, Monica Sorensen (still listening to Mecano?), Howard Wachtel, Brian Yates, and I am sure numerous others whose names I forgot.

After my undergraduate years at American University, the next three years in the doctoral program at the University of Iowa were undoubtedly the intellectually most stimulating period in my life. Again, there are too many people to thank, but just a few that helped me navigate my way through the doctoral program, in addition to my dissertation committee members noted earlier, were: Joyce Bono, Kevin Carlson, Randy Hirokawa, Brian McNatt, Gay Mikelson, Barney Olson, Skip Owen, Chris Quinn-Trank, Steve Scullen, Amy Wenzel, and Kuh Yoon.

When I finished my dissertation in Washington, DC in 1997–98, Cynthia McSwain and Mark Starik helped me realize that there were so many other interesting organizational phenomena to explore. My time in Sydney, one of the greatest cities in the world, consisted of five unforgettable years during which the following people were helpful and supportive: Eddie Anderson, Prithviraj Chattopadhyay, Maggie DeVane, Tim Devinney, Lex Donaldson, Graham Dowling, Geoffrey Eagleson, Sheena and Steve Frenkel, Elizabeth George, Markus Groth, Siggi Gudergan, Anna Gunnthorsdottir, Ujwal Kayande, Bob Marks, Susanne Nottage, Laura-Kate Quartermaine, Geoff Waring, and Bob Wood. In New Zealand, Peter Boxall, Ljiljana Erakovic, Nigel Haworth, Peter Haynes, Darl Kolb, Ross MacDonald, Suchi Mouly, Debbie Shepherd, Peter Smith, Rachel Wolfgramm, and Christine Woods helped me adjust to life at the University of Auckland Business School.

At the moment, many people at Nottingham University Business School have helped me develop and maintain a schedule that allowed me to finish several research projects for the International Centre for Corporate Social Responsibility *as well as* this book. Particular thanks belong to: Laure Cabantous, Wendy Chapple, Janet Cooke, Anna Cortens, Kate Gosser, Karen Maltby, Jeremy Moon, Judy Muthuri, David Owen, Maggie Royston (Byron), and especially Jean-Pascal Gond, who helped me come up with ideas for Chapter 10, and Glen Whelan, who helped me improve my writing in Chapters 8 and 10.

My professional development benefited greatly from correspondence with the editors and associate editors at the *Academy of Management Journal* and countless other Academy members.

The foundation for my contributions to this book was established in Rosenheim where some unforgettable teachers and friends used to live, including Angela Altendorfer, Sonja Altmutter, Frau Asenbeck, Herr Bertram Auer, Olaf Brückmann, Andrea and Dalio Despot, Guido Distler, Herr Dieter Dworak, Herr Ellmann, Stephanie Erdmann, Frau Brigitte Eschbaum, Herr Forstmeier (especially on the funny bus trip to our 8th grade ski camp), Antje Fudickar, Brigitte and Iris Gagel, Anja Gaschott, Cornelia Gromann, Frau Heindl, Sascha Hoch, Ingo Höller, Herr Gernot Kirsch, Frau Christel Koch, Frau Dr. Annemarie Lutz, Frau Roswitha Millkreiter-Stahl, Regina & Oki Nagy, Harry Purainer, Maren and Andreas Riedrich, Dagmar Ritthammer, Herr Roppel, Carola Schmied, Herr Franz Seiler, Herr Dr. Helmut Tribus, Ursel von der Weiden, Iris Wagner, Christian Wellner, Frau Dr. Jolanda Wieser, Vanessa Ziegler, and last but certainly not least the Wiedemann family.

Family members that deserve special thanks: My grandparents Ulla and Hans Mayrl who spoiled me more than anyone, Dr. Walter and Gilda Orlitzky, Marlies, Walter & Christine Schindler, my parents (Ursula and Rainer Orlitzky), Evi, Bill, Manuel, Frank, and Bill(y) Dawson, and last but not least my sister Julia.

My apologies to all those people who have been inadvertently omitted from these acknowledgments.

Most importantly, this book is dedicated foremost to my Omuttl, who was *always* there for me in the 1980s and 1990s with all her advice, love, and an unparalleled sense of humor. Our bond was very special.

Diane Swanson: I have many people to thank for assisting me with my intellectual journey, a journey partly reflected in my contributions to this book. First and foremost, I am indebted to the Business Ethics and Public Policy scholars who at one time spearheaded a critical mass of business and society research at the Katz School of Business at the University of Pittsburgh in Pennsylvania. It is no exaggeration to say that these remarkable scholars were at the forefront of helping to establish the foundations for inquiry into the nature of corporate social responsibility and corporate social performance. Among them, I was extremely fortunate to study with William C. Frederick, a renowned founder of corporate social responsibility and business ethics research, who chaired my dissertation committee. Without Bill's encouragement and generosity in sharing his remarkable wisdom, I would not have endeavored to publish the two *Academy of Management Review* articles that constitute Chapters 1 and 2. I am grateful to the members of the International Association for Business and Society Award Committee for selecting the 1999 *Academy of Management Review* article for 'Best Article' in 2001.

I also benefited greatly from studying with Barry Mitnick, whose expertise in public policy and regulation is unparalleled, and Jim Wilson who is uncommonly skillful in applying insights drawn from psychology and history to organizational dynamics.

To complement my doctoral studies in Business Administration, I minored in Sociology of Organizations in the Department of Sociology at the University of Pittsburgh. While doing so, I was extremely lucky to get intellectual guidance from Pat Doreian and the late Bob Avery. Both professors helped deepen my understanding of the cultural and bureaucratic aspects of organizations and the nature of their environments. My informal studies with the late Rolf von Eckartsberg at Duquesne University helped me grasp the existential aspects of organizational life. Jim Weber, a skillful business ethicist, also at Duquesne, assisted me in my efforts to apply moral analysis to corporate social performance.

Prior to my doctoral studies at the University of Pittsburgh, I received a Masters of Arts in Economics from the University of Missouri at Kansas City where I studied institutional economics along with other variants of economic thought. This particular educational background proved to be very instrumental in preparing me for exploring business and society issues at the University of Pittsburgh. I particularly want to thank Jack Ward for his kind mentorship at the University of Missouri at Kansas City and also Ross Shepherd, Bob Brazelton, and the late John Hodges for their roles in preparing me for further graduate studies.

I am fortunate to be in an environment in the College of Business Administration at Kansas State University supportive of ethics education and research. For this I thank Yar Ebadi, Dean, and Brian Niehoff, Management Department Head. Other colleagues at K-State who have demonstrated uncommon leadership shaping a climate conducive to ethics education and research include Dann Fisher, Marne Arthaud-Day, and Tom Marini. Cheryl May, Director of Media Services, deserves recognition for helping to spread the news of our college's distinctive competency in ethics to regional, national and international audiences. I am especially grateful to Dennis and Sally von Waaden, distinctive friends of the college and university, for supporting a professorship that I am honored to hold in their name.

Prior to joining the faculty at Kansas State University, where I currently teach Business, Government, and Society and Professional Ethics, I taught Strategic Management at Robert Morris University while pursuing my doctoral degree at the University of Pittsburgh. Without the support of George Biles, then Dean of the Business College at Robert Morris University, and Nell Hartley, Head of Management at that time, my efforts in juggling full time teaching and doctoral studies would have been much more difficult.

In a more personal arena, I want to express gratitude for a family culture in Kansas marked by a respect for educational pursuits. Without that, I would not have persevered in academia. My sister and brother, Marsha Swanson and Hal Swanson, have supported my academic endeavors in very practical ways. My parents, Harold and Betty Jo Swanson have always provided help and support far beyond the call of duty. My son, Christopher Scott, has carried on the tradition of teaching that he first learned from my mother, who taught in the public school system and then subsequently founded her own private Montessori schools. She, in turn, was following in the tradition of teaching established by her mother, Minta Starr, and great uncle, Phillip Starr. The message imparted has always been to give educational endeavors a very high priority. For that, I am very appreciative.

Of special note, the late Reverend John Guice of Kansas City, Missouri taught me early on to strive to think clearly and deliberately about moral issues in society.

I am also lucky to have close friends who support my academic journey, including Diane Adams, Mary Ash, Bruce Balkenhol, Cora Cooper, Jane Gilbert, Tammie Hartwick, Jinna Long, Maria Marshall, Matt Moline, and Clark Petersen.

Finally, this book is dedicated in part to my dear grandmother who immigrated to the United States from Sweden and showed uncommon strength in helping her extended family establish roots in another country, always with the goal of assisting others in the community as well.

Introduction

Given the increased impact of nonmarket forces on business reputation and success, there has never been a greater need to grasp corporate social performance from a theoretically sound, integrative perspective. This involves understanding the responsibilities that business firms have to society, the means by which they respond to stakeholder demands, and the impacts these actions have on social and natural environments. Indeed, interest in these aspects of the business and society field continues to abound, particularly in light of the findings, presented in Part II of this volume, which substantiate the proposition that responsible corporate conduct can pay financially. Given these findings, it can be to a firm's advantage to incorporate social responsibility into strategic planning proactively as well as to influence and adhere to voluntary codes of ethical conduct in an industry. In short, corporate social responsibility can represent a strategic opportunity. Conversely, not attending to this area can invite public scrutiny. Notably, the public's concern about a lack of business responsibility, fueled by a wave of business scandals, has culminated in increased investigations by the press and new, expensive oversight mechanisms, such as the regulatory response of Sarbanes-Oxley in the United States, a Code of Corporate Governance in the United Kingdom shaped by the Smith and Higgs Reports, and a legion of ethics consultants charged with assisting firms with compliance.

This scrutiny is increasingly directed at multinational corporations that operate across sovereign boundaries to encounter ethical quandaries, many of which stem from cultural relativism manifest as different legal and cultural norms. The stakes for understanding what constitutes socially responsible corporate performance are raised further by claims that business needs to be part of the solution to large-scale environmental issues that challenge the ability of humans and other species to survive and flourish on this planet. These issues include ozone depletion, global warning, deforestation, and endangerment of biological diversity, all of which are affected by corporate activity. In an age of globalization, there is an opportunity to address these issues proactively and strategically (Hart, 2007). For instance, partnering with civil society groups such as the Global Reporting Initiative, Human Rights Watch, Council of Institutional Investors, Business for Social Responsibility, and Amnesty International can help shape norms of responsible business conduct globally.

As authors of this book, we have long endeavored to help shape inquiry into these issues. In fact, this book can be viewed as a culmination of our two closely related research programs. We are grateful that some of these efforts have been recognized by our peers. For instance, in 2001 Diane Swanson received the Best Article Award from the International Association for Business & Society for her contribution to corporate social performance theorizing, specifically for her 1999 *Academy of Management Review* article (see Chapter 2). This contribution and her 1995 *Academy of Management Review* article on a similar topic (Chapter 1) are widely cited in several related fields.

In 2004 Marc Orlitzky won two different awards for his meta-analyses. First, he received the Moskowitz Prize for outstanding quantitative research relevant to the social investment field, (revised and updated in Chapter 4), an award he shares with co-authors Frank Schmidt and Sara Rynes. As background, the Moskowitz Prize is awarded each year to the research paper that best meets the criteria of (1) practical significance to practitioners of socially responsible investing, (2) appropriateness and rigor of quantitative methods, and (3) novelty of results. It is sponsored by Calvert Group, First Affirmative Financial Network, KLD Research & Analytics Inc., Nelson Capital Management, Rockefeller & Co., and Trillium Asset Management Corporation. Since then, this research has been cited more often than any other most-cited article published in the same year (2003) in the most prestigious management journals. Specifically, as of this writing, the study presented in Chapter 4 outperformed other top-cited articles in *Academy of Management Journal*, *Academy of Management Review*, *Strategic Management Journal*, and *Administrative Science Quarterly* by a minimum of ten citations in terms of citations garnered in the *Social Science Citations Index*. Even researchers with contrary views of the corporate social-financial performance relationships, summarized in Part II of this book, deemed this study 'influential' (e.g., Vogel, 2005, p. xvi). In fact, this study has been referred to as the 'mother of all studies' in the *Australian Financial Review* (O'Halloran, 2005). In addition, Marc Orlitzky, along with John Benjamin, won the Best Article Award from the International Association for Business & Society for a study of business risk and corporate social performance (revised and updated in Chapter 5).

This book provides an overview of these award-winning articles as well as other research efforts.

As the book's title suggests, we approach corporate citizenship from an integrative perspective. Consistent with Carroll's (1998) definition, 'corporate citizenship' refers to the extent to which organizations are able to fulfill four broad responsibilities: economic, legal, ethical, and philanthropic. The only conceptual adjustment that we would like to note here is that 'philanthropy' is too narrow a term for voluntary, or supererogatory, acts of business (going above and beyond the law and ethics) because it connotes charitable donations (Porter & Kramer, 2002), whereas discretionary organizational activities can also be designed to meet broader community needs, including those related to ecological imperatives (Carroll, 1998, 1999; Porter & Kramer, 2006; Porter & van der Linde, 1995). It is these broad community needs that this book addresses.

This conceptualization of our core topic alerts the reader that our approach is *integrative* in several ways. First, the theoretical perspective in Part I of the book reconciles some normative and descriptive aspects of extant corporate social performance research. Second, based on meta-analytic methodology, Part II conveys the accumulated evidence that complementary relationships between corporate citizenship and other important organizational constructs exist. Consistent with our theme of integration, a widely used synonym for 'meta-analysis' is 'integrative literature review' (Cooper, 1998; Cooper & Hedges, 1994; Hunter & Schmidt, 2004). Third, throughout the book, but especially in Part III, we assume that since organizational performance is multidimensional, only an integrative, multilevel perspective on corporate citizenship can shed light on how to bring about desired consequences for business and society. Specifically, economic, social, and ecological goals should not be treated *a priori* as contradictory either/or decisions since they often exhibit affinities (see also Orlitzky, 2006), particularly if organizational decision makers are broadminded and strategic in their approach to these multifaceted issues (Porter & Kramer, 2006).

Such an integrative approach to corporate citizenship places at least two demands on good research. First, integration in this context means that theory and methodology should inform each other. In this vein, this book represents an effort to demonstrate that sound theory and rigorous methodology are both important for intellectual progress in this burgeoning field. By definition, this kind of integration requires an incorporation of extant theoretical and empirical research relevant to organizational decision making, which we have attempted to do. The second demand that an integrative approach places on research is that relevance not be sacrificed to rigor. Just as our research shows that there is not necessarily a tradeoff between 'the descriptive' and 'the normative' (Part I) and financial and social goals (Part II), we eschew a tradeoff between rigor and relevance. According to this standard, we deliberately prescribe means by which companies can navigate and manage their environments more effectively (see, for examples, Chapters 4, 5, 6, and 8), prompted by the belief that theory and empirical-functionalist research can help in the development of more effective and rational business practices (see Bazerman, 2005).

In line with this prescriptive organizational focus, the viewpoint stressed in Part I and reflected in the other parts of this book is that of being inside a firm looking out, so to speak. Essentially, we focus on the internal organizational decision processes that must be in place for firms to grasp stakeholder interests and respond constructively to them while also pursuing financial goals. Given this focus, there is no attempt to develop a decision orientation for public policy makers, government regulators, social activists, or other public interest actors who may seek a constructive business and society relationship, although we welcome such complementary research. Nor is there an examination of citizenship from the purview of political science as loci of protections granted by nation states. Although such research is important in light of globalization that can result in less influence exerted by nation states and more expectations placed on corporations to compensate (Matten & Crane, 2005; Wood, Logsdon, Lewellyn & Davenport, 2006), our research is on a continuum with the understanding that a firm's quest for citizenship involves activities related to corporate social responsibility (Carroll, 1998), meeting legitimate stakeholder expectations of these activities (Maignan & Ferrell, 2001), and ultimately forging collaborative partnerships with community members (Marsden, 2000; Vidaver-Cohen & Altman, 2000; Waddock & Smith, 2000). From this vantage point, we are interested in a firm's posture toward the external environment, particularly as a tone set by top executives to drive processes of engagement with stakeholders that inform day-to-day operating practices (see Marsden & Andriof, 1980; Waddock, 2002). As conveyed in Chapters 1, 2 and 3, if this posture is neglectful, then there is no possibility for citizenship, however defined. More affirmatively, a firm's ability to exhibit an 'attuned' relationship with its stakeholder environment is presented in Part I as a precondition for corporate citizenship. Hence, we use the qualifying phrase 'toward integrative corporate citizenship' in the title of this book. Moreover, the empirical evidence conveyed in Part II suggests that this kind of attuned relationship can pay financially, which points to the possibility of a mutually reinforcing relationship between, or integration of, social and financial goals in many instances.

The book is structured as follows. Part I integrates various theoretical contributions to the literature in reoriented models of corporate social performance while the four chapters of Part II summarize several empirical, meta-analytic advances. The final three chapters of Part III conclude with suggestions for improved measurement of integrative corporate citizenship, executive-level predictors of corporate social performance, and some thoughts on implementation.

References

Bazerman, M. H. (2005). Conducting influential research: The need for prescriptive implications. *Academy of Management Review, 30*(1), 25–31.

Carroll, A. B. (1998). The four faces of corporate citizenship. *Business and Society Review, 100*(1), 1–7.

Carroll, A. B. (1999). Corporate social responsibility: Evolution of a definitional construct. *Business and Society, 38*(3), 268–295.

Cooper, H. M. (1998). *Synthesizing research: A guide for literature reviews.* Thousand Oaks, CA: Sage.

Cooper, H. M. & Hedges, L. V. (1994). *The handbook of research synthesis.* New York: Russell Sage Foundation.

Hart, S. L. (2007). *Capitalism at the crossroads: Aligning business, Earth, and humanity* (2nd ed.). Upper Saddle River, NJ: Wharton School Publishing.

Hunter, J. E. & Schmidt, F. L. (2004). *Methods of meta-analysis: Correcting error and bias in research findings* (2nd ed.). Thousand Oaks, CA: Sage.

Maignan, I. & Ferrell, O. C. (2001). Antecedents and benefits of corporate citizenship: An investigation of French businesses. *Journal of Business Research, 51,* 37–51.

Marsden, C. (2000). The new corporate citizenship of big business: Part of the solution to sustainability? *Business and Society Review, 105,* 9–25.

Marsden, C. & Andriof, J. (1980). Toward an understanding of corporate citizenship and how to influence it. *Citizenship Studies, 2*(2), 329–330.

Matten, D. & Crane, A. (2005). Corporate citizenship: Toward an extended theoretical conceptualization. *Academy of Management Review, 30,* 166–179.

Orlitzky, M. (2006). Links between corporate social responsibility and corporate financial performance: Theoretical and empirical determinants. In J. Allouche (ed.), *Corporate social responsibility, Vol. 2: Performances and stakeholders* (Vol. 2, pp. 41–64). London: Palgrave Macmillan.

O'Halloran, L. (2005, April 21). SRI – The new investment style. *Australian Financial Review*, 20.

Porter, M. E. & Kramer, M. R. (2002). The competitive advantage of corporate philanthropy. *Harvard Business Review, 80*(12), 56–68.

Porter, M. E. & Kramer, M. R. (2006). Strategy & society: The link between competitive advantage and corporate social responsibility. *Harvard Business Review, 84*(12), 78–92.

Porter, M. E. & van der Linde, C. (1995). Green and competitive: Ending the stalemate. *Harvard Business Review, 73*(5), 120–134.

Vidaver-Cohen, D. & Altman, B. (2000). Concluding remarks: Corporate citizenship in the new millennium: Foundation for an architecture of excellence. *Business and Society Review, 105*, 145–168.

Vogel, D. (2005). *The market for virtue: The potential and limits of corporate social responsibility*. Washington, DC: Brookings Institution Press.

Waddock, S. (2002). *Leading corporate citizens: Vision, values, value added*. New York: McGraw-Hill Irwin.

Waddock, S. & Smith, N. (2000). Relationships: The real challenge of corporate global citizenship. *Business and Society Review, 105*, 47–62.

Wood, D. J., Logsdon, J. M., Lewellyn, P. G. & Davenport, K. (2006). *Global business citizenship: A transformative framework for ethics and sustainable capitalism*. New York: M. E. Sharpe.

Part I

Theories of Corporate Social Performance: Toward a New Vision of Theoretical Integration of Value-Based Business Leadership

Introduction to Part I

Is corporate social performance theorizing capable of dealing with the complex, ponderous concerns presented in the Introduction of this book? Our view is that corporate social performance, as typically understood, is too narrowly construed to provide a framework for articulating, assessing, and guiding corporate actions on such a vast scale. More pointedly, corporate social performance is marred by an unwieldy tension that precludes an integration of its research topics, mainly because it embodies two inherently contradictory approaches, discussed in Chapter 1, as *economic-focused* and *duty-aligned perspectives*. Neither is particularly well suited to serve as a basis for theory capable of addressing large-scale, complicated social issues. Briefly, the economic perspective that has shaped the business and society field at large and corporate social performance research in particular tends to equate corporate social responsibility with the efficient and profitable production of goods and services. Mostly utilitarian in nature, it judges economic activity in terms of these consequences while accepting a narrow formulation of self-interest that prompts a pursuit of them. This perspective contrasts rather sharply with that aligned with duty. Influenced by business ethics research, the dutiful view eschews a focus on consequences and an elevation of narrow self-interest to formulate rules based on a motivation of respect for moral personhood aligned with standards of human rights and justice, ultimately expressed as duties to others.

We do not claim that the first three chapters in Part I resolve this theory-building dilemma or the tension between the two perspectives, but rather that core problems are explicated and ameliorated in order to provide an integrative approach that can better inform theoretical and empirical research in corporate social performance. That this integrative approach is grounded in organizational theory is important to note, since the economic and dutiful perspectives do not take full advantage of developments in social science expressed in organizational theory. Indeed, a reliance on social science marks this volume, consistent with our belief that incorporating advances in organizational theory and methodology can ultimately inform better research and practice, as noted in the Introduction.

Chapter 1 demonstrates that while the economic and dutiful perspectives overlap in a common interest in the social control of business, such as that posed by government regulation and stakeholder pressure, they are not integrated. A more complete understanding of theory-building problems is accomplished by analyzing what is commonly known as 'the corporate social performance model', which is reoriented so that it can be used to explore a synthesis of the two perspectives which are revised in terms of the three main categories of the model – principles of corporate social responsibility, processes of corporate social responsiveness, and outcomes of corporate behavior. This reframing is macro-oriented in that it addresses theory-building problems by proposing a new synthesis of business and society topics overall. Ultimately, however, it points to a revitalization of corporate social performance by emphasizing the importance of executive leadership, which is the subject of Chapter 2 where the lack of integration between the economic and dutiful perspectives is explicated in terms of a stubborn tension between 'the descriptive' (what corporations do or can do) and 'the normative' (what corporations should or should not do).

Informed by the reorientation of research topics laid out in the first chapter, the second chapter shows how normative-descriptive unification is possible in terms of executive decision making that does not bracket ethical values (the normative) from facts (the descriptive) but rather integrates both in an attempt to direct a firm's relationship with its social environment in terms of value-aware organizational decision processes. The potentiality for this type of executive leadership culminates in an organizational posture toward society dubbed 'attunement'. The main proposition is that executives' receptivity toward understanding and leveraging constructive personal and organizational values is a necessary condition for aligning corporate behavior with broad-based expectations of responsible organizational conduct. This *normative receptivity* is compared to *normative myopia*, stipulated as the propensity of executives to ignore or downplay the role of ethical values in their decision making. Normative myopia, in turn, can lead to *corporate neglect* of social concerns, a form of conduct exemplified by the eruption of corporate scandals referred to in the Introduction.

Chapter 3 further explores the proposition that executives' receptivity to values is necessary for aligning corporate behavior with social expectations of responsible organizational conduct. This exploration is threefold. One, the importance of identifying organizational values relevant to an attuned relationship between business and society is underscored. Two, the possibility that pressure from special interest groups can in fact constrain an executive's inclination to foster and encourage the organizational values that serve the collective good is explored. Three, the potential for a trustful dialogue between organizational representatives and community constituents that helps align corporate conduct with the expressed needs of community is presented as an important part of the attunement process. Indeed, trustful dialogue is formulated as a linchpin for extending corporate social performance into the domain of corporate citizenship writ large, as reflected in the title of this book. After all, one of the first principles of business ethics is that the corporation is a citizen of the larger community. Understanding the responsibilities of such citizenship means that corporations need to go beyond forced compliance with social control to willingly and proactively monitor and attend to community interests by engaging in a form of communication that, according to the dutiful perspective, is based on a respect for stakeholders that helps build trust. Since research presented in Part II suggests that economic goals may be accomplished in the process, the extension of topics in Chapter 3 points to the potential for blending the economic and duty-aligned perspectives in theory and practice, consistent with our quest to forge an integrative approach to corporate citizenship.

This value-based, integrative approach to corporate citizenship, which relies on the possibility of forging the attuned relationship with society described in Chapter 2, is also considered in Part III in terms of executive preference for compensation, strategic planning, social and environmental accounting, and fit and flexibility in human resource management. The integrative review of cutting-edge empirical research linking corporate social performance and corporate financial performance in Part II, and the implications for measurement and practice in Part III, substantiates our view that the blending of theoretical and empirical advances represented in this monograph, and their reliance on advances in social science, can enhance value-based organizational leadership that effectively integrates financial, social, and environmental concerns in decision making.

1

Addressing a Lack of Theoretical Integration in Corporate Social Performance

As indicated in the Introduction to Part I, the business and society field at large and corporate social performance topics in particular have been shaped by two dominant orientations, referred to here as *economic-focused* and *duty-aligned* perspectives. The purpose of this chapter is to describe the two perspectives, demonstrate their lack of integration, and identify the problems posed for integrative theory development. To preview, their lack of integration means that restraining unethical behavior by social control that is normatively undefined is emphasized to the detriment of a more forward-looking, affirmative view of business's role in society. Practically speaking, this fuels the misperception among practicing managers that economics and ethics do not mix, as indicated by the familiar refrain that 'business ethics is an oxymoron' (Swanson, 2002; 2008). One goal of integration is to point managers to a holistic approach that counteracts this myth.

The economic-focused perspective, largely expressed through the field's management research, encompasses many social and ethical issues. It never, however, loses sight of the firm's inviolable economic responsibility to efficiently and profitably produce goods and services for society. This perspective accepts some tenets of the utilitarian ethic in neoclassical economics, including a teleological approach to ethics that judges economic activity by its consequences or outcomes. Overall, neoclassical economics maintains that the consequence of greatest

This chapter originally was published in 1995 as Diane L. Swanson, 'Addressing a theoretical problem by reorienting the corporate social performance model', *Academy of Management Review, 20*, 43–64. It was revised for publication in this book. The material of the original chapter was used with permission of the Academy of Management.

social satisfaction or good occurs when individuals are free to pursue their own self-interest in economic activity. It prizes not only efficient and profitable outcomes, but also autonomy and economic freedom. Further, because it factors power behavior and ill-will toward others out of economic activity and into the political realm, it takes self- and other interest to be mutually beneficial (Hirshman, 1981; March, 1992; Vogel, 1991). Consequently, it sees no compelling reason to account for benevolence or duty-based morality (Etzioni, 1988; Hausman, 1992; Sen, 1987). Neoclassical theory does, however, accept restraints from the public to the direction self-interest takes in business activity. In this spirit, Friedman (1962, 1970), a contemporary spokesperson for this view, argued that managers need not be moral agents because their actions are already restrained by standards of public policy, the law, and ethical custom.[1]

Lindblom (1977) referred to such restraints as forms of social control called 'authority and persuasion'. Authority, or legitimized power, is expressed in law and public policy (Harris & Carman, 1987). Persuasion can be based on morality and generally accepted norms and expectations embedded in social custom or tradition and reinforced by habit (Scott, 1987; Selznick, 1992). Like neoclassical theory, the economic perspective in the business and society field accepts these forms of restraints to business activity, taking them to be means by which society directs business activity to be compatible with useful ends, i.e., those consequences consistent with sociocultural values (Buchholz, 1982, 1985; Chamberlain, 1973, 1977; Frederick, 1986; Jones, 1983; Steidlmeier, 1987).

The duty-aligned perspective, largely expressed through the field's business ethics research, includes many managerial and economic issues. It never, however, loses sight of its primary interest in formulating rules for corporate moral behavior and expressing these rules as obligations or duties. Typically, it uses two closely related ethical approaches to do so: rights and justice. The first approach, a rights-based ethic, seeks protections or extensions of individual entitlements. More specifically, protections of entitlements are negative rights to be free from harm; extensions of entitlements are positive rights to have or pursue a benefit (Velasquez, 1982; Werhane, 1985). These rights invoke weak and strong forms of correlative duties. In weak form, negative duty protects negative rights by restraining action that can harm others. In strong form, positive duty supports positive rights by advocating a willing, active commitment to help others obtain their good. Both forms of duty reject a utilitarian assessment of action by consequences. Instead, they emphasize motivation, maintaining that ethical action requires the respect for the moral personhood of others described in Kant's duty-centered (or deontological) moral philosophy (Boatright, 1993; Brady, 1985; De George, 1990; Donaldson, 1989; Freeman & Gilbert, 1988; Velasquez, 1982).

The second approach, a justice-based ethic, prizes liberty, equality, and fairness of opportunity. It insists that an unfair distribution of harms and benefits be explained and defended on logical grounds (Frederick, 1987; Rawls, 1971). Standards of justice are closely related to those of rights because justice argues for the conditions that justify negative rights (the right to be free from harm) and positive rights (the right to have or pursue a benefit) (Beauchamp & Bowie, 1993). Concurrently, these conditions justify the negative and positive duties required by rights.

In other words, business ethics research typically aligns rights and justice standards with rules about duties. This alignment occurs because the provision of closely-related rights and justice standards for individuals usually requires duties from others (Collins, 1989; Donaldson, 1989; Freeman & Gilbert, 1988; Selznick, 1992; Velasquez, 1982), the ethical motivation being a respect called for by a duty-centered ethic (Rawls, 1971).

In principle, the economic and duty-aligned perspectives overlap significantly in a concern for the social control of business. Simply put, this topic is *the* central concept in the business and society field (Jones, 1983). Its centrality is due to the interest in negative duty or restraint to self-interest that the perspectives share. This mutual interest is not surprising because most ethical theories, including utilitarianism, agree on the importance of restraining self-interest (Selznick, 1992).

The next section in this chapter examines a well known corporate social performance model to show how this overlap has historically been expressed in the business and society field. This examination demonstrates that, even in their shared interest in social control, the two perspectives are antagonistic. Or, as Brady (1985) put it, they represent 'Janus-headed' ethical views of business and society issues.

Frederick (1987) described this antagonism in terms of 'tradeoff and moral justification problems'. The first problem occurs when the field's theorists argue for compliance with social controls because it is required by the law or public policy and because business may lose its much prized autonomy and economic freedom if it does not respond assuredly to social pressure. When such compliance seems costly, it invokes a tradeoff between corporate economic goals and negative duty. For corporations to go beyond complying with social pressure and accept positive duty to society can appear even more costly. Put simply, a tradeoff problem exists when profits and duty seem to collide. Part II of this volume takes up this issue by examining important research that suggests that corporate social performance and corporate financial performance can go hand in hand, a state of affairs that mitigates the tradeoff problem.

The moral justification problem occurs when social control, and perhaps even positive duty, seems to serve corporate economic goals. Then the defense for corporate social responsibility can be that it *pays* or is strategically wise (see Ackerman & Bauer, 1976; Mitnick, 1981; Preston & Post, 1975; Wood & Jones, 1994). However, ethicists never justify morality by economic criteria, even when the two happen to coincide (Beauchamp & Bowie, 1993; Donaldson, 1989; Frederick, 1987). Consequently, even when the economic and duty-aligned perspectives do not pose a tradeoff problem, they can fail to reveal the reasons *why* corporations should be socially responsible. This absence of clear moral directive is the moral justification problem.

Given the tradeoff and moral justification problems, the field's dominant research orientations are not theoretically integrated, in spite of their strong shared interest in social control. The next section examines this lack of integration as expressed in corporate social performance.

Corporate social performance revisited

A consolidated classification of research can be an important step toward theory development, especially for a field as eclectic as business and society. Discussed again in Chapter 2, such a framework can show interrelationships among diverse topics and provide a unifying theme and an agenda for future research (Jones, 1983). Wood's corporate social performance (CSP) model (see Table 1.1) is a well known classification that demonstrates interrelationships among three topics:

1. Principles of corporate social responsibility expressed on the institutional, organizational, and individual levels.
2. Corporate processes of responsiveness as environmental assessment, stakeholder management, and issues management.
3. Outcomes of corporate behavior as social impacts, social programs, and social policies.

Wood's CSP model extends and revises Wartick and Cochran's (1985) model, which is, in turn, based on Carroll's (1979) work. These works

Table 1.1   A Classification of Corporate Social Performance

Principles of Corporate Social Responsibility (CSR)

Institutional principle: legitimacy (Origin: Davis, 1973)
Organizational principle: public responsibility (Origin: Preston & Post, 1975)
 Individual principle: managerial discretion (Origin: Carroll, 1979; Wood, 1990)

Processes of Corporate Social Responsiveness

Environmental assessment
Stakeholder management
Issues management

Outcomes of Corporate Behavior

Social impacts
Social programs
Social policies

From 'Corporate Social Performance Revisited,' by D. J. Wood, 1991a, Academy of *Management Review, 16,* 694. Copyright 1991 by the Academy of Management. Adapted with permission of the author.

are primarily shaped by the field's longstanding management research. As a result, the model does not give similar weight to the business ethics research that influenced the field later. This imbalance needs to be redressed because responsibility is a well-developed concept in business ethics (see Steidlmeier, 1987). Consequently, this ethics research has the potential to develop critically the normative dimensions of corporate social responsibility (CSR).

Argued below, because the CSR principles illustrated in Table 1.1 lack this kind of normative development, they restrain corporate economic activity with social control that is normatively undefined. Further, they formulate corporate positive duty as optional altruism or philanthropy. These undeveloped interpretations of duty pose two major difficulties for comprehensive theory development. First, these interpretations invoke tradeoff and moral justification problems in the CSR principles that render incompatible the economic and duty-aligned perspectives. Second, these interpretations render the CSR principles normatively inadequate for assessing processes of corporate social responsiveness and outcomes of corporate behavior. Essentially, the development of a general theory for the field awaits the integration of its dominant perspectives into one that is normatively adequate for assessing corporate social performance.

The institutional principle of legitimacy

The institutional principle originated with Davis's (1973) Iron Law of Responsibility. It states that business is a social institution that must use its power responsibly. Otherwise, society may revoke it. On this, Davis wrote:

> Society grants legitimacy and power to business. In the long run, those who do not use power in a manner which society considers responsible will tend to lose it. (Davis, 1973, p. 314)

Sethi (1979) also held that if corporations ignore social expectations, they are likely to lose control over their internal decision making and external dealings. More recently, Vidaver-Cohen and Altman (2000) have observed that corporate citizenship research tends to emphasize that firms engaged in global business should strengthen ties with local communities in order to preserve legitimacy in the public eye.

The invocation of legitimacy is not necessarily misplaced. The problem is one of proportionality. As Wood (1991a) observed, the institutional principle expresses a prohibition rather than a positive duty. It implies that business should act on the threat of social control instead of on a positive commitment to society that disregards or downplays self-interest and consequences. Indeed, even if society expects positive duty from business, this expectation is contradicted if it is gained by threat of social coercion. Reinforcing such threat, Freeman's (1984) widely used stakeholder concept emphasizes that groups in society that can affect or are affected by an organization can *block* corporate goals. Related research describes how stakeholders can retaliate against questionable corporate practices (see Collins, 1989).

By emphasizing negative duty, the institutional principle fails to legitimate the positive duty found in ethics research. Furthermore, it demonstrates the field's moral justification problem. Shaped by the economic perspective, it justifies social control by the threat of loss of autonomy and economic freedom so valued by the business sector (see Cavanagh, 1990). By contrast, the duty-aligned perspective would instead justify social control by advocating that corporations be motivated to restrain certain business activity out of respect for their stakeholders. In sum, the institutional principle neither promotes positive duty nor advocates the moral motivation of respect. Thus, it is not infused with the sense of moral responsibility found in business ethics.

The organizational principle of public responsibility

Originating with Preston and Post's (1975) model that takes business and society to be interpenetrating systems, the organizational principle limits corporate duty to those social problems that can be traced to a firm's economic operations. Wood defined this principle:

> Businesses are responsible for outcomes related to their primary and secondary areas of involvement [i.e., economic impact] with society. (Wood, 1991a, p. 697)

Based on the neoclassical economic concept of an 'externality', the organizational principle says that corporations are responsible only for solving the direct and indirect problems they cause. Solving these problems is their public responsibility. Despite its premise that business and society are symbiotic and mutually adaptive systems, this principle draws an economic boundary to corporate responsibility. Further, because it defines and enforces this responsibility with public policy, it emphasizes social control.

The concept of public responsibility is not entirely negative. Because it speaks of a mutually adaptive relationship between business and society, it has a constructive tone. Even so, it holds positive corporate duty to society at bay in three ways. First, it treats responsibilities beyond the problem-defined boundary as optional. Second, by linking corporate conduct to public policy, it emphasizes social control while it de-emphasizes a positive commitment to community that might be expressed in business-government partnerships. Similarly, it overlooks the possibility that such partnerships could be inclusive of civil society groups, particularly when corporations operate globally in different economic and social environments (see Waddock, 2002; Waddell, 2000). Third, the concept of public responsibility does not address how corporate duty to society can be incorporated into managerial decision making so that social problems are minimized in the first place.

The individual principle of managerial discretion

Although the individual principle in the CSP model does not resolve the latter concern, it does acknowledge that individual managers have moral discretion in decision making. Wood explained that

> managers are moral actors. Within every domain of corporate social responsibility, they are obliged to exercise such discretion as

is available to them, toward socially responsible outcomes. (Wood, 1991a, p. 698)

This principle originated with Carroll's (1979) hierarchy of corporate responsibilities, which describes voluntary managerial duties that are not specifically prohibited or demanded of companies because of their other economic, legal, and ethical responsibilities (Wood, 1991a). This hierarchy means that managerial positive duty is discretionary because it is ranked last in importance, after the firm's known economic, legal, and ethical responsibilities.

The individual principle emphasizes social control in two ways. First, its legal category represents explicit social control of economic activity. Second, ethical responsibility invokes the threat of social control based on ethical custom. It does so by appealing to social expectations that corporations avoid 'questionable' practices (see Carroll, 1979). So far, it is consistent with the contemporary articulation of neoclassical economics because it accepts restraints to economic activity from the law, public policy, and ethical custom. Even so, the individual principle goes beyond these forms of social control by addressing managers' discretion to choose positive duty. Yet, this discretionary range is narrow and *per se* voluntary compared to the more pervasive restraint to their behavior from social control.

Normative difficulties posed by CSR principles

Tradeoff and moral justification problems. The economic and duty-aligned perspectives are not compatible in these three CSR principles. Rather, they are subject to tradeoff and moral justification problems. The first problem occurs when negative duty appears costly in one of two ways. First, social control suggests implicit costs: Corporations forego profits when public policy, the law, and ethical custom restrain their pursuit of all economic opportunities. Second, social control suggests explicit costs: Corporations bear out-of-pocket costs when public policy, the law, and ethical custom require that they rectify the direct and indirect problems they cause. Because positive duty is formulated as discretionary and optional to social control, largely as altruism or philanthropy, it can appear even more costly. Also, because it is optional, it can be harder to justify, especially in difficult economic times.

Some CSP scholars take the tradeoff problem seriously and counter it by asserting that, under certain conditions, corporate social responsibility can *pay*. Social control and positive duty may coincide with or even serve economic goals, as the findings presented in Part II suggest.

Yet, a sole reliance on this argument implicitly accepts the primacy of economic standards in the CSR principles and judges negative and positive duty against such standards.[2] This kind of justification alone is not acceptable from the duty-aligned perspective because it fails to address the importance of moral motivation. More specifically, it fails to deal with an attitude of respect toward others that would properly motivate corporate social responsibility. Arguably, a field that purports to incorporate ethics research must grapple with this view, as we do in Chapter 3 where we propose that an attitude of respect may help motivate managers to establish a trustful dialogue with stakeholders aimed at aligning corporate goals with community interests.

Inadequate normative criteria for responsiveness. The CSR principles lack adequate normative criteria for evaluating processes of responsiveness. These processes are corporate tools for assessing the environment and managing stakeholder issues. They are the action counterparts to responsibility (Wood, 1991a). The social control standard in the principles cannot effectively be used to assess these actions because it is normatively unclear in two ways. First, the principles do not identify what sociocultural values are at stake in social control issues. Instead, like Friedman's (1970) contemporary neoclassical view, the principles take these values to be embedded in public policy, the law, and ethical expectations, especially those of stakeholders who affect or are affected by business organizations. Thus, the CSR principles cannot answer what Jones (1983) asserted are two fundamental social control questions: How congruent are existing social control mechanisms with social values? How can they be made more congruent?

Corporations can provide answers to these questions when they use their tools of responsiveness to *change* social controls, to which they then adjust. Then they can be deemed responsible, according to the CSR principles. Clearly, corporations influence public policy, the law, and ethical expectations, and this influence is increasing (Jacobs, 1999; Wood, 1987). Quite simply, corporate economic power can become political power (Brady, 2001; Etzioni, 1988). Corporations can seek this power by lobbying Congress, building coalitions, using mass media, providing Congressional testimony, establishing political action committees, and using their public affairs function to manage social issues (Chomsky, 1987; Epstein, 1969; Sethi, 1982; Wartick & Cochran, 1985; Wartick & Rude, 1986).

The second way the CSR principles lack normative clarity is related to the moral justification problem. Eschewing a theoretical ethics base, the principles do not address the moral motivation of respect that supports duty. They instead rely on control and coercion. Although corporate social responsibility may be motivated by several factors, including respect for stakeholders, it may also be strategically defensive and diversionary (see Sethi, 1982; Weidenbaum, 1977). Further, what appears to be corporate responsibility can be a paternalistic expression of corporate power instead of a responsible interaction with society (Frederick, 1987). Because the CSR principles do not deal with ethical motivation, they lack adequate criteria for making such distinctions.

Inadequate normative criteria for outcomes. Outcomes of corporate behavior are subject to similar problems. For social impacts (e.g., pollution, payment of taxes, provision of jobs), it is a question of whether firms adhere to public policy, the law, and ethical expectations. Again, because corporations can influence these forms of social control, their adherence to them cannot be the primary standard for corporate social performance. The same holds for social programs and policies. They institutionalize motives and decision-making processes for managing social impacts (Wood, 1991a). In them, corporations house the means to influence their standards of social control. Again, the principles do not clarify a firm's moral motivation for doing so.

To recapitulate, the economic and duty-aligned perspectives are not compatible in CSR principles because they encounter stark tradeoff and moral justification problems that prevent their theoretical integration. Additionally, the principles restrain corporate economic responsibilities through normatively unclear social controls that can be influenced by a corporation's own response mechanisms. Moreover, the principles do not clarify the moral motivation for this influence and other corporate social behavior.

The need for broader CSR principles

The emphasis on corporate economic responsibility in CSR principles is not misplaced. The vital social function of business is economic (Committee For Economic Development, 1971; Donaldson, 1989; Frederick, 1992; Preston & Post, 1975). Even so, business decisions consist of continuous, interrelated economic and moral components (Etzioni, 1988; Frederick, 1986). The CSR organizational and individual principles divide this interrelatedness, functionally, then hierarchically, with the standard of social control. This standard emphasizes negative duty or restraint to economic responsibility based on control. In turn, this control standard de-emphasizes positive duty. On the institutional level, positive duty is not addressed; on the organizational level, it is not functionally linked to economic responsibilities; on the individual level, it is optional. Further, the principles do not address the moral motivation that would motivate a voluntary corporate commitment to both negative and positive social duties.

All of this renders these principles too narrow for comprehensive theory development. They do not articulate the field's primary interest in what constitutes a complete sense of corporate responsibility to society. The field's theorists recognize that the modern corporation operates on an expanded scale that requires a new business and societal relationship (see Epstein, 1987; Frederick, 1986; Sethi, 1982; Wartick & Cochran, 1985; Wood, 1991b; Zeitlin, 1978). From the beginning, many researchers have been interested in defining corporate responsibility for social progress that matches an expanded agenda of human issues and needs (Bowen, 1953, 1978; Chamberlain, 1977; Davis, 1964; Eells, 1960; Frederick, 1986; Lodge, 1975; Preston, 1986; Steiner, 1983; Votaw & Sethi, 1969). This larger agenda requires broad standards for corporate social involvement, commitment, and responsibility to community (Buchholz, 1989; Frederick, 1986; Preston, 1986). To accommodate these broad standards, the CSP field needs to develop a larger theoretical perspective (Wood & Jones 1994).

The CSR principles reviewed in this chapter are not answering what Wood (1991c) argued is the field's most pressing question: How can and do corporations contribute to constructing 'the good society'? To do so, their normative dimensions need to be developed in the following ways. First, the principles need to hold social control to normative standards. Second, they need to incorporate positive duty across their institutional, organizational, and individual levels. Finally, they need to address the moral motivation that supports both negative and positive expressions of duty. In other words, the CSR principles need to integrate the field's economic and duty-aligned perspectives into broader standards that can adequately assess corporation social performance by normative criteria.

Theory-building problems in corporate social performance

It has been argued that the economic and duty-aligned perspectives resist integration, despite their shared interest in social control. Indeed, recent attempts to integrate these two perspectives indicate that they are largely incompatible. For example, Donaldson (1989), a philosopher, restrained some corporate moral duties with economic cost standards, and Etzioni (1988), a sociologist, restrained economic activity within a duty-bound community. Certainly, it is unusual for a philosopher to yield to economic precepts and a sociologist to philosophic ones. This unusual situation occurs because the two perspectives, as presently formulated, resist blending for three interrelated reasons.

The obstacles to integrating the perspectives

Incompatible value outcomes. The first reason the two perspectives resist blending is that they prize incompatible value outcomes. The utilitarian reasoning expressed in corporate social performance focuses on gain for *self*. It uses cost-benefit calculus to measure efficiency and to determine whether a net gain accrues to individuals in markets or to stockholders *vis-à-vis* corporate profits. Focused on this self-centered end, it de-emphasizes questions of rights and justice for others (see Wood, 1991a). In contrast, the duty-aligned perspective focuses on *duty to others* and, despite its emphasis on motivation, it weighs morality by the extent to which others are treated dutifully by standards of rights and justice.

Because the economic and duty-aligned perspectives prize different value outcomes, they encounter the tradeoff or moral justification problem. As noted in the CSR principles, the tradeoff problem occurs when duty appears costly. This problem is also demonstrated by a proposed algorithm for ethical decision making, whereby economic, rights, and justice standards are tradeoffs, except for those instances where they seem to coincide (Cavanagh, Moberg & Velasquez, 1981). Even then, the economic and duty-aligned perspectives do not agree on the moral rationale for choice, the first judging by consequences and the second by moral motivation. Hence, they still encounter the moral justification problem.

Focus on individual choice. The second reason the perspectives resist blending stems from the first. In their emphasis on gain or duty, both perspectives focus mainly on the logic of individual choice (Steidlmeier, 1987). This focus on individual dynamics is misplaced because it de-emphasizes how self- and other interests are played out in large, complex organizations and how group-influenced behavior affects the business and societal relationship. In these organizations, people function interdependently on an unprecedented scale (Lindblom, 1977). The logic of individual action does not necessarily explain their behavior, especially as it is expressed in groups (Cohen, March & Olsen, 1972). Essentially, corporate social responsibility, responsiveness, and outcomes occur in tandem with organizational dynamics, not logical rules for individual choice. The disproportionate importance that both perspectives grant to the individual is not appropriate for a field interested in explaining social phenomena.

Narrow value orientations. Finally, because both perspectives focus on individual gain or duty, neither gives a broad accounting of social values. These values are well recognized and include communitarian standards like social justice (Jones, 1983; Steidlmeier, 1987). As some scholars observe, business research continues to formulate these standards individualistically (see Aram, 1993; Preston, 1986). This narrow value orientation is consistent with a reported lack of research in the business and society field on the social dimensions in the business environment (see Reed *et al.*, 1990).

Although self-interested gain and other-interested duty are important and deserve study, they co-exist with other value variations that operate dynamically across the individual, organizational, and societal levels (Rokeach, 1973; Williams, 1979). Neither the economic nor duty-aligned perspectives account for all the sociocultural values that can be expressed in business and societal interaction and the social control of it. Notably, neither develops the role of power as a sociocultural value that affects this interaction. This situation suggests that the field has not completely replaced the neoclassical separation of economic activity from politics, despite its organizational principle that takes them to be interpenetrating systems. The point is that the field lacks a broad account of sociocultural values and how they can be expressed in the business and society relationship. Instead, its economic and duty-aligned perspectives narrowly focus on the value of individual gain or duty to others, reinforcing the field's tradeoff and moral justification problems.

The inadequacies of both perspectives for theory development

The two perspectives are not easily integrated because of their (a) incompatible value outcomes, (b) emphasis on individual choice, and (c) narrow value orientations. For these reasons, neither is an adequate foundation for more comprehensive business and society theory development. Because of their relative simplicity, they cannot adequately account for the ongoing interaction between large, complex, and powerful business organizations and their complex, dynamic, and turbulent social environments. This interaction can be interwoven and adaptive. It involves complex value relationships across the individual, organizational, and societal levels. It involves power. The field needs a research perspective that can accommodate these dimensions of the business and societal relationship.

A research strategy

Despite shortcomings, the economic and duty-aligned perspectives bring important understandings to the field. Neither should be discarded. The first emphasizes vital corporate economic responsibility and the social expectation that it be carried out. Through managerial research and corporate experience, it has been sharpened into an organizational pragmatism that provides effective tools for corporate social responsiveness. Although these tools can influence social control, they can also enhance corporate economic survival in complex, dynamic, and turbulent environments (see also Part II). On the other hand, the duty-aligned perspective emphasizes the importance of the humanizing standards of rights and justice and the social expectation that business adhere to them. It also advocates a moral motivation for this adherence. Further, it provides reflective moral reasoning for examining these aspects of corporate duty.

Although the CSR principles demonstrate the field's central theoretical problem, they also demonstrate that the field may be poised to integrate its two dominant perspectives by reformulating and broadening its theoretical base. For instance, the principles diverge from neoclassical economics by recognizing the importance of three research topics. First, the institutional principle recognizes that business has power that affects its relationship with society. Second, the organizational principle recognizes that this power relationship is not partitioned but is interpenetrating and can be interwoven and adaptive. Third, the individual principle recognizes that managers are moral agents who can exercise positive duty. All in all, these topics acknowledge a relationship between business and society that involves more than economic restraint. It also involves power, collaboration, and positive duty. This acknowledgement hints that the field may be ready to broaden its CSR principles into more adequate standards for assessing corporate social performance. To do so, it needs to bring together the economic and duty-aligned perspectives in theoretically sound ways.

The proposed research strategy reformulates the perspectives so that they are normatively compatible and adequate for theory development. This strategy involves three overlapping approaches: (a) bridge the perspectives with the topic of decision making, (b) formulate decision making in terms of social processes, and (c) formulate social processes as ethical and value processes.

Bridge the perspectives with decision making

What is considered 'ethical' in business must be assessed within the context of reasoning that invokes actions (Weber, 1993). As a research topic, decision making can address reasoning that invokes action by addressing the motivation that prompts decisions. It can also address the consequences of these decisions. Thus, the topic of decision making has the potential to accommodate both moral motivation and economic consequences. Put differently, this topic may be a bridge between the duty-aligned and economic perspectives because it can accommodate the emphasis on moral motivation of the former and the economic consequentialism of the latter.

Formulate decision making in terms of social processes

Decision makers in organizations can occupy different roles and hierrchical positions. Their decisions create ongoing organizational and environmental consequences that influence further decisions. Epstein (1987) described this interaction as a social policy process, and its features suggest that decision making be formulated as processes that can be linked across the individual, organizational, and societal levels. Consistent with general systems theory, this formulation is a powerful way to account for dimensions in business and societal interaction (Preston & Post, 1975). Consequently, it renders the two basic perspectives better candidates for theory development. Further, it rectifies two obstacles to their integration. One, it removes their undue emphasis on the individual (while keeping it as an important level of analysis). Two, it removes their fixed-ended reasoning or singular emphasis on the finality of certain results. In the case of the economic perspective, this singular emphasis equates to targeting gain for self; in the case of the duty-aligned approach, it amounts ultimately to weighing justice and rights for others.

Based on historical evidence, Boulding (1978) proposed three major social organizers or processes that have evolved to link individuals to productive organizations. These processes have been cross-validated by other research, including Lenski's (1966) large cross-cultural study of societies ranging from hunting and gathering to advanced industrial states (see also Capra, 1982; Harris, 1979). Briefly, these social processes are:

1. *Exchange process*: Involves an invitation to trade based on reciprocity. It is undergirded by production that is based on specialization and division of labor.
2. *Threat process:* Involves the use of force or dominance.
3. *Integrative process:* Involves co-operation that is based on shared identities among people in communities.

Formulate social processes as ethical and value processes

Boulding asserted that ethics and values are bound up in the social processes. Ethics in the foregoing discussion has already been accounted for as negative and positive duty. Because values help explain action and its motivation (Freeman & Gilbert, 1988; Rokeach, 1973), it is particularly important to account for their role in the social processes. That done, values and ethics can be formulated as interactive processes in decision making that span the individual, organizational, and societal levels.

Frederick (1995) accounts for those values in the social processes relevant to business organizations. For the purpose at hand, this accounting broadens the concept of value beyond narrow gain or duty standards. Briefly, these value processes are:

1. *Economizing*: Refers to the ability of organizations to convert inputs to outputs efficiently through competitive behavior. This process provides the goods and services for exchange in markets.
2. *Power aggrandizing* or *power seeking*: Refers to status-enforced, self-centered behavior in organizations that seeks to acquire and use coercive power through hierarchical arrangements.
3. *Ecologizing*: Refers to symbiotic, integrative linkages between organizations and their environments that function adaptively to sustain life. These linkages are based on co-operative, collaborative behavior.

In terms of how these values are bound up in the social processes, economizing is necessary for exchange; power seeking is part of threat systems; and ecologizing is part of the integrative process. Frederick also proposes a separate value set consisting of the personal values held by individuals in business organizations. Research on these values indicates that they are far too numerous to list here (see, England, 1967; Frederick & Weber, 1987; Posner & Schmidt, 1984). Even so, it is important to note that they include the extent to which individuals prize economic, rights, and justice standards.

Reorienting corporate social performance

According to the research strategy, the reoriented CSP model (Figure 1.1) formulates decision making in terms of ethical and value processes that are linked across the (a) individual (e.g., executive, managerial, and employee), (b) organizational, and (c) societal levels. As such, it discards the assumption that the CSR principles are hierarchical. This reorientation suggests a theoretical picture that is interactive across principles, processes, and outcomes (see Wood 1991a). The model organizes this inter-

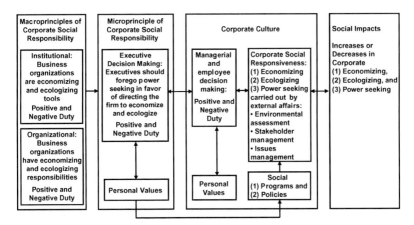

Figure 1.1 The Reoriented CSP Model

action in terms of four broad research topics: (a) CSR macroprinciples, (b) CSR microprinciple, (c) corporate culture, and (d) social impacts. In Figure 1.1, the research topics are in boxes; their interrelationships or linkages are denoted by arrows.

Macroprinciples of corporate social responsibility

Institutional level. Organizations are special-purpose tools. When they adapt to social values beyond technical requirements, they become institutions (Selznick, 1957, 1992). As such, the institutional principle in Figure 1.1 states that corporations are economizing and ecologizing tools, a description that is congruent with the social contract conclusion that corporations are legitimate because they enhance the social good. They do so by producing goods and services on a scale that would otherwise be unattainable (Donaldson, 1989). That is, corporations can economize. Further, corporate legitimacy rests on their ability to adapt production to life-sustaining social needs and be integrated into society (Sethi, 1979). This integration requires that they forge co-operative, collaborative linkages with it (Etzioni, 1988; Waddock, 2002). In this way, corporations can ecologize.

As a research topic, the institutional principle invites an examination of the interrelationships among (a) economizing, (b) ecologizing, and (c) negative and positive duty. Both the economic and duty-aligned perspectives agree that negative duty is a restraint to corporate action that harms society. The institutional principle implies that these harms are economic (e.g., industrial relocation that brings unemployment) and ecological (e.g., pollution), and the duty-aligned perspective insists that they are also violations of rights (e.g., the right to subsistence) and justice (e.g., fair and equitable on-the-job treatment). Additionally, the duty-aligned perspective views positive duty as a willing, constructive corporate commitment to provide rights and justice benefits to stakeholders. The institutional principle implies that these benefits can take economic and ecological forms. Supporting the importance of the latter, Selznick (1992) asserted that the integration of institutions into society is a major social benefit. In this vein, interest in corporate volunteerism (positive duty) continues, although some are careful to point out that volunteerism alone is not sufficient for corporate social responsibility. Oversight mechanisms in the form of public policy, public pressure and media attention are also needed to direct corporate conduct toward beneficial social outcomes (see Frederick, 2006; Prakash & Potoski, 2006; Swanson, 2000).

Organizational level. Given the restated institutional principle, it follows that corporations have responsibilities to economize and ecologize and provide negative and positive duties to society. A more specific description of these organizational responsibilities awaits future research. In particular, this research would address how the interrelationships among economizing, ecologizing, and negative and positive duties can be manifest in *specific* industrial and social environments.

Microprinciple of corporate social responsibility

Executive decision making, ethics, and personal values. The microprinciple in Figure 1.1 states that executives should forego or limit power seeking as a personal or an organizational goal. Instead, they should make decisions that direct the firm to economize and ecologize. This principle is consistent with Davis's Iron Law of Responsibility; however, it is more concrete. It places the responsibility for legitimate use of power with the decision makers at the top of the corporate hierarchy.

Organizations have been described by some as tools of power for leaders whose interests are bound up with the expansion of corporate capital (Perrow, 1986; Zeitlin, 1978). The microprinciple distinguishes between illegitimate and legitimate use of executive power. Illegitimate use, or 'power seeking', relies on coercion and rank-order status. Its motivation is self-interested empire-building. In contrast, legitimate power involves the motivation and ability to direct organizational resources toward economizing and ecologizing. Negative and positive duties are important components of responsible executive decision making. Broadly, they provide a distinction between directing the firm to (a) restrain action that harms stakeholders and (b) provide action that promotes their good or benefit. Making these distinctions is related to executives' motives and personal values. Again, the latter includes economic, rights, and justice standards.

Corporate culture and normative processes

Morality is inseparable from culture (Feldman, 2002). Executives manage the belief systems or corporate cultures out of which organizations respond to their environments (Schein, 1985). Thus, the reoriented model links executive decision making to corporate culture. Figure 1.1 indicates that when corporate culture is understood in terms of normative processes, it allows interrelationships among several research topics, including:

1. Linkages among normative executive decision making, corporate social programs and policies, and value-defined responsiveness carried out by an external affairs strategy. These linkages are consistent with Miles' (1987) finding that executive philosophy drives a firm's external affairs strategy.
2. Linkages between normative managerial and employee decision making and value-defined corporate social responsiveness.

Overall, the new model is capable of addressing two questions that Epstein (1987, p. 100) proposed are basic to understanding corporate management as a normative social policy process. They are:

1. How can the leaders of a large, complex business organization best incorporate into their firm's decision-making processes the difficult but essential task of defining (and redefining), evaluating, and institutionalizing the values that underlie its policies and practices as well as determine its unique culture?
2. What conceptual contributions can management thought make to business practitioners seeking to institutionalize value considerations into ongoing decision-making processes?

Social impacts

Finally, the reoriented model allows linkages between normative processes occurring in corporate cultures and the social impacts of a company. Social impacts are depicted as increases or decreases in corporate economizing, ecologizing, and power seeking. Two-way arrows between research topics indicate that executive decision making, as well as social programs and policies, can be influenced by a firm's external affairs assessment of its social impacts.

Conclusion and prospects for integration

The reoriented CSP model presented in this chapter is consistent with Wood's (1991a) assertion that the CSR principles are analytical forms to be filled with value content that can be operationalized. These operational processes – (a) economizing, ecologizing and power-seeking values; (b) ethics as negative and positive duty; and (c) personal values – are interrelated research topics. The new model can be used to develop these topics and to assess whether the field's economic and duty-aligned perspectives can be integrated into an adequate normative theory for corporate social performance. Chapter 2 takes up this challenge by emphasizing the role that executive decision making can have in aligning constructive personal, organizational, and societal values in questing for responsible corporate social performance.

Notes

1. Economic theory represents a vast body of knowledge, including much research that explicitly addresses the ethical dimensions of economic activity (e.g., Arrow, 1951; Hirsch, 1976; Hirschman, 1985; Myrdal, 1970; Polanyi, 1944; Robinson, 1962; Sen, 1977, 1987). This chapter does not address these normative strands of economic thought. Nor does it delve into discussions of psychological, ethical, or economic egoism (e.g., Beauchamp & Bowie, 1993). Rather, it deals with the extent to which a particular interpretation of neoclassical economics has impacted the business and society field, as evidenced by the analysis of Wood's (1991a) model, which has served as baseline for a preponderance of corporate social performance research.
2. The studies covered in Part II do not accept the primacy of economic goals over other duties. Instead, they describe statistical correlations between corporate social performance and corporate financial performance. The implications of these findings for integrative theory and practice will be explored in the final chapter.

References

Ackerman, R. W. & Bauer, R. A. (1976). *Corporate social responsiveness: The modern dilemma*. Cambridge, MA: Harvard University Press.
Aram, J. D. (1993). *Presumed superior*. Englewood Cliffs, NJ: Prentice Hall.
Arrow, K. (1951). *Social choice and individual values*. New York: Wiley.
Beauchamp, T. L. & Bowie, N. E. (1993). *Ethical theory and business*. Englewood Cliffs, NJ: Prentice Hall.

Boatright, J. R. (1993). *Ethics and the conduct of business.* Englewood Cliffs, NJ: Prentice Hall.

Boulding, K. (1978). *Ecodynamics.* Beverly Hills, CA: Sage Publications.

Bowen, H. R. (1953). *Social responsibilities of the businessman.* New York: Harper.

Bowen, H. R. (1978). Social responsibilities of the businessman – Twenty years later. In E. M. Epstein & D. Votaw (eds), *Rationality, legitimacy, responsibility; Search for new directions in business and society* (pp. 116–130). Santa Monica, CA: Goodyear.

Brady, F. N. (1985). A Janus-headed model of ethical theory: Looking two ways at business/society issues. *Academy of Management Review, 10,* 568–576.

Brady, R. A. (2001). *Business as a system of power.* New Brunswick, NY: Transaction Publishers.

Buchholz, R. A. (1982). *Business environment and public policy.* Englewood Cliffs, NJ: Prentice Hall.

Buchholz, R. A. (1985). *Essentials of public policy for management.* Englewood Cliffs, NJ: Prentice Hall.

Buchholz, R. A. (1989). *Business ethics.* Englewood Cliffs, NJ: Prentice Hall.

Capra, F. (1982). *The turning point.* New York: Simon and Schuster.

Carroll, A. B. (1979). A three-dimensional model of corporate social performance. *Academy of Management Review, 4,* 497–505.

Cavanagh, G. F. (1990). *American business values.* Englewood Cliffs, NJ: Prentice Hall.

Cavanagh, G., Moberg, D. & Velasquez, M. (1981). The ethics of organizational politics. *Academy of Management Review. 6,* 363–368.

Chamberlain, N. (1973). *The place of business in America's future: A study in social values.* New York: Basic Books.

Chamberlain, N. (1977). *Remaking American values.* New York: Basic Books.

Chomsky, N. C. (1987). *The Chomsky reader.* (J. Peck, ed.). New York: Pantheon Books.

Cohen, M., March, J. & Olsen, J. (1972). A garbage can model of organizational choice. *Administrative Science Quarterly, 17,* 1–25.

Collins, D. (1989). Organizational harm, legal condemnation and stakeholder retaliation: A typology, research agenda and application. *Journal of Business Ethics, 8,* 1–13.

Committee for Economic Development. (1971). *Social responsibilities of business corporations.* New York: Author.

Davis, K. (1964). The public role of management. *Proceedings of the Annual Meeting of the Academy of Management, 3–9.*

Davis, K. (1973). The case for and against business assumption of social responsibilities. *Academy of Management Journal. 16,* 312–322.

De George, R. T. (1990). *Business ethics.* New York: Macmillan.

Donaldson, T. (1989). *The ethics of international business.* New York: Oxford University Press.

Eells, R. (1960). *The meaning of modern business.* New York: Columbia University Press.

England, G. W. (1967). Personal value systems of American managers. *Academy of Management Journal, 10,* 107–117.

Epstein, E. M. (1969). *The corporation in American politics.* Englewood Cliffs, NJ: Prentice Hall.

Epstein, E. M. (1987). The corporate social policy process: Beyond business ethics, corporate social responsibility, and corporate social responsiveness. *California Management Review, 29*(3), 99–114.

Etzioni, A. (1988). *The moral dimension: Toward a new economics.* NY: Free Press.

Feldman, S. P. (2002). *Memory as a moral decision: The role of ethics in organizational culture.* New Brunswick, NJ: Transaction Publishing.

Frederick, W. C. (1986). Toward CSR3: Why ethical analysis is indispensable and unavoidable in corporate affairs. *California Management Review, 28*, 126–141.

Frederick, W. C. (1987). Theories of corporate social performance. In S. P. Sethi & C. Falbe (eds), *Business and society: Dimensions of conflict and cooperation* (pp. 142–161). New York: Lexington Books.

Frederick, W. C. (1992). Anchoring values in nature: Toward a theory of business values. *Business Ethics Quarterly, 2*, 283–303.

Frederick, W. C. (1995). *Values, nature, and culture in the American corporation.* New York: Oxford University Press.

Frederick, W. C. (2006). *Corporation, be good! The story of corporate social responsibility.* Indianapolis, IN: Dog Ear Publishing.

Frederick, W. C. & Weber, J. (1987). The values of corporate managers and their critics. In W. C. Frederick & L. E. Preston (eds), *Research in corporate social performance and policy* (vol. 9, pp. 131–152). Greenwich, CT: JAI Press.

Freeman, R. E. (1984). *Strategic management: A stakeholder approach.* Boston, MA: Pitman/Ballinger.

Freeman, R. E. & Gilbert, D. R. (1988). *Corporate strategy and search for ethics.* Englewood Cliffs, NJ: Prentice Hall.

Friedman, M. (1962). *Capitalism and freedom.* Chicago: University of Chicago Press.

Friedman, M. (1970, September 13). The social responsibility of business is to increase its profits. *New York Times Magazine, 33*, 122–126.

Harris, M. (1979). *Cultural materialism.* New York: Random House.

Harris, R. G. & Carman, J. M. (1987). Business-government relations. In S. P. Sethi & C. Falbe (eds), *Business and society: Dimensions of conflict and cooperation* (pp. 177–190). New York: Lexington Books.

Hausman, D. M. (1992). *The inexact and separate science of economics.* New York: Cambridge University Press.

Hirsch, F. (1976). *Social limits to growth.* Cambridge, MA: Harvard University Press.

Hirshman, A. O. (1981). *Essays in trespassing: Economics to politics and beyond.* New York: Cambridge Press.

Hirschman, A. O. (1985). Against parsimony: Three easy ways of complicating some categories of economic discourse. *Economic Philosophy, 1*, 7–21.

Jacobs, D. C. (1999). *Business lobbies and the power structure in America: Evidence and arguments.* Westport, CT: Quorum Books.

Jones, T. M. (1983). An integrating framework for research in business and society: A step toward the elusive paradigm? *Academy of Management Review, 8*, 559–564.

Lenski, G. (1966). *Power and privilege.* New York: McGraw-Hill.

Lindblom, C. E. (1977). *Politics and markets.* New York: Basic Books.

Lodge, G. (1975). *The new American ideology.* New York: Knopf.

March, J. (1992). The war is over and the victors have lost. *The Journal of Socio-Economics, 21*, 261–267.

Miles, R. A. (1987). *Managing the corporate social environment.* Englewood Cliffs, NJ: Prentice Hall.

Mitnick, B. M. (1981). The strategic uses of regulation – and deregulation. *Business Horizons, 24*(2), 71–83.

Myrdal, G. (1970). *The challenge of world poverty.* New York: Pantheon Books.

Perrow, C. (1986). *Complex organizations: A critical essay.* New York: McGraw-Hill.

Polanyi, K. (1944). *The great transformation.* New York: Farrar & Rinehart.

Posner, B. Z. & Schmidt, W. H. (1984). Values and the American manager: An update. *California Management Review, 2*(3), 202–215.

Prakash, A. & Potoski, M. (2006). *The Voluntary environmentalists: Green clubs, ISO 14001, and voluntary environmental regulations.* Cambridge, UK: Cambridge University Press.

Preston, L. E. (1986). Social issues management: An evolutionary perspective. In D. A. Wren & J. A. Pearce II (eds), *Papers dedicated to the development of modern management: Celebrating 100 years of modern management: 50th anniversary of the Academy of Management* (52–57). Academy of Management.

Preston, L. E. & Post, J. E. 1975. *Private management and public policy: The principle of public responsibility.* Englewood Cliffs, NJ: Prentice Hall.

Rawls, J. (1971). *A theory of justice.* Cambridge, MA: Harvard University Press.

Reed, L., Getz, K., Collins, D., Oberman, W. & Toy, R. (1990). Theoretical models and empirical results: A review and synthesis of JAI volumes 1–10. In L. E. Preston (ed.), *Corporation and society research: Studies in theory and measurement* (pp. 27–62). Greenwich, CT: JAI Press.

Robinson, J. (1962). *Economic philosophy.* Chicago: Aldine.

Rokeach, M. (1973). *The nature of human values.* New York: Free Press.

Schein, E. H. (1985). *Organizational culture and leadership.* San Francisco: Jossey-Bass.

Scott, R. W. (1987). *Organizations: Rational, natural, and open systems.* Englewood Cliffs, NJ: Prentice Hall.

Selznick. P. (1957). *Leadership in administration.* New York: Harper & Row.

Selznick, P. (1992). *The moral commonwealth.* Berkeley: University of California Press.

Sen, A. (1977). Social choice theory: A reexamination. *Econometrica, 45,* 53–89.

Sen, A. (1987). *On ethics and economics.* Oxford, England: Blackwell Publishing

Sethi, S. P. (1979). A conceptual framework for environmental analysis of social issues and evaluation of business response patterns. *Academy of Management Review, 4,* 63–74.

Sethi, S. P. (1982). Corporate political involvement. *California Management Review. 24*(3), 32–42.

Steidlmeier, P. (1987). Corporate social responsibility and business ethics. In S. P. Sethi & C. Falbe (eds), *Business and society: Dimensions of conflict and cooperation* (pp. 101–121). New York: Lexington Books.

Steiner, G. A. (1983). *Business and society.* New York: Macmillan.

Swanson, D. (2000). Codetermination: A business and government partnership in procedural safety for ecological sustainability. *Systems Research and Behavioral Science, 17,* 527–542.

Swanson, D. L. (2002) Business ethics and economics. In R. Frederick. (ed.), *A companion to business ethics* (pp. 207–217). Malden, MA: Blackwell Publishing.

Swanson, D. L. (2008). Normative/descriptive distinction. In R. Kolb (ed.), *Encyclopedia of Business Ethics and Society*. Thousand Oaks, CA: Sage.

Velasquez, M. G. (1982). *Business ethics: Concepts and cases*. Englewood Cliffs, NJ: Prentice Hall.

Vidaver-Cohen, D. & Altman, B. (2000). Concluding remarks: Corporate citizenship in the new millennium: Foundation for an architecture of excellence. *Business and Society Review, 105*, 145–168.

Vogel, D. (1991). The ethical roots of business ethics. *Business Ethics Quarterly, 1*, 101–120.

Votaw, D. & Sethi, S. P. (1969). Do we need a new corporate response to a changing social environment? *California Management Review. 12*(1), 3–31.

Wartick, S. L. & Cochran, P. L. (1985). The evolution of the corporate social performance model. *Academy of Management Review, 10*, 758–769.

Waddell, S. (2000). New institutions for the practice of corporate citizenship: Historical, intersectoral, and developmental perspectives. *Business and Society Review, 105*, 107–126.

Waddock, S. (2002). *Leading corporate citizens: Vision, values, value added*. New York: McGraw-Hill Irwin.

Wartick, S. L. & Rude, R. E. (1986). Issues management: Corporate fad or corporate function? *California Management Review, 29*(1), 124–140.

Weber, J. (1993). Institutionalizing ethics into business organizations. *Business Ethics Quarterly, 3*, 419–436.

Weidenbaum, M. (1977). *Business, government, and the public*. Englewood Cliffs, NJ: Prentice Hall.

Werhane, P. H. (1985). *Persons, rights, and corporations*. Englewood Cliffs, NJ: Prentice Hall.

Williams, R. (1979). Change and stability in values and value systems: A sociological perspective. In M. Rokeach (ed.), *Understanding human values* (pp. 15–46). New York: Free Press.

Wood, D. I. (1987). Strategic uses of public policy. In S. P. Sethi & C. Falbe (eds), *Business and society: Dimensions of conflict and cooperation* (pp. 75–100). New York: Lexington Books.

Wood, D. I. (1991a). Corporate social performance revisited. *Academy of Management Review, 16*, 691–718.

Wood, D. J. (1991b). Social issues in management: Theory and research in corporate social performance. *Journal of Management, 17*, 383–406.

Wood, D. J. (1991c). Toward improving corporate social performance. *Business Horizons, 34*(4), 66–73.

Wood, D. J. & Jones, R. E. (1994). *Research in corporate social performance: What have we learned?* Paper presented at the Conference on Corporate Philanthropy, sponsored by the Center for Corporate Philanthropy, University of Indiana, and the Mandel Center of Case Western Reserve University, Cleveland.

Zeitlin, M. (1978). Managerial theory vs. class theory of corporate capitalism. In L. E. Preston (ed.), *Research in corporate social performance and policy* (vol. 1, 255–263). Greenwich CT: JAI Press.

2
Toward an Integrative Theory of Value-based Leadership

This chapter takes up where the last left off. Specifically, corporate social performance topics are further reformulated to move inquiry beyond problems of integration and toward a coherent approach that can inform theory and practice, keeping in mind that the mission of the business and society field is to find and develop a constructive business relationship with society. This search is inherently normative, because it seeks to explain what corporations should or should not do on behalf of the social good (Buchholz, 1989; Frederick, 1986; Waddock, 2002; Wood, 1991b). The endeavor necessarily involves factual accounts of corporate activity as well. However, the normative (what corporations should or should not do) and the descriptive (what corporations do or can do) are difficult to blend into one theoretical perspective for corporate social performance, although the approach taken in Chapter 1 can be seen as an important first step toward reconciliation. This dilemma parallels the antagonism between the duty-aligned approach (influenced by ethics research) and the economic perspective (shaped by management research) detailed in that chapter. The conundrum is serious. Many prominent scholars hold that a coherent theory of business and society will be kept at bay until an integration of the normative and descriptive is forged (Donaldson & Dunfee, 1994; Donaldson & Preston, 1995;

This chapter originally was published in 1999 as Diane L. Swanson, 'Toward an integrative theory of business and society: A research strategy for corporate social performance', *Academy of Management Review 24*, 506–521. In 2001 it was selected to receive the 'Best Article Award' from the International Association for Business and Society with sponsorship from *California Management Review*. It was revised for publication in this book. The material of the original chapter was used with permission of the Academy of Management.

Frederick, 1994; Freeman, 1994; Jones & Wicks, 1999; Quinn & Jones, 1995).[1]

This chapter considers the 'integration dilemma' in terms of the lack of unification of the normative and the descriptive by first analyzing how this dilemma manifests in business and society research in general and in corporate social performance literature in particular. As part of this analysis, certain theory-building problems that illuminate the persistent nature of this dilemma and its threat to the aims of business and society inquiry are identified. Second, theory-building problems are addressed *vis-à-vis* a research strategy that organizes corporate social performance topics according to the concept of value. Third, a research strategy is employed that yields two *ideal types* of corporate social interactions: *value neglect* and *value attunement*. Value neglect elaborates on the theory problems posed by the lack of integration. In comparison, value attunement demonstrates the potential for a normative-descriptive unification and its theory-building advantages. In other words, *neglect* is a theoretical devise that reflects the logical implications of the integration dilemma while *attunement* seeks to move inquiry beyond these problems. In the fourth and final section of this chapter, some implications of attunement for future research aimed at coherent theory development are examined.

A theoretical dilemma in business and society research

Generally speaking, business and society literature has been shaped by two kinds of inquiry. The most long-standing is that by management theorists and social scientists; the more recent comes from business ethicists or applied philosophers. The following discussion demonstrates that the two groups have habits of inquiry different enough to resist blending. That is, the normative concerns of ethicists are very often in conflict with the focus on description of management theorists. Jones and Wicks (1999) hold that this conflict poses methodological problems for the stakeholder model of the firm in that it detracts from understanding how managers can create workable, moral business environments for stakeholders. Later it is shown how the integration dilemma is evident in business and society literature called 'corporate social performance'.

Normative versus descriptive business ethics

Philosophers who analyze business and society are concerned with its normative dimensions. This concern, however, does not blend easily with the interests of management theorists and social scientists who describe the facts of business. Indeed, an entire issue of Business Ethics Quarterly (1994) is devoted to the antagonism between normative and empirical approaches to business ethics. In that issue Treviño and Weaver (1994) elaborate on some reasons for the tension. They observe that normative philosophy is centered on moral evaluation, judgment, and prescription of human action (see also Treviño & Weaver, 2003).

By comparison, empiricism seeks explanation, measurement, and prediction: it assumes that observable causal relationships exist among variables and that they are subject to influence or intervention (Treviño & Weaver, 1994, p. 115). So too does management science in its search to describe how behavior in organizations can be directed toward certain goals (e.g., wealth maximization). Such elevation of instrumental reasoning and consequences is typical of social science-based theory, which contrasts sharply with the primacy granted to moral principles in formal ethics (Jones & Wicks, 1999).

Brady (1985) describes the contrast between consequentialism and formalism in ethical analysis as a 'Janus-headed' view of business and society. On the one hand, consequentialism looks forward to focus on the best results through innovative means. From this viewpoint, managers are considered instrumentally ethical if their moral conduct pays off in terms of owners' wealth maximization (Quinn & Jones, 1995). Consequentialism of this kind is ethically relative because the value of ends can justify different means.

On the other hand, ethical formalism looks backward to ethical tradition for principles that are absolute and have universal application. It is assumed that morality is intrinsic and cannot be legitimized by goals (Quinn & Jones, 1995). Since both views (consequentialism and formalism) have claimed to possess exclusive decision procedures, they are not easy to reconcile (Brady, 1990). In sum, the integration dilemma is well recognized in business ethics as a predicament of blending factual diagnosis and moral prescription.

Normative versus descriptive approaches to corporate social performance

The longitudinal view. It is also possible to distinguish between normative and descriptive approaches to business and society by taking a longitudinal perspective. Frederick (1987, 2006) has delineated three historic phases. The first phase called for corporate responsibility to society, the second elaborated on managerial tools for responsiveness, and the third phase is concerned with ethics and values. The second phase of corporate social responsiveness is mostly descriptive, whereas the first and third are markedly normative. Taken as a whole, these three phases constitute the bulk of research on corporate social performance. Yet the normative and descriptive approaches to this research have not been theoretically integrated (Mitnick, 1995), a dilemma that can be brought into sharper focus by examining the consolidation of corporate social performance topics into organizing schemes for research.

The consolidated view. Classifications of corporate social performance topics, referred to as 'CSP models', include works by Carroll (1979), Wartick and Cochran (1985), Wood (1991a), and Swanson (1995). Each taxonomy extends and revises earlier conceptions of business and society. As a consolidated classification of research, the CSP model can enhance theory-building efforts; it can show interrelationships among diverse topics and provide coherent structures for assessing their relevance to central questions in the field (Jones, 1983; Mitnick, 1993).

That most CSP models emphasize corporate social responsibility as a normative restraint to corporate social responsiveness is perhaps an unintended artifact of Carroll's taxonomy. Carroll drew on initial research in the field to categorize hierarchically society's expectations of business responsibilities. In order of decreasing importance, these responsibilities are economic, legal, ethical, and discretionary.

The firm's fundamental economic obligation is attenuated first by the laws and regulations that comprise the legal category. Economic obligations are then further tempered by ethical responsibilities or social expectations and norms not yet codified into law. These legal and ethical restraints on corporate activity constitute social control of business (Friedman, 1970), now taken into account even by staunch supporters of the wealth maximization view of the firm (Quinn & Jones, 1995). This state of affairs was discussed in Chapter 1 as a shared interest in social control or negative duty expressed by the economic and duty-aligned perspectives. Discretionary responsibilities go beyond those required by social control; included are activities that help society, such as corporate philanthropy and programs that address social problems (e.g., corporate training programs for disadvantaged workers, in-house day care centers, and so on). Unlike social restraint, the discretionary category refers to positive duty or the willingness of decision makers to exercise affirmative obligations. These duties, however, are entirely voluntary and of smallest importance in a hierarchy of controls on corporate economic activity.[2]

Subsequent models by Wartick and Cochran (1985) and Wood (1991a) continue the hierarchical presentation of responsibility and the emphasis on restraint. Wartick and Cochran's categories of responsibility are sub-sumed into 'principles' buttressed by aspects of social contract and moral agency arguments. According to the first argument, society not only confers legitimacy on business because of its economic role but enters into a contract with business, by which its behavior is brought into conformity with social expectations (Donaldson, 1983). Moral agency reinforces the normatively freighted tone of the contract view by holding that if corporations have moral status, they should, like people, assume moral burdens (Donaldson, 1983; Werhane, 1985).

Wood (1991a) argues that since principles of corporate social respon-sibility express social values that can motivate societal, organizational, and individual action, one must specify their levels of application. Her model identifies three distinct levels for the categories of responsibility: institutional, organizational, and individual. Across these levels and consistent with previous models, responsibility is still formulated mostly as social control. On the institutional level, Wood uses Davis's Iron Law of Responsibility (1973) to codify the Institutional Principle of Corporate Social Responsibility: society grants legitimacy and power to business; if business does not use this power responsibly, society may revoke it. Again, this threat is consistent with the emphasis on social control as a central theme in the field (Jones, 1983; Mitnick, 1981; Wood, 1991c), reinforced by interpretations of social contract and moral agency arguments.

Social curbs on business activity are yet further stressed in Wood's (1991a) articulation of the organizational principle. Based on Preston and Post's (1975) view of business and society as interpenetrating sys-tems, this principle limits corporate duty to those social problems that can be related to a firm's economic operations. Since this system's view does not propose how business activity should be conducted so that social restraint is not so necessary, its rendition of organizational responsibility has a *post hoc* quality.

The *post hoc* tone is continued in Wood's identification of the indi-vidual principle of responsibility: managers are obliged to exercise their discretion toward socially responsible outcomes. This principle ori-ginated with what has been described as Carroll's hierarchy of corporate responsibilities. Again, it addresses the voluntary duties of managers not specifically prohibited or demanded of their companies because of their known economic, legal, and ethical responsibilities. Although social restraint is still stressed, the individual principle accommodates affirm-ative or positive duty as well. Nevertheless, since affirmative duty is last in a hierarchy of other responsibilities, it is granted lesser importance in a narrowed range of managerial decision making. The possibility is not acknowledged that factoring affirmative duty into managerial decisions concurrently with other criteria may alleviate the need to curb business activity with social control. Thus, the discretionary category does little to alleviate the otherwise bridled intonation of responsibility.

Unlike the restraint associated with responsibility, corporate social responsiveness refers more to how organizations actively interact with and manage their environments. For example, Carroll's (1979) model, based on Sethi's (1975) earlier work, shows responsiveness correlated with concepts of identification, analysis, capacity, change, and development. These are specific means by which corporations can respond to identifiable social issues. The response styles and the degrees of managerial action implied range on a continuum from no response (do nothing) to a proactive response (do much).

Besides academic uses, Carroll's model is a 'diagnostic problem-solving tool' for planning, aimed at assisting managers in their conceptualization and analysis of social issues (1979, p. 503). Its instrumentalism hints at a means-ends continuum embedded in subsequent models. Wartick and Cochran express the continuum by linking means of responsiveness to goal-oriented policies of social issues management. Wood's model reinforces the means-ends continuum by identifying outcomes of corporate behavior as social (1) impacts, (2) programs, and (3) policies. These outcomes result from means of responsiveness as (1) environmental assessment, (2) stakeholder management, and (3) issues management.

Corporate social performance theory-building problems

To recap, most CSP models emphasize the social obligations of business as responsibilities. Responsiveness, however, is cast as the way corporations interact with and manage their environments. The moral restraint of responsibility (what corporations should not do) contrasts uneasily with the prospective action of responsiveness (what corporations can do). As core concepts in business and society, responsibility and responsiveness should, ideally, have continuity of meaning (Sethi, 1975). That they do not recalls the antagonism between normative and descriptive approaches to business ethics and the Janus-headed model of business and society. Like ethical formalism, responsibility tends to look backwards, relying on traditions of social control embodied in law and ethical custom. This retrospection diverges from responsiveness, which looks forward to pick the best possible means, innovations, and practices for achieving desired results. This divergence of views goes hand in hand with the integration dilemma or the lack of unification of normative and descriptive approaches (Swanson, 2008a). The following discussion clarifies why the dilemma persists and how it can undermine the very aims of business and society inquiry.

The self-perpetuating nature of the integration dilemma

Mutually reinforcing dichotomies. The integration dilemma persists because it is self-perpetuating. This occurs for two interrelated reasons. The first is that comparable dichotomies legitimate the segregation of research along normative and descriptive lines. This segregation, in turn, supports the continued use of the dichotomies for research. In this way the lack of integration continually reproduces itself or is self-perpetuating.

Consider, for example, the distinction between 'what should be' and 'what is' in the field's corporate governance literature (Wartick & Cochran, 1985). Although used to identify governance issues, the distinction ultimately serves to maintain separate domains for normative and descriptive inquiry. This is true also of research on corporate social investment, which distinguishes between two seemingly unrelated goals: making value judgments about desirable investments and describing objectively what corporations will do under various circumstances (Keim, 1978).

Moreover, the separation of 'should' and 'is' manifests as three distinct groupings of stakeholder research: normative, descriptive, and instrumental (Donaldson & Preston, 1995). The first is concerned with why stakeholder interests should be taken into account, the second reports on whether and how they are taken into account, and the last assesses the effects of stakeholder management on the achievement of corporate goals. Instead of being complementary, the three groupings function more as alternative approaches to stakeholder theory (Donaldson & Preston, 1995). Typically, the normative is associated with ethical theory, whereas the instrumental subsumes empirical and descriptive research (Jones & Wicks, 1999). Hence, the stakeholder groupings can perpetuate, rather than challenge, the separation of normative and descriptive approaches.

It is possible that the various forms of dichotomy represent an illegitimate bifurcation of values from facts in business and society research (Buchholz & Rosenthal, 1995; Freeman, 1999; Victor & Stephens, 1994; Wicks, 1996). The fact-value separation becomes taken for granted and perpetuated as scholars segregate their findings accordingly. Research proceeds as if dichotomies were real rather than intellectually invented and deserving of scrutiny (Frederick, 1994). The danger is that dichotomies can become habits of inquiry that reinforce one another and seemingly legitimate the very fact-value separation on which they are based.

The immunization of means-ends logic from normative evaluation. A corollary to the first is the second reason the integration dilemma is self-perpetuating. When research is dichotomized according to fact-value distinctions, means-ends (instrumental) logic becomes immunized from normative evaluation (Dewey, 1939). This 'immunization problem' is articulated in a well-known proclamation, often posed as a question: Isn't business ethics an oxymoron? Inherent in this query is the perception that business and ethics are contradictory terms and that normative evaluation of business practice is neither possible nor desirable (Wicks, 1996). This perception, in turn, perpetuates the bifurcation of research into normative and descriptive domains.

The significance of the immunization problem has long been recognized by organizational theorists. Notably, Max Weber (1922/1947) held that organizations can be tools for instrumental rationality or the empirically-based selection of means for stated goals. However, these goals should ideally be defined by substantive or affirmative human purposes. Along these lines, some business and society scholars have conceptualized normative considerations as fully embodied in instrumental efforts (e.g., Buchholz & Rosenthal, 1995; Donaldson & Preston, 1995; Frederick, 1995; Freeman, 1999; Gilbert, 1996; Quinn & Jones, 1995). Yet, normative purposes are not guaranteed by the instrumental actions of organizations (Scott & Hart, 1979), just as responsibility is not guaranteed by responsiveness, although the instrumentalism of responsiveness should ideally serve the normative standards represented by responsibility. When it does not, an inversion of business and society aims is possible, discussed next.

An inversion of research aims

It has been argued that the absence of integration is self-perpetuating for two interrelated reasons: one, dichotomies reinforce it; two, instrumental reasoning becomes immunized from normative evaluation. For these reasons, a third problem can occur: an inversion of the aims of business and society inquiry. Again, these aims are to find and develop a normatively constructive business and society relationship. The inversion problem means that responsibility as social control can be defined by vested interests instead of by values that serve the broader social good. Responsiveness involves very effective means (e.g., lobbying) by which business organizations can shape and influence the law, public policy, and ethical expectations. Hence, what constitutes social control can be shaped by a variety of special interest groups (Brady, 2001; Frederick, 1986; Jacobs, 1999; Matten, Crane & Chapple, 2003; Weidenbaum, 1977). Obviously, it does not serve the mission of the business and society field for responsibility to be defined by shifting political aims.

The point is that the integration dilemma means that responsiveness lacks clearly understood normative direction. The problem is hardly alleviated by the possibility that certain positive duties can serve the social good, because these duties are de-emphasized in the examined principles of responsibility. Arguably, the discretionary category of responsibility fits better with the forward-looking analysis of responsiveness, in that it supports a more prospective interpretation of the social contract: that business should display an affirmative willingness to enhance social welfare and search for opportunities to do so (Donaldson, 1983, 1989).

The idea that corporations should anticipate social expectations has always been implicit in responsiveness (Sethi, 1975). Yet, the closely related notion of positive duty lacks strong reinforcement from principles of responsibility when it is de-emphasized by the assignment of a narrow range of discretion. This assignment is consistent with the lack of attention to a prospective sense of responsibility in management research (Quinn & Jones, 1995). The research strategy developed next addresses such theory-building deficiencies.

A research strategy

Research in business and society has been described as largely fractured along normative and descriptive lines. The lack of integration and the concomitant fixation on social control instead of prospective responsibility does not promote coherent theory-building. What business organizations should do and what they can do are but complementary aspects of one unifying theme: corporations have as one of their principal functions the serving of the social good (Selznick, 1957; Swanson, 1995).

Presented next is a three part research strategy that reformulates responsibility and responsiveness so that they can be granted their inherent continuity of meaning. To that end, CSP topics are (1) organized according to values, (2) conceptualized as decision-based value processes and (3) interpreted as two ideal types of responsiveness or contrasting frames of reference for theory development.

Organize responsibility and responsiveness according to values

The first part of the research strategy is to organize topics related to responsibility and responsiveness according to values. This method is consistent with theory development based on grouping objects of investigation according to relationships based on similarities (Kuhn, 1962). If the objects have concepts in common, then logical associations can be made more easily (Jones, 1983; Stogdill, 1970).

The unifying potential of the 'value concept' is conveyed by Kluckholn's (1951) definition of a value as a belief – implicit or explicit – that influences the selection from available modes, means, and ends of actions. As beliefs, values are already implicit in principles of responsibility. Wartick and Cochran (1985) base their principles on the conviction that corporations must behave in a manner consistent with social values.

Values are also embodied in CSP models as goal orientations. Wood's (1991a) principles convey that values can motivate corporate behaviors that result in social outcomes. Detailed in Chapter 1, Swanson (1995) subsequently modeled values as bound up in processes of responsiveness, which lead to social impacts.

Conceptualize responsibility and responsiveness as decision-based value processes

The second part of the research strategy is to conceptualize responsibility and responsiveness as decision-based value processes. Values operate dynamically across individual, organizational, and societal levels of analysis to influence decision making (Etzioni, 1988; Williams, 1979). Weick (1969) describes three decision processes that can be used to conceptualize the role of values across these levels. These processes – selection, retention, and enactment – represent ways information variety gets introduced into organizational decision making. Selection involves the filtering of data by decision makers so that the equivocality or lack of clarity regarding information is reduced. Retention determines what information decision makers can recall for further use. Finally, enactment means that the processing of information by organizational participants ultimately creates the environment to which an organization adapts (Scott, 1987).

Weick's perspective can be applied to responsibility and responsiveness as follows: the social values pertaining to responsibility are subject to decision processes, which result in the enactment of environments to which organizations respond. Based on this view, 'enacted responsiveness' involves (1) the executive's normative orientation to social policy, (2) formal organizational decision making, (3) informal organizational decision making, and (4) external affairs management. The importance of these categories to the research strategy is outlined below, starting with the executive level of analysis.

The executive's normative orientation to social policy. The personally held values of senior managers strongly influence their formulation of corporate social policy (Frederick & Weber, 1987; Guth & Tagiuri, 1965; Waddock, 2002). The implementation of policy, in turn, significantly affects society's perception of the legitimacy of the business as an institution (Miles, 1987). Hence, the executive's normative orientation to policy can influence the extent to which a firm is deemed socially responsible (Swanson, 2008b). This policy orientation also can influence enacted responsiveness by impacting the selection and retention of values by other organizational actors, starting with decision making in the formal organization.

Formal organizational decision making. In the formal organization, executive value premises are communicated to subordinates along a chain of command, setting the range for the subordinates' decision-making discretion (Simon, 1957). This occurs as decisions at each hierarchical level are directed toward a value-derived goal set by a higher level of administration (Perrow, 1986). Although specific values vary from organization to organization, England (1967) categorizes three general types that can become part of formal decisions.

The first category of operative values is that which decision makers rank as highly important, and these values are deemed successful in organizational life. Operative values have the greatest impact on decisions: organizational actors act directly on them by channeling information into defined responses to problems. Taking Weick's (1969) view, when subordinates select and activate the value premises of executives, the equivocality of information is reduced.

The second set of adopted values is those that subordinates observe as being successful in organizational life, but they do not rank them as highly important. Although these values are not internalized, they still will be selected and activated along the chain of command.

The third grouping of intended values is considered highly important; however, these values do not fit the subordinate's organizational experience. Because these professed values are seen as being neither permissible nor useful, they are rarely selected to be instrumental in problem solving (Argyris & Schon, 1978). Professed values, therefore, are not activated in hierarchical decision processes. They are retained, instead, as inactive or latent.

Informal organizational decision making. Operative, adopted, and intended values also pertain to the more informal domain of organizational culture. Schein (1985) observes that, in this realm, values strongly influence the processes by which groups in organizations try to solve problems and tasks posed by the environment. In other words, organizational culture helps determine enacted responsiveness. Similarly, Feldman (2002, pp. 4–5) presents culture as a 'chain of memory' that morally regulates relationships.

Schein describes primary and secondary means as the methods executives use to signal which values should be selected (as operative and adopted) or suppressed. Primary means are what executives pay attention to and are their criteria for recruitment and promotion. Secondary means are the design of organizational structure, systems, and procedures, as well as executive statements about organizational philosophy. Executives can also seek to influence retention through the positive sanctioning of desirable values in rituals and ceremonies. Schein refers to this form of retention as 'maintenance'.

External affairs management. Because external affairs management spans the boundary between organizations and their environments, one can view it as pivotal to enacted responsiveness. External affairs subordinates are charged with detecting information about the environment, which they relay to senior managers and other employees (Ackerman & Bauer, 1976; Waddock, 2002). This information is selected yet again if factored into hierarchical and group-based decision processes. When retained in this manner, the value-laden information determines an organization's response to the external environment (Schein, 1985). Thus, external affairs can be viewed as a value-detecting instrument that strongly influences enacted responsiveness.

Interpret the value processes as ideal types of responsiveness

The third part of the research strategy is to cast the value processes of selection, retention, and enactment according to the ideal type. This method accentuates a one-sided view, allowing a researcher to consider what characteristics a pure criterion would have (Bailey, 1994). Weber (1922/1947) vaulted the ideal type into prominence by using it to capture the distinctive elements of bureaucratic organizations, the interrelationships among these elements, and their logical implications. As a result, classifications and ideal types are now considered complementary steps in theory-building.

Classifications identify distinct research subjects that yield logical implications when formulated as ideal types (Bailey, 1994). Accordingly, the research subjects classified in CSP models will be used to formulate two ideal types of responsiveness: neglect and attunement. Again, the first will illustrate more concretely the logical fallacies posed by the integration dilemma, and the second will explore the potential for blending the normative and descriptive approaches to business and society. Obviously, the two heuristics *do not* represent actual organizations, nor do they constitute theory. It is important to keep in mind that the ideal types, developed next, are designed as contrasting frames of reference for further theory development.

The ideal type of value-neglect responsiveness

According to the research strategy, the first ideal type conceptualizes value processes in terms of (1) the executive's normative orientation to social policy, (2) formal organizational decision making, (3) informal organizational decision making, and (4) external affairs management.

Across these categories, theory-building problems are accentuated as (1) *normative myopia*, (2) the *hierarchical circumscription* of value information, (3) the role of *value-inert culture*, and (4) *value-restricted* external affairs. Value neglect responsiveness is implied. In Figure 2.1 these characterizations of theory-building problems are placed in boxes, with related topics bracketed. Interrelationships among them are shown by arrows.

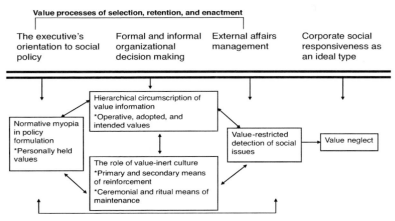

Figure 2.1   Value Neglect

Normative myopia

Normative myopia typifies corporate social policy consistent with the integration dilemma. In this instance a myopic executive would perceive values as irrelevant to a factual diagnosis of policy. Yet, as indicated in Figure 2.1, executives do, in fact, hold personal values that strongly influence their decisions (Frederick & Weber, 1987; Guth & Tagiuri, 1965; Waddock, 2002). Paradoxically, then, *myopic* policy making would be distorted by the misperception that it is value free.

Scott and Hart (1979) refer to this dilemma as 'unexamined determinism'. That is, executives who dismiss normative philosophy as irrelevant end up referencing certain personally held values without examination. Moreover, the values most referenced are those supporting narrow organizational goals – not broader community interests. According to Scott and Hart, this downplaying of community values is the organizational imperative of the modern corporation.

Consistent with unexamined determinism, executives who exhibit *myopia* would not recognize social interests in the firm as valid unless those interests happen to coincide with their personally held beliefs. The organizational imperative suggests that this intersection of interests simply would legitimize the *status quo* of myopic policy. Myopia recalls the immunization problem, in that it denotes corporate policy invulnerable to the influence of broader social values. According to the logic in the examined principles of responsibility, the typical solution to myopia would be social control.

In other words, this solution implies that if corporate policy diverges from social expectations, it should be forced to conform to the law, public policy, and ethical custom. The inversion problem is ever present in this rendition of responsibility because the values that could serve the social good are not clearly identified. The principles are remarkably silent on the possibility that myopic executives could influence the social control of their own firms.

The hierarchical circumscription of value information

Myopia portends a scarcity of value information available for problem solving in the formal organization. This follows from previous descriptions of how operative, adopted, and intended values are selected and retained in organizations. Value information would be circumscribed as subordinates seek conformity with myopia, selecting the executive-held values viewed as successful and suppressing those deemed otherwise.

Said differently, formal organizational decision processes would align with executive normative myopia. Two-way arrows in Figure 2.1 depict the alignment as mutually perpetuating: executives would receive information feedback that merely restates their own narrow, unexamined beliefs. This 'hierarchical circumscription' could not be offset by employees' intended values, because they would be retained in latent state – unavailable for problem solving.

According to previous analysis, the individual principle of responsibility does not address how the normative discretion of subordinates can be restricted by executive beliefs. Again, the principle's discretionary range is defined by standards of social control, which themselves can be immunized from normative evaluation.

The role of value-inert culture

In terms of ideal typing, 'value-inert culture' denotes the reinforcement and maintenance of value circumscription in the informal organization. Executives may, for instance, reinforce circumscription by promoting employees who exhibit like-minded myopia. Using Schein's (1985) lexicon, the criteria for such promotions would be primary reinforcers and the procedures for them secondary. Myopic executives may also seek to maintain circumscription by the positive sanctioning of rituals and ceremonies that publicly acclaim myopia and circumscription. An example is company-wide meetings at which myopic employees are recognized affirmatively.

Value-restricted external affairs

The above decision processes would hamper the ability of external affairs to detect the values driving social interests in the firm. In lieu of a comprehensive analysis of these values, external affairs employees would adhere to a myopia that is reinforced by prerogatives of status and maintained by ceremonial rituals. Social values perceived as incongruent with the *status quo* would be de-emphasized, misconstrued, not communicated to the executive office, or simply not detected in the first place.

Two-way arrows in Figure 2.1 indicate that value restriction can be systematically reinforced when deficient information is transmitted back and forth among external affairs employees and other decision makers. The long feedback loop indicates that the dearth of information would logically perpetuate myopia, as executives receive and transmit insufficient information about corporate social policy.

Value-neglect responsiveness

Research suggests that the self-referenced and inward-looking organization described so far will not be able to adapt effectively to social
values that diverge from its own narrowly conceived ones (Dutton &
Dukerich, 1991; Purser, Park & Montouri, 1995; Swanson, 1992). Nor
is such an organization poised to learn about complex and dynamic
environments. Basic learning depends on a system's incorporation of
information that deviates from operating norms; it denotes an ability
to respond to feedback that is different from previously processed
information (Weiner, 1961). To go beyond basic learning and to 'learn
to learn' requires that the relevance of operating norms be questioned
(Argyris & Schon, 1974; Bateson, 1972; Pondy & Mitroff, 1979).

The value-neglect organization illustrated in Figure 2.1 is not well
equipped to engage in basic and advanced learning about social values.
Instead, its enacted environment would be defined by a narrow set of
unexamined beliefs. That these beliefs could incidentally correspond to
some social expectations would not necessarily constitute responsibility.
Discussed later, corporate policy can be aimed at economic efficiency
and yet be neglectful of other important social values.

At any rate, the implication that neglectful organizations could easily
deviate from social expectations corresponds to a form of the immunization problem as a failure of business to adhere to evaluative norms.
Ironically then, social control would be especially pertinent to organizations exhibiting neglect. That such organizations could influence
what counts as social control recalls the inversion problem. In short,
value-neglect responsiveness accentuates the theory-building obstacles
posed by the integration dilemma.

The ideal type of value-attuned responsiveness

The second ideal type also models value processes in terms of (1) the
executive's normative orientation to social policy, (2) formal organizational decision making, (3) informal organizational decision making,
and (4) external affairs management. In contrast to neglect, Figure 2.2
depicts these categories as (1) *normative receptivity*, (2) the *hierarchical
expansion* of value information, (3) the role of *value-discovery* culture,
and (4) *value-expanded* external affairs. The value-attuned responsiveness implied should properly be viewed as a reformulation of CSP
topics for the purpose of exploring theoretical integration. Like value
neglect, value attunement is an ideal type that captures the distinctive
elements of the topics under consideration, the interrelationships

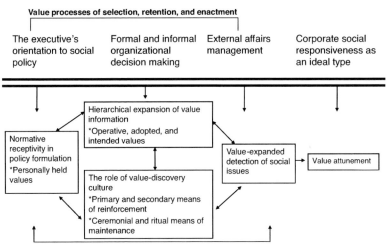

Figure 2.2 Value Attunement

among these elements, and their logical implications. As a pure type of logic, it provides a contrasting benchmark to value-neglect for the purposes of integrative theory-building.

Normative receptivity

In contrast to the normative myopia associated with neglect, normative receptivity denotes a perception that values and facts are inseparable in policy formulation. It follows that the executive with such perception may consciously acknowledge the influence of his or her personally held values on policy and that the values held by others deserve consideration. A senior manager with this broadened orientation may potentially direct an organizational expansion of value information, beginning with formal or hierarchical decision making.

The hierarchical expansion of value information

The *receptive* executive may encourage the examination of many values along the decision-making chain of command. During this process, some latent values may be activated, increasing the organization's potential for value variety. Hence, 'expansion' refers to the enlargement of an organization's inventory of values for instrumental endeavors.

Two-way arrows in Figure 2.2 depict the mutually sustaining feasibility of expansion: receptive executives might receive information feedback that enhances their understanding of the values pertinent to policy. Notwithstanding this prospect, the filtering of data by hierarchy means that some deficiencies in policy making are inevitable (March & Simon, 1958; Simon, 1957). Ultimately, then, hierarchy would be a recalcitrant tool for value expansion – a limitation discussed later as a problem of organizational design.

The role of value-discovery culture

'Discovery' refers to the reinforcement and maintenance of value expansion in organizational culture. For instance, the recruitment of employees adept at identifying and analyzing values may function as a primary reinforcer of expansion. The selection of employees with such skills is consistent with the 'person-organization fit' approach to human resource management. According to this view, the skills of employees should match the overall demands of the organization's work environment, instead of that of a narrow job description (Bowen, Ledford & Nathan, 1991). If corporations and society are interpenetrating value systems, as suggested by previous analysis, then value considerations permeate the work environment of organizations. It follows that the ability to identify and analyze values is an important skill for employees to possess or develop. We revisit this point in Chapter 10 in terms of hiring employees with relatively high levels of moral development.

Primary reinforcement for discovery may also mean rewarding employees for selecting and conveying all pertinent value data to executives, instead of only those which support current policy. Secondary reinforcement could come from systems and procedures supportive of expansion, such as training sessions aimed at improving employee value selection and analysis. Finally, maintenance may be provided by executive-sanctioned rituals and ceremonies that celebrate ways to bring about expansion, including public promotions of employees adept at value analysis.

Value-expanded external affairs

Two-way arrows in Figure 2.2 indicate that discovery goes along with a value expansion in external affairs. A culture that attends to value analysis may potentially support the detection of a wide range of social values by external affairs employees and the transmittal of this information to other organizational decision makers. The long feedback loop represents the prospect of a mutually reinforcing dynamic between the executive office and external affairs: executives who exhibit receptivity may receive more information about the values pertinent to social policy.

Value-attuned responsiveness

The expansion phenomenon points to value-attuned responsiveness. Attunement denotes the possibility that organizations can select and recall many values for learned responses to their environments. That organizations should respond affirmatively to positive social goals is a long-standing exemplar in business and society research. Many analysts have promoted corporate activity that is attuned to or aligned with values that can enhance community flourishing (e.g. Buchholz & Rosenthal, 1995; Committee for Economic Development, 1971; Eells, 1960; Frederick, 1987; Freeman, 1984; Steidlmeier, 1987).

Value attunement ameliorates theory-building problems in several ways. The immunization problem is redressed because instrumental means of policy, such as external affairs management, are not severed from normative considerations. As a result, responsiveness acquires a moral tone previously stressed for responsibility. Whereas attuned responsibility is not fixated on social control, it becomes more forward looking, prospective, and open ended. Corporations exhibiting attunement will seek to understand social values instead of reflexively warding them off or merely complying with social pressure. This typification of responsiveness renders an inversion of business and society aims less problematic. In these ways attunement demonstrates the potential for theoretical integration.

Research implications

It has been argued that value attunement brings responsibility and responsiveness closer together so that integration is possible. That this ideal type relies on means-ends logic is consistent with Freeman's (1999) call for instrumental frameworks that address normative-descriptive linkages across research topics. The potential for unification is 'symbiotic', which Treviño and Weaver (1994, 1999, 2003) hold is the reliance of the normative and descriptive upon each other for the purpose of setting research agendas. Likewise, attunement points to research needed for coherent theory development, including, first and foremost, a theory of values.

The need for a theory of values

Although attuned organizations process a wide range of value information, not all values serve the social good. For an obvious example, genocide represents a disrespect for human life antithetical to the terms of the social contract between business and society. Attunement needs to be based on an understanding of the values that can enhance community flourishing.

Such research was scarce during the first two phases of business and society research, but it is a significant part in the third, more normative phase. A notable example is Frederick's (1992, 1995, 2006) conceptualization of five value clusters relevant to business. One, economizing values refers to the ability of organizations to efficiently convert inputs to outputs. Two, ecologizing denotes symbiotic, integrative linkages between organizations and their environments that function adaptively to sustain life in communities. Three, power aggrandizing is status-enforced, self-centered corporate behavior that seeks to exercise dominance through hierarchical structure. Four, technological values represent tool-use logic by which organizations use instrumental means to reach other value goals. Finally, 'X-factor' is the set of all values held by individuals in organizations. Although it is outside the scope of this chapter to elaborate on these value clusters, it is important to note that they can take many forms of interactions characteristic of complex systems (Frederick, 1998, 2006). For example, Frederick proposes that economizing and ecologizing can be complementary in sustaining life or, as discussed next, can be subject to tradeoffs.

To understand how a theory of values can provide attunement with explanatory power, consider the long-standing controversy surrounding Nestle's sales of infant formula. For more than two decades this corporation faced social opposition to its marketing of infant formula in developing countries. Several groups, including the World Health Organization (WHO), have claimed that adverse conditions – for example, unsanitary water and low rates of literacy – render the sale of infant formula in those countries life threatening (Sethi, 1994). For these reasons the WHO, comprising more than 100 member nations, has pressured Nestle to comply with an international code meant to restrict the sales of infant formula in international markets.

According to Frederick's theory, the Nestle case can be understood as a clash of economizing and ecologizing. It appears that Nestle executives, referencing certain personally held values and using instrumental tools of marketing, directed the organization to pursue economizing at the peril of broader community values. In the absence of enforceable international law, corporate power prerogatives were exercised, instead of a proactive responsibility to sustain community life through ecologizing. In short, neglect was exhibited rather than attunement.

To reiterate, social control is a central topic in business and society research. That economizing and ecologizing can clash and that power aggrandizing can be exercised to the detriment of the community help explain why social control of business occurs. Broadly speaking, the eruption of corporate misconduct in the first part of this century and the response of Sarbanes Oxley in the U.S. can be understood in this manner. A pursuit of economic goals that risks other life-affirming values does not necessarily serve the overall good of society. And power aggrandizing or pursuing bloated corporate growth for the sake of personal gain or status is even more problematic. As an exemplar, attunement can encourage managers to factor a broad range of community interests into their decision making so that social control of business is not so necessary. A theory of values is necessary for understanding those interests that serve the social good.

Understanding the personally held values of executives. A theory of values for attunement also needs to identify the personally held beliefs that can prompt executives to deal with community interests in a willing and positive manner. Social control as massive public pressure eventually forced Nestle executives to reckon with the sales of infant formula to developing countries. Attunement suggests that some set of personally held values could have induced the executives to deal willingly and proactively with the dispute in its early stages, or to have prevented the problem in the first place.

The identification and promotion of such managerial values could mitigate the historic, hollow tenor of responsibility as social control. It could also put the integration dilemma into proper perspective – as an issue needing more psychological research than philosophical arguments. In reality, the 'glue' that holds the normative and descriptive together is in the mindsets of practicing managers (Donaldson, 1999). If managers believe that they should carry out certain ethical duties and responsibilities, then values and facts can simply represent different ways of talking about their decisions. For example, if Nestle executives had decided early on to end the sales of infant formula to developing nations, they could have justified the decision both in terms of the sanctity of life and in statistics on infant mortality.

Accounting for value relativism. A theory of values for attunement necessarily will come to terms with the relative nature of corporate social responsibility. To repeat, formalism looks for absolute principles that have universal application; consequently, it holds that ethical relativism is not valid. A more realistic position is that value relativism is inevitable in corporate social policy (Buchholz & Rosenthal, 1995; Epstein, 1987; Frederick, 1987; Wood, Logsdon, Lewellyn & Davenport, 2006). In the case of Nestle's sales of infant formula, the sobering issue of harm (infant death) existed precisely because of the circumstances of the product's use: consumer illiteracy in developing nations and the lack of access to a sanitary water supply. The dangers associated with these adverse conditions are not present for more affluent users.

Such value relativism needs to be accounted for. Otherwise, a wide range of corporate social problems could be immunized from normative analysis, which takes the facts of human experience into account. Ultimately, such a theoretic problem impacts practice. Unless moral analysis can accommodate the complexities of social phenomena, managers simply will not view ethical arguments as having credibility (Gioia, 1999).

Exploring corporate normative awareness

The moral agency argument of ethical formalism holds that the assignment of moral responsibility to corporations depends ultimately on whether intention and blame can be applied to them. Some ethicists hold that the application is not valid, and, consequently, they conclude that corporations do not have moral obligations (see Velasquez, 1983). Yet, attunement theorizing need not be stymied by philosophical arguments that organizational morality is moot. If corporate decision makers can be conscious of value selection, retention, and enactment, then the salient issue is whether normative awareness can be imbued in corporate decision processes.

This line of inquiry is not new. Some sociologists have described organizations as, essentially, vehicles of consciousness (e.g., Berger, Berger & Kellner, 1973). Indeed, analysts long have recognized that business's awareness of social values is a necessary condition for corporate responsibility (Committee for Economic Development, 1971; Epstein, 1979; Frederick, 1987; Votaw, 1972; Waddock, 2002). Research on attunement would take this normative awareness to be first and foremost an executive's responsibility. The logical alternative is some form of corporate social neglect. An extension of this line of inquiry would be to understand the neural impulses that can be expressed in individual decision making that enacts power and domination over others rather than reciprocal values that sustain attunement, especially since corporate culture can mitigate or amplify such impulses (Frederick, 2006).

Designing organizations for value expansion

The design of structures and information systems constitutes a secondary means of reinforcing value expansion in corporate cultures. Frederick's (1995) theory suggests that flatter structures might mitigate the power-aggrandizing behaviors in organizations that detract from the selection, retention, and enactment of constructive values. It stands to reason that, all else being equal, flatter organizations could transmit information pertaining to values better than taller ones (Halal, 1994).

A communicative ethic or dialogue between corporate managers and community groups based on mutual respect could be an important source of value-based information. Such moral dialogue could provide corporate decision makers with pertinent feedback regarding their firm's social responsibilities (Waddock, 2002). As part of information systems, a communicative ethic might mitigate self-referencing tendencies of organizations, resulting in their increased awareness of social concerns (Bowen, Power & Clark, 1993; Calton & Kurland, 1996; Swanson, 1996). This possibility will be explored in Chapter 3 in terms of a 'trustful dialogue' between corporations and their stakeholders.

If social values are constantly brought to the attention of executives and other employees, then a variety of values will become available for organizational problem solving. Accordingly, a communicative ethic might deter hierarchy's vise on information. Since the executive's listening style is the model for the organization (Peters, 1987; Stodgill, 1974), his or her role in establishing and facilitating a communicative ethic could constitute an important aspect of value expansion.

Conclusion

The continuity between this chapter and the last is that they both address a lack of integration between normative and descriptive approaches to corporate social performance. The theory-building problems posed by this dilemma and exemplified as value neglect substantiates the importance of avoiding fact-value fallacies in research. By comparison, value attunement demonstrates the potential for a normative-descriptive unification and theory-building advantages in terms of executive policy making, formal and informal organizational decision making, and external affairs management as instrumental, interrelated value processes. This reformulation is addressed further in the next chapter, which extends attunement theorizing while underscoring the importance of values to it.

Notes

1. Noted in this chapter, the lack of integration between normative and descriptive inquiry also mars the field of business ethics, according to Treviño and Weaver (1994, 1999, 2003). The difference between their view and the

one taken here is that Treviño and Weaver are concerned with business ethics research at large, whereas Chapters 1 and 2 in this volume address the normative-descriptive divide specifically in terms of corporate social performance literature.

2. While it is outside the scope of this discussion to delve into the pros and cons of corporate philanthropy, this chapter takes the view that positive duty should be reformulated more generally as decision-making processes that facilitate a collaborative, attuned posture toward the stakeholder environment. Chapter 3 proposes that a trustful dialogue between managers and stakeholders can be an important ongoing mechanism for seeking such positive attunement.

References

Ackerman, R. W. & Bauer, R. A. (1976). *Corporate social responsiveness: The modern dilemma.* Cambridge, MA: Harvard University Press.

Argyris, C. & Schon, D. A. (1974). *Theory in practice.* San Francisco: Jossey-Bass.

Agyris, C. & Schon, D. A. (1978). *Organizational learning: A theory of action perspective.* Reading, MA: Addison-Wesley.

Bailey, K. D. (1994). *Typologies and taxonomies.* Belmont, CA: Sage.

Bateson, G. (1972). *Steps to an ecology of mind.* New York: Ballentine Books.

Berger, P., Berger, B. & Kellner, H. (1973). *The homeless mind.* New York: Vintage Books.

Bowen, D. E., Ledford, G. E. & Nathan, B. R. (1991). Hiring for the organization, not the job. *Academy of Management Executive*, 5(4), 35–51.

Bowen, M. G. & Power, F. C. (1993). The moral manager: Communicative ethics and the Exxon Valdez disaster. *Business Ethics Quarterly*, 3, 97–115.

Brady, F. N. (1985). A Janus-headed model of ethical theory: Looking two ways at business/society issues. *Academy of Management Review*, 10, 568–576.

Brady, F. N. (1990). *Ethical managing: Rules and results.* London: Macmillan.

Brady, R. A. (2001). *Business as a system of power.* New Brunswick, NY: Transaction Publishers.

Buchholz, R. A. (1989). *Business ethics.* Englewood Cliffs, NJ: Prentice-Hall.

Buchholz, R. A. & Rosenthal S. B. (1995). Theoretical foundations of public policy: A pragmatic perspective. *Business & Society*, 34, 261–279.

Calton, J. & Kurland, N. (1996). A theory of stakeholder enabling: Giving voice to an emerging postmodern praxis of organizational discourse. In D. M. Boje, R. P. Gephart, Jr. & T. J. Thatchenkery (eds), *Postmodern management and organizational theory* (pp. 154–177). Thousand Oaks, CA: Sage.

Carroll, A. (1979). A three-dimensional model of corporate social performance. *Academy of Management Review*, 4, 497–505.

Committee for Economic Development. (1971). *Social responsibilities of business corporations.* New York: Author.

Davis, K. (1973). The case for and against business assumption of social responsibilities. *Academy of Management Journal*, 16, 312–322.

Dewey, J. (1939). *Theory of valuation.* Chicago: University of Chicago Press.

Donaldson, T. (1983). Constructing a social contract for business. In T. Donaldson & P. Werhane (eds), *Ethical issues in business* (pp. 153–165). New York: Oxford University Press.

Donaldson, T. (1989). *The ethics of international business.* Englewood Cliffs, NJ: Prentice-Hall.

Donaldson, T. (1999). Making stakeholder theory whole. *Academy of Management Review, 24,* 237–241.

Donaldson, T. & Dunfee, T. W. (1994). Towards a unified conception of business ethics: Integrative social contracts theory. *Academy of Management Review, 19,* 252–284.

Donaldson, T. & Preston, L. E. (1995). The stakeholder theory of the corporation: Concepts, evidence, and implications. *Academy of Management Review, 20,* 65–91.

Dutton, J. & Dukerich, J. (1991). Keeping an eye on the mirror: Image and identity in organizational adaptation. *Academy of Management Journal, 34,* 517–554.

Eells, R. (1960). *The meaning of modern business.* New York: Columbia University Press.

England, G. W. (1967). Personal value systems of American managers. *Academy of Management Journal, 10,* 107–117.

Epstein, E. M. (1979). Societal, managerial, and legal perspectives on corporate social responsibility – product and process. *The Hastings Law Journal, 30,* 1287–1320.

Epstein, E. M. (1987). The corporate social policy process: Beyond business ethics, corporate social responsibility, and corporate social responsiveness. *California Management Review, 29*(3), 99–114.

Etzioni, E. (1988). *The moral dimension: Toward a new economics.* New York: Free Press.

Feldman, S. P. (2002). *Memory as a moral decision: The role of ethics in organizational culture.* New Brunswick, NJ: Transaction Publishing.

Frederick, W. C. (1986). Toward CSR3: Why ethical analysis is indispensable and unavoidable in corporate affairs. *California Management Review, 28*(2), 126–141.

Frederick, W. C. (1987). Theories of corporate social performance. In S. P. Sethi & C. M. Falbe (eds), *Business and society: Dimensions of conflict and cooperation* (142–161). New York: Lexington Books.

Frederick, W. C. (1992). Anchoring values in nature: Toward a theory of business values. *Business Ethics Quarterly, 2,* 283–303.

Frederick, W. C. (1994). The virtual reality of fact vs. value: A symposium commentary. *Business Ethics Quarterly, 4,* 171–173.

Frederick, W. C. (1995). *Values, nature, and culture in the American corporation.* New York: Oxford University Press.

Frederick, W. C. (1998). Creatures, corporations, communities, chaos, complexity: A naturological view of the corporate social role. *Business & Society, 37,* 358–389.

Frederick, W. C. (2006). *Corporation be good! The story of corporate social responsibility.* Indianapolis, IN: Dog Ear Publishing.

Frederick, W. C. & Weber, J. (1987). The values of corporate managers and their critics. In W. C. Frederick & L. E. Preston (eds), *Research in corporate social performance and policy* (vol. 9, pp. 131–152). Greenwich, CT: JAI Press.

Freeman, R. E. (1984). *Strategic management: A stakeholder approach.* Boston, MA: Pitman/Ballinger.

Freeman, R. E. (1994). The politics of stakeholder theory: Some future directions. *Business Ethics Quarterly, 4,* 409–421.

Freeman, R. E. (1999). Divergent stakeholder theory. *Academy of Management Review, 24*, 233–236.

Friedman, M. (1970, September). The social responsibility of business is to increase its profits. *New York Times Magazine, 33*, 122–126.

Gilbert, D. R. (1996). *Strategy and ethics.* New York: Oxford University Press.

Gioia, D. A. (1999). Practicability, paradigms, and problems in stakeholder theorizing. *Academy of Management Review, 24*, 228–232.

Guth, W. & Tagiuri, R. (1965, September–October). Personal values and corporate strategies. *Harvard Business Review, 43*, 123–132.

Halal, W. H. (1994). From hierarchy to enterprise: Internal markets are the new foundation of management. *Academy of Management Executive, 8*(4), 69–83.

Jacobs, D. C. (1999). *Business lobbies and the power structure in America: Evidence and arguments.* Westport, CT: Quorum Books.

Jones, T. M. (1983). An integrating framework for research in business and society: A step toward the elusive paradigm? *Academy of Management Review, 8*, 559–564.

Jones, T. M. & Wicks, A. C. (1999). Convergent stakeholder theory. *Academy of Management Review, 24*, 206–221.

Keim, G. D. (1978). Corporate social responsibility: An assessment of the enlightened self-interest model. *Academy of Management Review, 3*, 32–39.

Kluckholn, C. (1951). Values and value-orientations in the theory of action. In T. Parsons & E. A. Shils (eds), *Toward a general theory of action* (pp. 388–433). New York: Harper & Row.

Kuhn, J. (1962). *The structure of scientific revolutions.* Chicago: University of Chicago Press.

March, J. G. & Simon, H. (1958). *Organizations.* New York: Wiley.

Matten, D., Crane, A. C. & Chapple, W. (2003). Behind the mask: Revealing the true face of corporate citizenship. *Journal of Business Ethics, 45*, 109–120.

Miles, R. A. (1987). *Managing the corporate social environment.* Englewood Cliffs, NJ: Prentice-Hall.

Mitnick, B. M. (1981). The strategic uses of regulation – and deregulation. *Business Horizons, 24*(2), 71–83.

Mitnick, B. M. (1993). Organizing research in corporate social performance: The CSP system as core paradigm. *International Association for Business and Society Conference Proceedings* (pp. 2–15).

Mitnick, B. M. (1995). Systematics and CSR: The theory and processes of normative referencing. *Business & Society, 34*, 5–33.

Perrow, C. (1986). *Complex organizations: A critical essay.* New York: McGraw-Hill.

Peters, T. (1987). *Thriving on chaos: Handbook for a management revolution.* New York: Harper & Row.

Pondy, L. R. & Mitroff, I. I. (1979). Beyond open system models of organizations. In B. M. Staw (ed.), *Research in organizational behavior* (vol. 1, pp. 3–39). Greenwich, CT: JAI Press.

Preston, L. E. & Post, J. E. (1975). *Private management and public policy: The principle of public responsibility.* Englewood Cliffs, NJ: Prentice-Hall.

Purser, R., Park, C. & Montouri. A. (1995). Limits to anthropocentrism: Toward an ecocentric organization. *Academy of Management Review, 20*, 1053–1089.

Quinn, D. P. & Jones, T. M. (1995). An agent morality view of business policy. *Academy of Management Review, 20*, 22–42.

Schein, E. H. (1985). *Organizational culture and leadership*. San Francisco: Jossey-Bass.

Scott, W. G. & Hart, D. K. (1979). *Organizational America*. Boston, MA: Houghton Mifflin.

Scott, W. R. (1987). *Organizations: Rational natural and open systems*. Englewood Cliffs, NJ: Prentice-Hall.

Selznick. P. (1957). *Leadership in administration*. New York: Harper & Row.

Sethi, S. P. (1975). Dimensions of corporate social performance: An analytic framework. *California Management Review, 17*(3), 58–64.

Sethi, S. P. (1994). *Multinational corporations and the impact of public advocacy on corporate strategy: Nestle and the infant formula controversy*. Norwell, MA: Kluwer.

Simon, H. (1957). *Administrative behavior*. New York: Macmillan.

Steidlmeier, P. (1987). Corporate social responsibility and business ethics. In S. P. Sethi & C. M. Falbe (eds), *Business and society: Dimensions of cooperation and conflict* (pp. 101–121). New York: Lexington Books.

Stogdill, R. (ed.) 1970. Introduction. *The process of model-building in the behavioral sciences* (pp. 3-13). USA: Ohio State University Press.

Stogdill, R. (1974). *Handbook of leadership*. New York: Free Press.

Swanson, D. L. (1992). Dysfunctional conglomerates: An explanation provided by linking ontological individualism to social relations within an open systems context. *Behavioral Science, 37*, 139–154.

Swanson, D. L. (1995). Addressing a theoretical problem by reorienting the corporate social performance model. *Academy of Management Review, 20*, 43–64.

Swanson, D. L. (1996). Neoclassical economic theory, executive control, and organizational outcomes. *Human Relations, 49*, 735–755.

Swanson, D. L. (2008a). Normative/descriptive distinction. In R. Kolb (ed.), *Encyclopedia of Business Ethics and Society*. Thousand Oaks, CA: Sage.

Swanson, D. L. (2008b). Top managers as drivers for corporate social performance. In A. Crane, A. McWilliams, D. Matten, J. Moon & D. Siegel (eds), *The Oxford Handbook of CSR*. Oxford, UK: Oxford University Press.

Treviño, L. & Weaver, G. (1994). Business ethics: One field or two? *Business Ethics Quarterly, 4*, 111–125.

Treviño, L. & Weaver, G. (1999). The stakeholder research tradition: Converging theorists – not convergent theory. *Academy of Management Review, 24*, 222–227.

Treviño, L. & Weaver, G. (2003). *Managing ethics in business organizations: Social science perspectives*. Stanford, CA: Stanford University Press.

Velasquez, M. (1983). Why corporations are not responsible for anything they do. *Business & Professional Ethics Journal, 2*(3), 1–18.

Victor, B. & Stephens, C. (1994). Business ethics: A synthesis of normative philosophy and empirical social science. *Business Ethics Quarterly, 4*, 145–155.

Votaw, D. (1972). Genius becomes rare: A comment on the doctrine of social responsibility. Part 1. *California Management Review, 15*(2), 25–31.

Waddock, S. (2002). *Leading corporate citizens: Vision, values, value added*. New York: McGraw Hill.

Wartick, S. L. & Cochran, P. L. (1985). The evolution of the corporate social performance model. *Academy of Management Review, 10*, 758–769.

Weber, M. (1922/1947). *The theory of social and economic organization*. (Translated and edited by A. H. Henderson & T. Parsons.) NY: Oxford University Press.

Weick, K. E. (1969). *The social psychology of organizing.* Reading, MA: Addison-Wesley.

Weidenbaum, M. (1977). *Business, government, and the public.* Englewood Cliffs, NJ: Prentice-Hall.

Weiner, N. (1961). *Cybernetics.* Cambridge, MA: MIT Press.

Werhane, P. H. (1985). *Persons, rights, and corporations.* Englewood Cliffs, NJ: Prentice-Hall.

Wicks, A. C. (1996). Overcoming the separation thesis: The need for a reconsideration of business and society research. *Business & Society, 35,* 89–118.

Williams, R. (1979). Change and stability in values and value systems: A sociological perspective. In M. Rokeach (ed.), *Understanding human values* (pp. 15–46). New York: Free Press.

Wood, D. J. (1991a). Corporate social performance revisited. *Academy of Management Review, 16,* 691–718.

Wood, D. J. (1991b). Toward improving corporate social performance. *Business Horizons, 34*(4), 66–73.

Wood, D. J. (1991c). Social issues in management: Theory and research in corporate social performance. *Journal of Management, 17,* 383–406.

Wood, D. J., Logsdon, J. M., Lewellyn, P. G. & Davenport, K. (2006). *Global business citizenship: A transformative framework for ethics and sustainable capitalism.* New York: M. E. Sharpe.

3
Value Attunement: Exploring the Potential for Responsible Executive Decision Making

As mentioned in the Introduction, society increasingly expects corporations to respond affirmatively to a wide variety of social concerns (Butler, 2001; Grace & Cohen, 1998). This expectation is consistent with the origin of the business corporation as a creation of government to be held accountable for serving the public interest (Waddell, 2000). Yet this institutional mission has become increasingly complicated as large corporations operate across the globe and small firms develop worldwide stakeholder networks (Vidaver-Cohen & Altman, 2000). Faced with such complexity, it is difficult for corporate leaders to know how to proceed. Their hesitation is not helped by the widely-held fallacy, addressed in Chapter 2, that values – or normative beliefs about right and wrong – are subjective preferences that cannot be identified and analyzed (Frederick, 1986; Treviño & Weaver, 1994, 1999, 2003). Given this fallacy, it is not surprising that many executives place low priority on integrating policies of social responsibility into organizational cultures and core business practices (Birch & Batten, 2001;

This chapter was originally published in 2002 as Marc Orlitzky & Diane L. Swanson, 'Value attunement: Toward a theory of socially responsible executive decision making', *Australian Journal of Management, 27* (Special Issue), 119–128. It was revised for publication in this book. The material from the original chapter was used with permission of the University of New South Wales and Robert Marks, General Editor of the *Australian Journal of Management*. The project was supported by an Australian Research Council grant. A related co-authored empirical study was presented at the 2002 Academy of Management Conference in Denver: 'Exploring individual differences in *normative myopia*: Executives' personality factors, pay preferences, and ethics of care.' Professor Swanson also acknowledges institutional support from the Dean's Office in the College of Business Administration at Kansas State University.

Milne, Owen & Tilt, 2001). Accordingly, they may downplay social issues, unless the values at stake just happen to coincide with their own personally held beliefs (Swanson, 1999). And even this 'value coincidence' may be uncommon (see Birch & Batten, 2001).

The propensity for executives to downplay social values is not a trivial matter, especially since it risks a loss of competitive advantage (Ansoff, 1991; Orlitzky & Benjamin, 2001). From this point of view, corporate social responsibility and financial success can go hand in hand (MacGregor, 2001). Yet the correlation is not exactly straightforward. After three decades of research, most scholars have concluded that the relationship between firms' social and financial performance is highly variable and moderated by several factors (e.g., Barnett, 2007; McWilliams & Siegel, 2001; Orlitzky, 2001; Wood & Jones, 1995).[1] Executives' awareness of their own personally held values might be one.

It is important to consider that poor corporate social performance can prompt a loss of goodwill, the threat of regulation, and increased oversight in the form of public pressure. Consider the longstanding global controversy surrounding Nestle's practice of marketing infant formula to consumers in developing countries, described in Chapter 2. For more than two decades, Nestle's critics alleged that conditions in developing nations, such as unsanitary water and low rates of literacy, rendered sales of infant formula life-threatening in those countries. Eventually the World Health Organization pressured Nestle to restrict the sales of infant formula in international markets (Sethi, 1994). Even to this day, Nestle's international reputation remains tarnished by charges that the company once neglected a compelling social issue. Such tarnishing can lead to a reputational crisis that damages a firm's bottom line (Mitroff & Alpaslan, 2003) or depletes the reputational capital that could have helped a firm weather other crises (Fombrun, Gardberg & Barnett, 2000). Indeed, reputation tops the intangible asset list of most CEOs (MacMillan & Joshi, 1997), perhaps because they realize that an accrual of reputational capital today can be used to exploit emerging financial opportunities tomorrow (see Fombrun *et al.*, 2000). To neglect social issues and stakeholder concerns means risking this reputational capital, which brings us back to the link between corporate social responsibility and financial success (Orlitzky & Benjamin, 2001, the study updated and reprinted in Part II of this book in Chapter 5).

This chapter elaborates on Swanson's (1999) theoretical typification of *value attunement* as an alternative to corporate neglect. Modeled in

Chapter 2, *attunement* represents the possibility that executives who are receptive to values can direct their organizations to respond affirmatively to a variety of stakeholder concerns. Put differently, it stands for a potential alignment of organizational behavior with broad-based expectations of social responsibility. Ben & Jerry's mission statement illustrates a quest for such alignment, given the company's stated commitment to improve the quality of life in communities locally, nationally, and internationally. More collectively, scores of corporate managers have endorsed the sustainable use of natural resources as formulated by the Coalition for Environmentally Responsible Economies (better known as the CERES principles) and more than 1,400 firms are members of Business for Social Responsibility, an alliance that fosters socially responsible corporate policies (Carroll & Buchholtz, 2006). Clearly, attunement is relevant to theory and practice.

In this chapter we extend attunement theorizing in three main ways. One, we underscore the importance of identifying all the values relevant to it. Two, we propose that pressure from special interest groups can constrain an executive's inclination to facilitate those values that may serve the collective good. In short, attempts at attunement can be co-opted by vested interests. Three, we propose that the process of 'trustful dialogue' may help mitigate such undue influences while helping corporate decision makers align corporate conduct with the constructive needs of the community at large.

In sum, we set forth a research agenda aimed at understanding the mechanisms that make attunement sound in theory and possible in practice, concluding with implications for those areas.

A review of the theoretical foundations for attunement

Scholars have long investigated principles of corporate social responsibility and corporate social responsiveness as distinctive topics of corporate social performance (Frederick, 1987). Specifically, responsibility deals with principles that motivate societal, organizational and individual action, whereas responsiveness involves organizational processes by which corporations interact with their host environments (Wood, 1991). Building on this line of inquiry, Swanson (1999) brought responsibility and responsiveness closer together by conceptualizing *normative receptivity* as an executive's awareness of the inseparability of values and facts in corporate policy. As an individual-level construct, *receptivity* refers to the possibility that executives who display an awareness of values will be able to direct their organizations to exhibit attunement, or an affirmative responsiveness to broad-based social expectations. The contrasting case of *normative myopia* depicts executives who ignore the role of values and risk directing their firms to enact *value neglect*, or poor corporate social responsiveness (Swanson, 1999, p. 513). *Myopia* is consistent with the fallacy or misconstrued belief that values cannot be identified and analyzed in corporate policy making. *Neglect* is its logical corollary in terms of an organization's posture toward society.

It is important to keep in mind that attunement and neglect are two distinct 'ideal types' or pure systems of logic. Following in this tradition established by Max Weber (1922/1947), Swanson (1999) modeled these two systems as contrasting forms of relationships between business and society, shaped by the interactions of values across individual, organizational, and societal levels of analysis. Her overarching thesis is that organizational behavior can be enacted as processes of social responsiveness, with attunement and neglect representing the best and worst types possible. Executive receptivity and myopia are portrayed as important drivers of these two organizational processes, which essentially represent opposite poles of the same dimension of corporate social performance (Swanson, 2008).

Our adaptation of Swanson's model is based on her original portrayal of attunement as four interrelated organizational processes of: (1) normative receptivity in executive decision making, (2) *hierarchical expansion* of value information, (3) *value-discovery culture*, and (4) *value-expanded detection* of social issues by external affairs. Translating Figure 3.1, executives who display receptivity to values could conceivably convey this attitude to other employees via formal hierarchical channels (Box 2) and informal means of culture (Box 3). In terms of hierarchical structure, they can do so by communicating their value premises along the chain of command to set the range for employee decision-making discretion (Simon, 1976). More informally, executives can employ cultural mechanisms – such as mentoring relationships, company-wide ceremonies, and public statements of organizational mission – to signal which values they deem important (Schein, 1992).

Swanson augmented formal and informal organizational dynamics with Weick's (1969) idea that information variety gets introduced in organizations through processes of selection, retention, and enactment. According to this perspective, executives select or filter data so that the equivocality (lack of clarity) of information that subordinates retain for future reference is reduced. This occurs directly through structural means, such as superior-subordinate reporting systems (Jackall, 1988; Perrow, 1986), or more indirectly through the cultural mechanisms mentioned

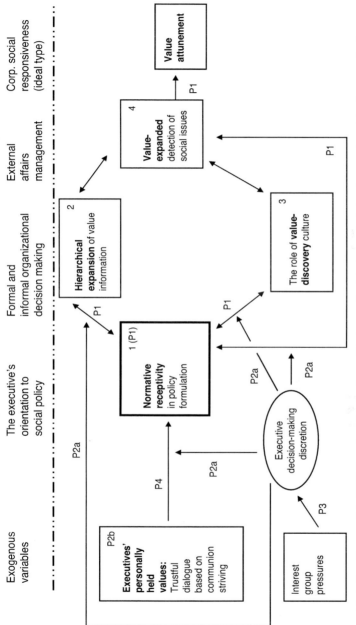

Adapted from Swanson, D. L. (1999). Toward an integrative theory of business and society: A research strategy for corporate social performance. *Academy of Management Review, 24*, 515. © Academy of Management. Reproduced with permission. All propositions (P1 through P4) are shown in the figure. The proposed moderator variable of executive decision-making discretion is shown in the oblong circle.

Figure 3.1 Value Attunement: Theoretical Extensions

previously. As information gets selected and retained over time, organizations ultimately create or enact the environments to which they adapt (Weick, 1969). During this process, certain values become more operative than others (England, 1967; Kabanoff, Waldersee & Cohen, 1995). If myopia prevails at the top, employees will be discouraged from recognizing values at all. In contrast, receptive executives can encourage a greater recognition of values throughout the organization.

As explained in greater detail in the previous chapter, two-way arrows in Figure 3.1 indicate that a hierarchical expansion of values becomes possible if employees select and retain information about values and convey this data to executives and other managers along the chain of command. Concurrently, employees in the informal organization may exhibit a greater recognition of values in response to cultural mechanisms that celebrate such awareness, a possibility shown as *discovery* culture (Box 3). Finally, when employees in external affairs (Box 4) follow suit by detecting information about social values and transmitting pertinent data to executives and other managers, then attunement becomes theoretically possible. In other words, an organization that assimilates sufficient information about values is logically capable of exhibiting a heightened sensitivity to those held by a variety of external stakeholders.

Our extension of Swanson's model is consistent with the idea that effective organizational behavior is a gestalt of structural and cultural synergies (Meyer, Tsui & Hinings, 1993). By implication, executive receptivity to values is a necessary but not sufficient condition for attunement. That is, if any of the synergistic structural or cultural processes depicted in Figure 3.1 are lacking, attunement is unlikely. On the other hand, the gestalt of impression management or a superficial image of corporate social responsibility might be enacted or projected onto the external environment instead (see Bozeman & Kacmar, 1997; Swanson & Niehoff, 2002). We will return to this possibility of impression management later, after qualifying Swanson's assertion that executive receptivity to values is an important determinant of attunement.

Proposition 1: An executive's receptivity to values is a necessary but not sufficient condition for attunement.

The centrality of Proposition 1 (P1) is shown under the heading of 'executive's orientation to social policy' in Figure 3.1. Although two-way arrows indicate that normative receptivity can strongly influence organizational dynamics, this type of executive decision making does not directly conflate to corporate behavior that serves the collective good. Nor did Swanson claim that it could. Again, she stressed that value attunement is an ideal type or theoretical point of reference that can be used to explore factors that affect corporate social performance (Swanson, 1999, p. 517). Discussed next, organizational decision processes can be shaped or constrained by many factors, including the nature of personally held values and pressures applied by special interest groups.

Theoretical extensions: executive discretion and personally held values

We have emphasized that an executive's receptivity to values does not guarantee attunement. Although the discretion that managers have at the apex of organizational structure plays an important role in determining organizational behavior (Hambrick & Finkelstein, 1987), executives can use this discretion to foster undesirable as well as desirable values. For instance, executives can act on egocentric self-serving beliefs to discourage subordinates from expressing views that contradict the *status quo* (Swanson, 1996). When this occurs, rank-and-file managers tend to fall in line with normative myopia as a matter of survival (see Jackall, 1988; Milgram, 1974). Conversely, less egocentric executives are more likely to encourage and comprehend a variety of views, including community-minded perspectives (Gilbert, 1996). The point is that executives can use their discretion to facilitate either neglect or attunement, depending on the nature of their own personally held values.

Proposition 2a: Executives can use their decision-making discretion to facilitate either value neglect or value attunement.
Proposition 2b: The nature of executives' personally held values influences their inclination to foster value attunement.

Proposition 2a is consistent with equifinality or the notion that outcomes in organizations are not unilaterally preordained by causal factors (Doty & Glick, 1994). Put in terms of neglect and attunement, executives can use their discretion to direct employees either to ignore or recognize a variety of value laden social issues. The latter instance was exemplified when Anita Roddick, founder of The Body Shop, reportedly encouraged her employees to work several hours a week on projects that enhanced community life. Alternatively, executives can just as easily signal a preference to neglect social issues. Given these equally possible outcomes, we have adapted Swanson's model to reflect Proposition 2a (P2a) that executive discretion moderates attunement processes (oblong circle, Figure 3.1). While executive discretion is inherent in Swanson's original model, we have added it here (P2a) to highlight the nature and influence of executives' personally held values (P2b) in terms of the discussion that follows.

According to Proposition 2b, it is not enough for executives to recognize the normative dimensions of social issues. Attunement also depends on the values they act upon and encourage employees to enact. Obviously, organizations can enact values that do not serve the greater good, such as executives' beliefs that it is acceptable to foster discrimination or ignore corporate contributions to environmental degradation. Hence, it is important to account for all personally held values that can shape organizational responses to society (Frederick, 1995), especially those held by executives. Indeed, Swanson (1999, p. 517) held that attunement theorizing cannot go forward without such accounting, a point we underscore in our concluding remarks to this chapter. For now, our refinement of her model indicates that executives who strive for attunement must necessarily display receptivity to the values that support community. In the next section, we elaborate on the nature of this receptivity as 'communion striving' that fosters 'trustful dialogue' between corporations and all stakeholders.

Returning to the role of decision-making discretion, certain forces can alter or circumscribe executive policies toward community, including pressure from internal whistle blowers, labor unions, shareholder activists, and attentive boards of directors (Johnson & Greening, 1999). External groups, such as regulatory bodies, lending institutions and highly organized consumer activists, can also exert influence over corporate conduct toward society (Rowley, 1997). To further complicate matters, dissatisfied stakeholders can invoke highly inflamed rhetoric to claim that executives do not properly represent their specific interests. Such allegations can dissuade executives from pursuing either extreme of neglect or attunement, resulting in less controversial 'middle of the road' corporate social performance.

Proposition 3: Pressures from internal and external stakeholders can circumscribe an executive's decision-making discretion.

That executive decisions can be affected by the influence of special interest groups renders the link between executive personally held values and corporate social responsibility more tenuous than it would be otherwise (see Agle, Mitchell & Sonnenfeld, 1999). The addition of Proposition 3 (P3) to Swanson's model allows for the fact that vested interests may drive executive decisions, issue by issue. Yet by definition, executives who strive for attunement must keep the needs of the whole community in mind. This brings us to our last agenda item of 'trustful dialogue' and the role it can play in attunement theorizing.

Bridging organizational behavior and social expectations with trustful dialogue

The propositions we have laid out constitute a research agenda of relational properties that require further investigation. Of these, it is paramount that all the values that can be enacted by organizations be identified. Although we do not undertake such accounting, we note that trust is a value that, if operative, can enhance the quality of relationships within organizations and between organizations and their social environments (Cohen & Prusak, 2001, Ring & Van de Ven, 1992). Notably, social complexity is easier to manage when trust is present (Calton & Lad, 1995; Luhmann, 1979). This is an important consideration, since value attunement depends on the accretion of information, which adds complexity to all decision processes. Under such conditions, trust, or confidence in the reciprocity and stability of social bonds, can function like glue, holding collective action together, even in the wake of unanticipated events (Barber, 1983; Feldman, 2002; Hosmer, 1995; Waddock, 2002). In this vein, Walker and Marr (2001) hold that viable relationships with stakeholders that benefit both the corporation and society depend on establishing trust and communication based on it. This type of dialogue involves honest articulation of core values and assumptions so that mutual concerns and issues can be discussed in a nonthreatening manner (Waddock & Smith, 2000). Consistent with attunement theorizing, such a collaborative, proactive approach can even preempt potential conflicts between a corporation and its constituents (see Scherer & Palazzo, 2007).

Yet another reason to highlight trust is that dialogue without it can easily deteriorate into superficial impression management that 'bends the truth' to serve narrow interests (see Bozeman & Kacmar, 1997; Swanson & Niehoff, 2002). Disentangling superficial rhetoric from trustful dialogue requires distinguishing between narrow self-interest and more other-regarding motives. The ethics of care can be a touchstone for this distinction, since it takes the focal point of morality to be a willingness to respond to another's needs and strive for the good of the whole community (Gilligan, 1982; Noddings, 1984). Given this focus, we propose that caring for others, or 'communion striving', is a valid motivation for trustful interpersonal dialogue, and by extension a necessary (micro) condition for attunement.

Proposition 4: The communion striving that fosters trustful dialogue is a necessary condition for attunement.

That communion striving and trustful dialogue must begin on the executive level is highlighted by Proposition 4 (P4) as a one-way arrow emanating from executives' personally held values in Figure 3.1.

Some implications for theory and practice

Value attunement poses many challenges to theory-building, especially since it blends individual decision making and organizational dynamics across several levels of analysis. Perhaps the most difficult task will be to account for all the values that can be selected, retained, and enacted by organizations (see Frederick 1995; Swanson, 1999, p. 517). Another challenge is to explain how certain values get embedded in small groups in the informal organization, leading to conflicting or recalcitrant subcultures that can thwart overall attunement, a possibility that Swanson did not raise.

In terms of practice, research suggests redesigning organizations to reduce the height of vertical structure or chain of command, a recommendation consistent with the notion that layers of hierarchy often discourage open discussions while encouraging habitual misinterpretations of messages (Jackall, 1988). Logically, hierarchy can get in the way of value attunement processes (Swanson, 1999), given that flatter organizations are thought to transmit information better than taller ones (Halal, 1994). Another implication for practice is that executives should implement policies aimed at recruiting and retaining employees adept at value analysis, communion striving and trustful dialogue. Indeed, these policies may mitigate the possibility of recalcitrant subcultures that thwart attunement, mentioned above. In particular, public affairs managers need to display skills of value analysis, communion striving and trustful dialogue, since the ability of organizations to enact attunement depends largely on the information they identify and transmit about the social environment (see Fleisher, 1998, Marsden, 2000). Along these lines, we will explore some implications for recruitment in Chapter 10.

Finally, a credible theory of corporate social performance must come to terms with cultural differences across national boundaries (Katz,

Swanson & Nelson, 2001). Demonstrated by the aforementioned example of Nestle, what counts as corporate social responsibility can depend on circumstances of culture and economic development. Consequently, executives who aim for value attunement should examine business practices through what amounts to an anthropological lens, using information gleaned from environmental scanning and trustful dialogues to try to align organizational conduct with community-minded cultural imperatives. In the case of infant formula, this could mean collaborating with local officials to educate consumers about product specifications, such as the importance of mixing the formula with sanitary water. Concurrently, public affairs officials should appraise the product's social impacts proactively and continuously. If the data suggest that the product remains unfit for general consumption in certain cultures, then attunement theorizing implies that marketing channels be reconfigured to preclude indiscriminate sales (see Austin & Kohn, 1990; Husted, 2000). This brings us back full circle to our introductory remark that executives increasingly are under pressure to respond to various stakeholder expectations in international business environments, a point we will revisit in Chapter 10. Our research program is aimed at shedding some light on this increasingly difficult responsibility from the perspective of organizational decision parameters. Along these lines, we have conducted a preliminary study of executives' values and personality in relation to high organizational pay dispersion and corporate social performance. We present this study and its relevance to our research program in Part III, Chapter 9, of this book.

Note

1. As explained in further detail in Part II, the variability of the relationship is often overstated, based on statistical misinterpretation of the evidence (Orlitzky, 2006, 2008; Orlitzky, Schmidt & Rynes, 2003, updated and revised in Chapter 4).

References

Agle, B. R., Mitchell, R. K. & Sonnenfeld, J. A. (1999). What matters to CEOs? An investigation of stakeholder salience, corporate performance, and CEO values. *Academy of Management Journal, 42*, 507–525.

Ansoff, H. I. (1991). Strategic management in a historical perspective. *International Review of Strategic Management, 2*(1), Chichester, UK: Wiley.

Austin, J. E. & Kohn, T. O. (1990). *Strategic management in developing countries: Case studies.* New York: Free Press.

Barber, B. (1983). *The logic and limits of trust.* New Brunswick, NJ: Rutgers University Press.

Barnett, M. L. (2007). Stakeholder influence capacity and the variability of financial returns to corporate social responsibility. *Academy of Management Review, 32*(3), 794–816.

Birch, D. & Batten, J. (2001, May 16). Corporate citizenship in Australia, Presentation at Museum of Sydney. Sydney, Australia.

Bozeman, D. P. & Kacmar, K. M. (1997). A cybernetic model of impression management processes in organizations. *Organizational Behavior and Human Decision Processes, 69,* 9–30.

Butler, R. (2001, June 12). Communism, socialism, capitalism: What next? Presentation at Australian Graduate School of Management (Distinguished Speaker Series), Sydney, Australia.

Calton, J. & Lad, L. (1995). Social contracting as a trust-building process of network governance. *Business Ethics Quarterly, 5,* 271–295.

Carroll, A. B. & Buchholtz, A. K. (2006). *Business & society: Ethics and stakeholder management.* Mason, OH: Thomson South-Western.

Cohen, D. & Prusak, L. (2001). *In good company: How social capital makes organizations work.* Boston, MA: Harvard Business School Press.

Doty, D. H. & Glick, W. H. (1994). Typologies as a unique form of theory building: Toward improved understanding and modelling. *Academy of Management Review, 19,* 230–251.

England, G. W. (1967). Personal value systems of American managers. *Academy of Management Journal, 10,* 107–117.

Feldman, S. P. (2002). *Memory as a moral decision: The role of ethics in organizational culture.* New Brunswick, NJ: Transaction Publishing.

Fleisher, C. S. (1998, July/August). The new public affairs. *Impact,* 1–3.

Fombrun, C. J., Gardberg, N. A. & Barnett, M. L. (2000). Opportunity platforms and safety nets: Corporate citizenship and reputational risk. *Business and Society Review, 105,* 85–106.

Frederick, W. C. (1986). Toward CSR3: Why ethical analysis is indispensable and unavoidable in corporate affairs. *California Management Review, 28,* 126–141.

Frederick, W. C. (1987). Theories of corporate social performance. In S. P. Sethi & C. Falbe (eds), *Business and society: Dimensions of conflict and cooperation* (pp. 142–161). New York: Lexington Books.

Frederick, W. C. (1995). *Values, nature, and culture in the American corporation.* New York: Oxford University Press.

Gilbert, D. (1996). *Strategy and ethics.* New York: Oxford University Press.

Gilligan, C. (1982). *In a different voice.* Cambridge, MA: Harvard University Press.

Grace, D. & Cohen, S. (1998). *Business ethics: Australian problems and cases* (2nd ed.). Melbourne, VIC: Oxford University Press,

Halal, W. H. (1994). From hierarchy to enterprise: Internal markets are the new foundation of management. *Academy of Management Executive, 8,* 69–83.

Hambrick, D. C. & Finkelstein, S. (1987). Managerial discretion: A bridge between polar views of organizational outcomes. *Research in Organizational Behavior, 9,* 369–406.

Hosmer, L. T. (1995). Trust: The connecting link between organizational theory and philosophical ethics. *Academy of Management Review, 20,* 379–403.

Husted, B. (2000). A contingency theory of corporate social performance. *Business & Society*, *39*, 24–48.

Jackall, R. (1988). *Moral mazes: The world of corporate managers*. New York: Oxford University Press.

Johnson, R. A. & Greening, D. W. (1999). The effects of corporate governance and institutional ownership types on corporate social performance. *Academy of Management Journal*, *42*, 564–576.

Kabanoff, B., Waldersee, R. & Cohen, M. (1995). Espoused values and organizational change themes. *Academy of Management Journal*, *38*, 1075–1104.

Katz, J., Swanson, D. & Nelson, L. (2001). Culture-based expectations of corporate citizenship: A propositional framework and comparison of four cultures, *International Journal of Organizational Analysis*, *9*, 149–171.

Luhmann, N. (1979). *Trust and power*. Chichester, UK: Wiley.

MacGregor, A. (2001, April 27). *Corporate social responsibility sells*. New South Wales Chamber of Commerce Press Release.

MacMillan, G. S. & Joshi, M. P. (1997, Summer). Sustainable competitive advantage and firm performance: The role of intangible resources. *Corporate Reputation Review*, *1*, 81–85.

Marsden, C. (2000). The new corporate citizenship of big business: Part of the solution to sustainability? *Business and Society Review*, *105*, 9–25.

McWilliams, A. & Siegel, D. (2001). Corporate social responsibility: A theory of the firm perspective. *Academy of Management Review*, *26*, 117–127.

Meyer, A. D., Tsui, A. S. & Hinings, C. R. (1993). Guest co-editors' introduction: Configurational approaches to organizational analysis. *Academy of Management Journal*, *36*, 1175–1195.

Milgram, S. (1974). *Obedience to authority*. New York: Harper & Row.

Milne, M. J., Owen, D. L. & Tilt, C. A. (2001, June 30). Environmental reporting in Australia and New Zealand: Corporate and stakeholder reactions to best practice, Presentation at Accountability Symposium, Accounting Association of Australia and New Zealand Conference, Auckland, New Zealand.

Mitroff, I. I. & Alpaslan, M. C. (2003, April). Preparing for evil. *Harvard Business Review*, 3–9.

Noddings, N. (1984). *Caring: A feminine approach to ethics and moral education*. Berkeley, CA: University of California Press.

Orlitzky, M. (2001). Does firm size confound the relationship between corporate social performance and firm financial performance? *Journal of Business Ethics*, *33*, 167–180.

Orlitzky, M. (2006). Links between corporate social responsibility and corporate financial performance: Theoretical and empirical determinants. In J. Allouche (ed.), *Corporate social responsibility, Vol. 2: Performances and stakeholders* (Vol. 2, pp. 41–64). London: Palgrave Macmillan.

Orlitzky, M. (2008). Corporate social performance and financial performance: A research synthesis. In A. Crane, A. McWilliams, D. Matten, J. Moon & D. Siegel (eds), *The Oxford Handbook of CSR* (pp. 113–134). Oxford, UK: Oxford University Press.

Orlitzky, M. & Benjamin, J. D. (2001). Corporate social performance and firm risk: A meta-analytic review. *Business & Society*, *40*(4), 369–396.

Orlitzky, M., Schmidt, F. L. & Rynes, S. L. (2003). Corporate social and financial performance: A meta-analysis. *Organization Studies*, *24*(3), 403–441.

Perrow, C. (1986). *Complex organizations: A critical essay*. New York: McGraw-Hill.

Ring, P. S. & Van de Ven, A. H. (1992). Structuring cooperative relationships between organizations. *Strategic Management Journal, 13*, 483–498.

Rowley, T. J. (1997). Moving beyond dyadic ties: A network theory of stakeholder influences. *Academy of Management Review, 22*, 887–910.

Schein, E. H. (1992). *Organizational culture and leadership*, San Francisco, CA: Jossey-Bass.

Scherer, A. G. & Palazzo, G. (2007). Toward a political conception of corporate social responsibility: Business and society seen from a Habermasian perspective. *Academy of Management Review, 32*, 1096–1120.

Sethi, S. P. (1994). *Multinational corporations and the impact of public advocacy on corporate strategy: Nestle and the infant formula controversy*. Norwell, MA: Kluwer.

Simon, H. A. (1976). *Administrative behaviour*. New York: Free Press.

Swanson, D. L. (1996). Neoclassical economic theory, executive control, and organizational outcomes. *Human Relations, 49*(6), 735–756.

Swanson, D. L. (1999). Toward an integrative strategy of business and society: A research strategy for corporate social performance. *Academy of Management Review, 24*, 506–521.

Swanson, D. L. (2008). Top managers as drivers for corporate social performance. In A. Crane, A. McWilliams, D. Matten, J. Moon & D. Siegel (eds), *The Oxford Handbook of CSR* (pp. 227–248). Oxford, UK: Oxford University Press.

Swanson, D. L. & Niehoff, B. (2002). Business citizenship outside and inside organizations: Toward a synthesis of corporate social responsibility and employee citizenship. In J. Andriof. & M. McIntosh (eds), *Perspectives on corporate citizenship: context, content and processes* (pp. 104–116). Sheffield, UK: Greenleaf Publishing.

Treviño, L. & Weaver, G. (1994). Business ethics: One field or two? *Business Ethics Quarterly, 4*, 111–125.

Treviño, L. & Weaver G. (1999). The stakeholder research tradition: Converging theorists – not convergent theory. *Academy of Management Review, 24*, 222–227.

Treviño, L. & Weaver, G. (2003). *Managing ethics in business organizations: Social science perspectives*. Stanford, CA: Stanford University Press.

Vidaver-Cohen, D. & Altman, B. (2000). Concluding remarks: Corporate citizenship in the new millennium: Foundation for an architecture of excellence. *Business and Society Review, 105*, 145–168.

Waddell, S. (2000). New institutions for the practice of corporate citizenship: Historical, intersectoral, and developmental perspectives. *Business and Society Review, 105*, 107–126.

Waddock, S. (2002). *Leading corporate citizens: Vision, values, value added*. New York: McGraw-Hill Irwin.

Waddock, S. & Smith, N. (2000). Relationships: The real challenge of corporate global citizenship. *Business and Society Review, 105*, 47–62.

Walker, S. F. & Marr, J. W. (2001). *Stakeholder power: A winning plan for building stakeholder commitment and driving corporate growth*. Cambridge, MA: Perseus Publishing.

Weber, M. 1922/1947. *The theory of social and economic organization*. (Translated and edited by A. H. Henderson & T. Parsons.) NY: Oxford University Press.

Weick, K. E. (1969). *The social psychology of organizing.* Reading, MA: Addison-Wesley.

Wood, D. J. (1991). Corporate social performance revisited. *Academy of Management Review, 16,* 691–718.

Wood, D. J. & Jones, R. E. (1995). Stakeholder mismatching: A theoretical problem in empirical research on corporate social performance. *International Journal of Organizational Analysis, 3,* 229–267.

Part II

Empirical Research Integration: Business Social Performance, Risk, and Financial Performance

Introduction to Part II

Part I of our monograph identified and addressed theory building problems in corporate social performance (CSP), arguing for a better foundation for corporate citizenship grounded in more rigorous social and organizational theories. These theoretical advances are important because they suggest that CSP can be shaped by organizational dynamics instead of the assumption of a strict dichotomy between economic performance and other important social goals (see the Introduction to Part I). In this vein, certain organizational processes were identified that may mitigate tradeoffs between economic and other social goals, theoretically aligning them to a greater extent than had been previously modeled.

Part II of this book shifts from theoretical to empirical integration by examining certain data in depth to assess whether, in general, corporate social and financial performance are contradictory organizational dimensions or, in fact, positively correlated. In particular, we highlight empirical analyses of business risk, quantitative CSP measurement, and possible contingencies as important considerations in a more comprehensive, strategic understanding of CSP. By *strategic* we mean a deeper understanding of CSP that takes into account empirical reality in the form of financial performance dimensions and economic drivers of business activity, thus allowing for a more complete analysis from a firm-level view. This strategic perspective on corporate citizenship, developed further in the last chapter of Part III, is informed not only by insights from empirical integration, but also by the holistic approach to organizational dynamics laid out in Part I. In this way, we point empirical and theoretical CSP research toward integrative corporate citizenship.

Generally speaking, the meta-analysis presented in Chapter 4 contradicts conventional assumptions about the empirical relationship between CSP and corporate financial performance (CFP). According to the orthodox view, the current evidence is simply too fractured or too variable to draw any generalizable conclusions about the relationship. However, the study presented in Chapter 4 shows the mainstream claim that there is little generalizable knowledge about CSP and CFP (which is still a very common and widespread theoretical and empirical assumption) is built on shaky grounds. Providing a methodologically more rigorous review than previous studies, a meta-analysis of 52 studies (which represent the population of prior quantitative inquiry) is conducted, yielding a total sample size of 33,878 observations. The meta-analytic findings suggest that corporate virtue in the form of social responsibility and, to a lesser extent, environmental responsibility is likely to pay off for firms economically, although the operationalizations of CSP and CFP also moderate the positive association. For example, CSP appears to be more highly correlated with accounting-based measures of CFP than with market-based indicators, and CSP reputation indices are more highly correlated with CFP than are other indicators of CSP. This meta-analysis establishes a greater degree of certainty about the CSP-CFP relationship than is currently assumed to exist by many researchers (e.g., Vogel, 2005).

Chapter 5 builds on Chapter 4 by focusing on the relationship between CSP and firm risk. Contrasting hypotheses derived from instrumental stakeholder theory and neoclassical economics, it shows that the higher a firm's corporate social performance, the lower its financial risk. Moreover, the relationship between CSP and risk appears to be one of reciprocal causality, since CSP is inversely related to subsequent risk and prior risk is inversely related to subsequent CSP. In other words, it seems that CSP at first reduces business risk, and over time, with decreasing risk, a firm is able to do more CSP. Additionally, CSP is more strongly correlated with market risk than accounting risk. Of all the different CSP operationalizations, reputation for social responsibility appears to be the most important in terms of its risk implications.

Chapter 6 examines the assumption that the positive relationship between CSP and corporate financial performance (CFP) is spurious and in fact caused by a third factor, namely large firm size. Three meta-analyses of more than two decades of research are integrated in a path model connecting (1) CSP and CFP, (2) firm size and CSP, and (3) firm size and CFP. The present study does not confirm size as a third factor which would confound the relationship between CSP and CFP. That is, even if firm size is controlled for across studies (comprising, on average, over 15,000 observations), CSP and CFP remain positively correlated, showing a 'true-score' corrected path coefficient p of .37.

Chapter 7 examines publication outlet variability as a contingency of how the relationship between corporate social performance (CSP) and corporate financial performance (CFP) is generally understood. The meta-analytic moderator analysis, based on a total sample size N of 33,878 observations, suggests that the complex interactions in the review process may affect findings. In economics, finance, and accounting journals, the average correlations found were only about half the value reported by Business Ethics or Business & Society journals (in which the mean observed correlation coefficient was $\bar{r}_{obs}$ = .11 vs. 25, respectively and the mean corrected correlation coefficient was $\rho = .22$ vs. .49, respectively). In general, (1) economists did not find null or negative CSP-CFP correlations as may have been expected and (2) average findings reported in general management outlets ($\bar{r}_{obs} = .21$; $\rho = .41$) were closer to Business Ethics/Business & Society results than those reported by economics, finance, and accounting researchers. As Chapter 7 shows, the second finding, which qualifies previous meta-analytic conclusions in important ways, is consistent with studies highlighting selective amplification in the manuscript review process and, more broadly, with sociology-of-science explanations.

With the empirical results of the next section (Part II) in mind, in the last section of the book (Part III) we will focus on issues of CSP measurement and implementation while pointing to the broader strategic implications for integrative corporate citizenship.

Reference

Vogel, D. (2005). *The market for virtue: The potential and limits of corporate social responsibility*. Washington, DC: Brookings Institution Press.

4
Corporate Social and Financial Performance: An Integrative Review

During the last decade, organizations (especially large corporations) have been facing ever-increasing stakeholder pressure demanding 'good corporate citizenship' from business. This pressure means that, among other things, nonmarket strategies are increasingly important for effective executive decision making (Baron, 2006). Nonmarket strategies can be observed and measured in a wide variety of ways. However, as is evident from Part I, corporate social performance (CSP) can be regarded as a central outcome of business nonmarket strategies. For the purpose of the empirical analysis presented in this chapter, CSP is defined as 'a business organization's configuration of principles of social responsibility, processes of social responsiveness, and policies, programs, and observable outcomes as they relate to the firm's societal relationships' (Wood, 1991a, p. 693). This is the definition that Swanson elaborated upon in her remodeling of CSP in Chapters 1 and 2 (where she conveyed these concepts as a means-end continuum).

This chapter, based on the first author's dissertation thesis in 1998, was originally published in 2003 as Orlitzky, M., Schmidt, F. L. & Rynes, S. L., 'Corporate social and financial performance: A meta-analysis', *Organization Studies, 24*(3), 403–441. *Organization Studies* is the official journal of the European Group for Organization Studies. The article was revised for publication in this book, and original material was used with permission of SAGE Publications. This study won the 2004 Moskowitz Award for outstanding quantitative research relevant to the social investment field. The Moskowitz Prize is awarded each year to the research paper that best meets the following criteria: 1) practical significance to practitioners of socially responsible investing; 2) appropriateness and rigor of quantitative methods; and 3) novelty of results. The sponsors of the Moskowitz Prize are Calvert Group, First Affirmative Financial Network, KLD Research & Analytics Inc., Nelson Capital Management, Rockefeller & Co., and Trillium Asset Management Corporation.

For several decades, researchers had been trying to find an answer to a question posed by *Business Week* in 1999: 'Can business meet new social, environmental, and financial expectations and still win?' ('The Next Bottom Line', 1999). The typical answer, so far, has been that the empirical evidence has been too variable to allow for any firm conclusions (e.g., Ullmann, 1985; Vogel, 2005). Weak theory construction (addressed in Chapters 1 and 2 of this book) and poor measures are often identified as causes of this apparent variability in findings (see also Griffin & Mahon, 1997; Roman, Hayibor & Agle, 1999; Rowley & Berman, 2000; Wood & Jones, 1995). The notion that this research stream is inconclusive has been a persistent assumption, which has resulted in the stipulation of a wide variety of contingencies between socially responsible actions and corporate financial performance (CFP) (e.g., Barnett, 2007; Godfrey, 2005; Mackey, Mackey & Barney, 2007; McWilliams & Siegel, 2001; Schuler & Cording, 2006). However, the empirical study presented in this chapter proposes that, before Business and Society researchers embark on a costly and time-consuming search for moderating variables, a theoretically and empirically meaningful integration of this area might be useful. In this chapter, we show that this line of inquiry leads to a number of empirically-supported conclusions that have hitherto been largely overlooked, downplayed, or ignored.

This chapter presents a meta-analytic review of prior quantitative studies of the CSP-CFP relationship. *Meta-analysis* has proven to be a useful technique in many other areas of research where multiple individual studies have yielded inconclusive or conflicting results (e.g., Damanpour, 1991; Datta, Pinches & Narayanan, 1992; Gooding & Wagner, 1985; Schwenk, 1989; see also Hedges, 1987, Hunt, 1997, Rosenthal & DiMatteo, 2001, and Schmidt, 1992 for broader reviews of the utility of meta-analysis). By statistically aggregating results across individual studies and correcting for statistical artifacts such as sampling error and measurement error, psychometric meta-analysis allows for much greater precision than other forms of research reviews. Ironically, some of the research that casts the most doubt on the existence of a positive relationship between CSP and CFP is based on the so-called 'vote-counting' technique, which has been shown to be flawed by many statistical experts (e.g., Hedges & Olkin, 1980; Hunter & Schmidt, 1990; Rosenthal, 1995; Schmidt, 1992). In vote counting, findings are coded and interpreted simply as significantly positive, negative, or statistically nonsignificant results in each study. Because the analysis of sample size and other influences, such as measurement error, is omitted, conclusions from such a 'vote counting' exercise are likely to be false (Hedges & Olkin, 1980; Hunter & Schmidt, 1990). In contrast, psychometric meta-analysis quantifies the impact of theoretical and methodological deficiencies in a given line of inquiry and is therefore, at present, the most sophisticated research integration technique.

The specific objectives of this meta-analysis are to: (1) provide a statistical integration of the accumulated research on the relationship between CSP and CFP; (2) assess the relative predictive validity of instrumental stakeholder theory in the context of the CSP-CFP relationship; and (3) examine several moderators, such as operationalization of CSP and CFP (i.e., measurement strategies) and timing of CSP and CFP measurement. In so doing, this chapter builds on earlier research by: (a) including market (stock) return measures in addition to accounting returns, (b) including CSP measures other than social-responsibility audits performed by Kinder, Lydenberg, Domini & Co., Inc., (c) responding to Waddock and Graves' (1997, p. 315) call for research on temporal consistency of results, independent of the time lag chosen between CSP and CFP measures, and (d) integrating empirical results across diverse study contexts, enabling us to look for theoretical moderators and statistical artifacts that might explain the highly variable results in previous studies.

Theory and hypotheses

Overall CSP-CFP relationship

Instrumental stakeholder theory (e.g., Clarkson, 1995; Cornell & Shapiro, 1987; Donaldson & Preston, 1995; Freeman, 1984; Mitchell, Agle & Wood, 1997) suggests a positive relationship between CSP and CFP. According to this theory, the satisfaction of various stakeholder groups is instrumental for organizational financial performance (Donaldson & Preston, 1995; Jones, 1995). Stakeholder-agency theory argues that the implicit and explicit negotiation and contracting processes entailed by reciprocal, bilateral stakeholder-management relationships serve as monitoring and enforcement mechanisms that prevent managers from diverting attention from broad organizational financial goals (Hill & Jones, 1992; Jones, 1995). Furthermore, by addressing and balancing the claims of multiple stakeholders (Freeman & Evan, 1990), managers can increase the efficiency of their organization's adaptation to external demands. We took this view in Chapter 3 by proposing that the creation and maintenance of a trustful dialogue between managers and stakeholders can enhance a firm's ability to enact an attuned relationship with its external environment.

Similar conclusions are derived from a firm-as-contract analysis (Freeman & Evan, 1990), which suggests that high corporate performance results not only from the separate satisfaction of bilateral relationships (see Hill & Jones, 1992), but also from the simultaneous coordination and prioritization of multilateral stakeholder interests. These strategic and tactical steps may be necessary to reduce the probability of an organization becoming stuck in a high-density network. (Network density refers to the proportion of actual ties in a network relative to the total number possible.) High network density can reduce CFP in a number of ways. For example, in a high-density network, firms may become stuck in the role of compromiser or subordinate, depending on the degree of the firm's network centrality (Rowley, 1997). Either of these roles may lead to further consumption of valuable firm resources such as time, labor, and capital. Conversely, high CSP (which was called 'value attunement' in Chapter 2) may bolster a company's competitive advantage due to the weighing and addressing of various constituent claims in a fair, rational manner, instead of enacting the default posture of the accommodative (compromiser) or defensive (subordinate) role. This perspective, derived primarily from instrumental stakeholder theory (Jones, 1995), has also been called the 'good management theory' (Waddock & Graves, 1997).

Hypothesis 1: Corporate social performance and financial performance are generally positively related across a wide variety of industry and study contexts.

Temporal sequence

Like the good management theory, the slack resources theory also points to a positive association between CSP and CFP. However, it proposes a different temporal ordering – namely, that prior CFP is directly associated with subsequent CSP. Prior high levels of CFP may provide the slack resources necessary to engage in corporate social responsibility and responsiveness (Ullmann, 1985; Waddock & Graves, 1997). Because CSP often represents an area of relatively high managerial discretion, the initiation or cancellation of voluntary social and environmental policies may, to a large extent, depend on the availability of excess funds (McGuire, Sundgren & Schneeweis, 1988).

To distinguish between the slack resources theory and the good management theory, the meta-analytic data set will be examined for three sets of temporal associations: (a) prior CSP related to subsequent CFP,

(b) prior CFP related to subsequent CSP, and (c) contemporaneous (cross-sectional) associations. If effect sizes are highly similar across all three meta-analytic subgroups, then Waddock and Graves' (1997) argument that there exists a virtuous cycle, or continual mutual reinforcement between CSP and CFP, would be supported irrespective of study context, sampling error, and measurement error (which invariably occur in primary studies). That is, there would be credence for the view that financially successful companies spend more on CSP because they can afford it and, in turn, CSP helps them become a bit more successful financially. Based on prior theoretical and empirical findings (e.g., McGuire, Schneeweis & Branch, 1990; Waddock & Graves, 1997), both instrumental-stakeholder and slack-resources views may be accurate descriptions of organizational reality, so that the two constructs are expected to be mutually reinforcing.

Hypothesis 2: There is reciprocal, or bi-directional, causality between corporate social performance and financial performance.

Mediating effects

CSP may be an organizational resource that provides internal and/or external benefits. Internally, investments in CSP may help firms develop new competencies, resources, and capabilities which are manifested in a firm's culture, technology, structure, and human resources (Barney, 1991; Russo & Fouts, 1997; Wernerfelt, 1984). Especially when CSP is preemptive (Hart, 1995) and a firm's environment is dynamic or complex, CSP may help build managerial competence because preventive efforts necessitate significant employee involvement, organization-wide coordination, and a forward-thinking managerial style (Shrivastava, 1995). Thus, CSP can help management develop better scanning skills, processes, and information systems, which increase the organization's preparedness for external changes, turbulence, and crises (e.g., Russo & Fouts, 1997), a view similar to the emphasis on internal responsiveness conveyed in Chapter 2. These competencies, which are acquired internally through the CSP process, would then lead to more efficient utilization of resources (Majumdar & Marcus, 2001). According to the 'internal resources/learning' perspective, whether or not CSP behaviors and outcomes are disclosed to outside constituents is largely irrelevant to the development of internal capabilities and organizational efficiency.

Additionally, CSP may have external effects on an organization's reputation for good citizenship. According to this view, an organization's communication with external parties about its level of CSP may help build a positive image with customers, investors, bankers, and suppliers (Fombrun, Gardberg & Barnett, 2000; Fombrun & Shanley, 1990). Firms high in CSP may use CSR disclosures as one of the informational signals upon which stakeholders base their assessments of corporate reputation under conditions of incomplete information (Fombrun & Shanley, 1990). Furthermore, firms with solid reputations for good corporate citizenship may improve relations with bankers and investors and thus facilitate their access to capital (Spicer, 1978). They may also attract better employees (Greening & Turban, 2000; Turban & Greening, 1997) or increase current employees' goodwill which, in turn, may improve financial outcomes (Davis, 1973; McGuire *et al.*, 1988; Waddock & Graves, 1997). In sum, the reputation perspective postulates reputational effects as mediators of the CSP-CFP linkage, while the internal-resources perspective proposes managerial competencies and learning as the intervening generative mechanism between a positive CSP-CFP association.

Hypothesis 3: Corporate social performance is positively correlated with corporate financial performance because it (a) increases managerial competencies, contributes to organizational knowledge about the firm's market, social, political, technological, and other environments, and thus enhances organizational efficiency, and (b) helps the firm build goodwill and a positive reputation with its external stakeholders.

Measurement strategy: an important moderator variable

Because both CSP and CFP are such broad meta-constructs, a given study's operationalization of each construct may act as an important moderator. To test this hypothesis, the entire meta-analytic set is broken down into different CFP and CSP subsets employing different measurement strategies. This breakdown can establish whether correlations between different CSP and CFP measures are similar across subgroups, or whether different operationalizations lead to systematically different effect sizes across studies. The following paragraphs provide a brief overview of how CFP and CSP have been measured in the past.

The three broad subdivisions of CFP consist of market-based (investor returns), accounting-based (accounting returns), and perceptual (survey) measures. First, market-based measures of CFP, such as price per share or share price appreciation, reflect the notion that shareholders are a primary stakeholder group whose satisfaction determines the company's financial fate (Cochran & Wood, 1984). The bidding and asking processes of stock market participants, who rely on their perceptions of past, current, and future stock returns and risk, determine a firm's stock price and thus market value. Alternatively, accounting-based indicators, such as the firm's return on assets (ROA), return on equity (ROE), or earnings per share (EPS), capture a firm's internal efficiency in some way (Cochran & Wood, 1984). Accounting returns are subject to managers' discretionary allocations of funds to different projects and policy choices, and thus reflect internal decision-making capabilities and managerial performance rather than external market responses to organizational (nonmarket) actions. Finally, perceptual measures of CFP ask survey respondents to provide subjective estimates of, for instance, the firm's 'soundness of financial position', 'wise use of corporate assets', or 'financial goal achievement relative to competitors' (Conine & Madden, 1987; Reimann, 1975; Wartick, 1988).

The construct of CSP is associated with the following four broad measurement strategies: (1) CSP disclosures; (2) CSP reputation ratings; (3) social audits, CSP processes, and observable outcomes; and (4) managerial CSP principles and values (Post, 1991). First, CSP disclosure measurement consists of content analysis of annual reports, letters to shareholders, 10Ks, and a number of other corporate disclosures to the public as surrogates of CSP. Content analysis is employed to compare units of text against particular CSP themes in order to draw inferences about an organization's underlying social performance (Wolfe, 1991).

A second approach to measuring CSP is the use of reputational indices, such as Moskowitz's (1972, 1975) tripartite ratings ('outstanding', 'honorable mention', and 'worst' companies; e.g., in Cochran & Wood, 1984; Sturdivant & Ginter, 1977) or *Fortune* magazine ratings of a company's 'responsibility to the community and environment' (e.g., Conine & Madden, 1987; Fombrun & Shanley, 1990; McGuire *et al.*, 1988). Other researchers (Alexander & Buchholz, 1978; Heinze, 1976; Vance, 1975) have developed their own reputational measures by surveying business professionals and business students. Reputational indices are based on the assumption that CSP reputations are good reflections of underlying CSP values and behaviors.

Social audits and concrete, observable CSP processes and outcomes are the third broad measurement category of CSP. Social audits consist of a systematic third-party effort to assess a firm's 'objective' CSP behaviors, such as community service, environmental programs, and corporate philanthropy. Objective data are the foundation for so-called 'behavioral' measures of CSP. However, behavioral measures based on social audits may still result in a ranking, such as the measure provided by the Council on Economic Priorities (CEP). Various studies have used the CEP social audit rankings of companies' pollution records (e.g., Bragdon & Marlin, 1972; Fogler & Nutt, 1975; Spicer, 1978). Although this subset of studies differs from the other subsets, it is still very broad. Therefore, this third group will be broken down further to examine the instrumental effectiveness of processes of social responsiveness, discussed in Chapters 1 and 2 as an important element of CSP.

The fourth measurement category of CSP assesses the values and principles inherent in a company's culture, the latter amplified in Chapter 2 as an important precursor to CSP. In terms of value-oriented principles, Aupperle (1984) developed a forced-choice survey of corporate social orientations, drawing on Carroll's (1979) corporate social responsibility construct with its four dimensions of economic, legal, ethical, and discretionary responsibilities. According to Aupperle, the last three elements comprise the construct 'concern for society'. Volume 12 of *Research in Corporate Social Performance and Policy* (Part III, pp. 265–401 in Post, 1991) reviews in greater depth the history and psychometric properties of the different CSP measures briefly delineated here (see Aupperle, 1991; Carroll, 1991; Clarkson, 1991; Gephardt, 1991; Wokutch & McKinney, 1991; Wolfe, 1991; Wolfe & Aupperle, 1991).

Differences in CSP-CFP statistical associations across these four measurement subsets may result from three sources. First, there might be 'real' or *substantive* cross-study variation in correlations between CSP and CFP, as predicted by Wood and Jones' (1995) mismatching thesis. Wood and Jones argued that effects would vary depending on expectations and evaluations of CSP, which differ from one stakeholder group to another. No positive correlations would be expected between measures that cannot be linked theoretically, such as CSP disclosures and accounting-based efficiency measures of CFP. Wood and Jones' review suggested that, for example, the match between market measures and market-oriented stakeholders (e.g., customers) would produce significant positive results, while the correlation between market measures and charitable contributions, for instance, would not.

Alternatively, differences in correlations across variable measurement subsets may simply be a function of at least two statistical artifacts. For example, if one measurement subgroup were found to contain many studies with very small sample sizes, this subgroup would show a relatively large random sampling error. Thus, differences in *sampling error* across measurement subgroups may explain CSP/CFP correlational differences in primary studies. In addition, *measurement error* of CFP and CSP (i.e., unreliability) might act as another artifactual source of cross-study variability in correlations. If, for example, CSP disclosure measures were plagued by comparatively low psychometric quality (see Abbott & Monsen, 1979; Ingram & Frazier, 1980; Wiseman, 1982), observed correlations between CSP disclosures and CFP would be systematically lower than the correlations between CFP and other, more reliable measures of CSP. In light of these difficulties, this meta-analysis hierarchically breaks down the overall data set to compare the relative magnitudes of correlations arising from different CSP and CFP measurement subcategories, and tests for three possible sources of cross-study variation of correlations, i.e., substantive differences, sampling error, and measurement error.

Hypothesis 4a: A large proportion of cross-study variance is due to statistical or methodological artifacts (sampling error and measurement error).
Hypothesis 4b: Consistent with stakeholder mismatching, after accounting for statistical artifacts, there will still be substantive differences in the statistical associations between different subdimensions of corporate financial performance and corporate social performance.

Figure 4.1 depicts the hypothesized relationships in a diagram.

Methods

Prior summaries of the CSP-CFP literature have relied mostly on narrative reviews or the vote-counting method of aggregation. Narrative reviews are literature reviews that attempt to make sense of past findings verbally or conceptually. The vote-counting method refers to the accumulation of significance levels or, in the simplest case, to the tabulation of significant and nonsignificant findings (Hunter & Schmidt, 1990; Light & Smith, 1971). Both of these research integration techniques tend to draw false inferences because they do not correct for sampling and measurement error, two important study artifacts (Hedges & Olkin, 1980; Hunter & Schmidt, 1990). In fact, the statistical errors in the typical vote-counting literature review tend to be more serious than in the average narrative review because the statistical power of the vote-counting procedure *decreases* with *increasing* number of studies reviewed (Hedges & Olkin, 1980; Hunter & Schmidt, 1990).

   In contrast, effect-size (r) meta-analysis is a rigorous approach to external validation, which calculates population parameter estimates (r) by correcting for the aforementioned artifacts. The effect of sampling error is important because sample sizes that are smaller than the population cause observed sample correlation statistics r to vary randomly from the

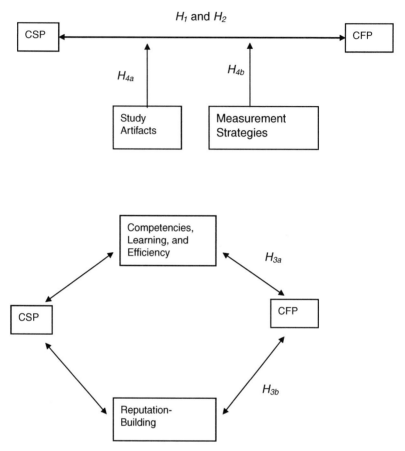

Figure 4.1   Hypothesized Relationships (H_i)
Note: CSP = corporate social performance; CFP = corporate financial performance.

population parameter, the true-score correlation ρ. Additionally, as mentioned before, measurement error (i.e., unreliability) systematically attenuates observed correlations (Nunnally & Bernstein, 1994).

Search for relevant studies

Computer searches of *ABI/Inform Global* and *PsycINFO* were conducted, using the keyword search 'organizational effectiveness and corporate social performance'. Synonyms for the former, used in separate computer searches, were 'organizational performance', 'profitability', 'economic success', and 'financial performance'. 'Corporate social performance' as a keyword search term was alternately substituted with 'corporate social responsibility', 'corporate environmental performance', 'responsiveness', and various abbreviations. *ABI/Inform Global* gives access to the full text and images of over 1,200 U.S. and international business and trade journal articles (1970-current), while *PsycINFO* indexes abstracts of journal articles and book chapters in psychology starting in 1974. To increase the scope of our search, cross-citations from previous narrative reviews (e.g., Aldag & Bartol, 1978; McGuire *et al.*, 1988, pp. 857–860; Preston, 1978a; Waddock & Mahon, 1991; Wood & Jones, 1995) were explored as well.

Criteria for relevance

The studies that were deemed relevant for the meta-analysis had the following characteristics. First, the studies quantitatively examined the relationship between CSP and CFP. The reported effect size did not have to be a Pearson's product-moment correlation *r*, but could also be a *t*-test statistic or effect size *d* (both *t* and *d* can be transformed to *r* according to Hunter & Schmidt, 1990). Second, the studies were concerned with at least one aspect of a firm's economic performance, as circumscribed by the definition of CFP. For the purpose of this study, CFP was defined as a company's financial viability, or the extent to which a company achieves its economic goals (Price & Mueller, 1986; Venkatraman & Ramanujam, 1986). Third, all retrieved studies were double-checked for conformance to Wood's (1991a) definition of CSP (see first paragraph of this chapter). Wood's (1991a) now classic definition is used because it is one of the most influential, helpful, parsimonious, and yet comprehensive conceptualizations of CSP. If the particular variable could not be classified as an example belonging to one of the nine subcategories of Wood's model, the study was excluded. In addition, unclear reporting of empirical results was also a reason for exclusion.

Note that this meta-analysis does not use Swanson's reconceptualization of CSP as presented in Chapters 1 and 2. Instead, it uses Wood's definition, which Swanson (1995) critiqued, remodeled, and extended. The older model of CSP was preferred for the purpose of statistical integration because Swanson's (1995, 1999) theoretical models are even broader than Wood's (1991a) conceptualization of CSP and thus more difficult to apply to previous quantitative measures of good corporate citizenship. In other words, for the purpose of our first quantitative meta-analysis, Wood's definition turned out to be empirically more tractable than Swanson's more comprehensive conceptualization. That said, Swanson's model may provide clues to theoretical moderators in future studies, a possibility we will explore in our final chapter.

Studies of environmental management and CFP are included in the meta-analysis for several reasons. First, several studies, especially earlier ones, used environmental performance as a proxy for social responsibility. Second, stakeholder proxies, such as environmental interest groups and government agencies, may in fact give voice to or claim a social 'stake' for, nonhuman nature (Starik, 1995). Finally, the business community tends to regard social responsibility as including both social and environmental performance (e.g., Willums, 1999). Still, the argument can be made that the literature on CSP differs from the one on corporate environmental performance in various aspects. To investigate differences between social and environmental performance, the entire set (k = number of effect sizes integrated = 388) is disaggregated into purely *social* performance measures only (i.e., excluding all environmental performance measures; k = 249) and environmental measures only (i.e., excluding all social performance measures; k = 139).

Characteristics of primary studies

Reliability is traditionally defined as the ratio of true-score variance to observed-score variance (Traub, 1994). Thus, classical measurement theory is concerned with the correspondence between observed scores and true scores. Some of the reliability coefficients used in this study are in the tradition of classical reliability theory, such as the coefficient alpha. Sometimes, however, it becomes necessary to count not only variation due to item sampling, but also day-to-day variation in scores as measurement error. In classical theory, one can accomplish this task by using an alternate-forms coefficient of reliability. In this regard, generalizability theory is less restrictive in its assumptions than classical theory (Cronbach, Gleser, Nanda & Rajaratnam, 1972). The coefficient of generalizability reflects the degree to which observed scores (of CSP or CFP in this case) allow for generalization about a firm's behavior in a defined universe of situations (Cronbach *et al.*, 1972; Shavelson, Webb & Rowley, 1989). Generalizability is estimated through 'alternate-forms' correlations between different CSP, and CFP, measures.

The present study estimates reliability by including coefficients of generalizability (76%), stability (4%), internal reliability (8%), and inter-rater reliability (12%). Both stability and generalizability coefficients are underestimates of reliability (Orlitzky, 1998). Because of the predominance of coefficients of stability and generalizability, the meta-analysis provides conservative estimates (i.e., lower-bound estimates) of the reliability of the CSP or CFP measurement instruments.

Depending on study context, both CSP and CFP were operational-ized in a wide variety of ways. From the vantage point of knowledge integration, this multiple operationism is an advantage because it helps determine whether a 'true' relationship exists in different industry con-texts with different operationalizations of the two focal constructs (Cook & Campbell, 1979; Cooper, 1989; Webb, Campbell, Schwartz, Sechrest & Grove, 1981). In past meta-analyses, integrated studies often contained broad meta-constructs as well, such as job or organizational performance, operationalized in many different ways (e.g., Gooding & Wagner, 1985; Ketchen, Combs, Russell, Shook, *et al.*, 1997; Roth, BeVier, Switzer & Schippmann, 1996; Wagner & Gooding, 1987). During data collection, the inclusion criteria for relevance (see the discussion above) served as constant checks on the operationalizations' consistency with the broad conceptual definitions of CSP and CFP.

Empirically, the standard deviation of r can serve as an indicator of cross-study heterogeneity. The percentage of cross-study variance explained by artifacts is another indicator of the degree of cross-study generalizability (Hunter & Schmidt, 1990).

Statistical conventions used in the meta-analysis

The meta-analysis uses Hunter and Schmidt's (1990) statistical aggrega-tion techniques for cumulating correlations and correcting for various study artifacts in order to estimate the true score correlation (r) between CSP and CFP. Meta-analysis arrives at a mean true-score correlation by correcting observed correlations for sampling error (which can be writ-ten as $\sigma_e = (1 - \rho^2) / (\sqrt{N - 1})$) and for measurement error. Since sampling error varies directly with sample size, all studies are weighted by sample size n_i before correcting for the average attenuation factor (Schmidt & Hunter, 1977).

Because measurement error data points are not always available for individual studies, study correlations cannot be corrected individually for measurement error. Instead, correlations are meta-analyzed using artifact distributions (for more details on artifact-distribution meta-analysis, see Hunter & Schmidt, 1990). The moderator analyses use Hunter and Schmidt's (1990) subgrouping algorithm, as described in the Results section.

Nonindependence in any meta-analytic data set can present certain problems. Therefore, sensitivity analyses were conducted by using two other aggregation techniques. In the first sensitivity analysis, we used only one independent correlation per study, i.e., com-posite scores. Furthermore, a second sensitivity analysis tested the stability of our transformations of effect sizes (reported t or d statistics into r).

Results

Overall CSP-CFP relationships

As shown in the first line of Table 4.1, the mean observed correlation (r_{obs}) for the total set of 388 correlations and a total sample size N of 33,878 observations is .18, with an observed variance of .06. The study artifacts of sampling and measurement error in CSP and CFP explain 24% of the cross-study variance of r_{obs}. After correction for sampling and measurement errors, the true score (corrected) correlation (ρ) was .36, which is twice the size of the observed correlation, with a variance (.19), which is slightly more than three times the size of the observed variance. As shown in the second line of Table 4.1, the relationship remains positive even after we removed studies that may be affected by response bias (survey measures of CFP) and a halo effect (see CSP reputation indices; Brown & Perry, 1994); the remaining meta-analytic set showed an average observed correlation of .08 and a true-score correlation of .15. Although this true score correlation is smaller than in the larger set including CSP reputation and CFP survey measures, it is not trivial. Thus, the meta-analytic findings support Hypothesis 1, which posits that corporate social performance and financial performance are generally positively related across a wide variety of industry and study contexts.

The sensitivity analyses tend to confirm this conclusion. The first sensitivity analysis, which uses only one effect size per study (thus, $k = 52$, $N = 4,924$), showed a mean observed correlation of .21 and a corrected correlation of .42. The second sensitivity analysis, on 210 product-moment correlations (k) with a total sample size of 22,218 observations (N), also showed slightly higher estimates ($r_{obs} = .20$; $\rho = .41$) than the overall meta-analysis reported in Table 4.1. Thus, in both sensitivity meta-analyses (not reported in the Tables), the mean observed and corrected correlations were positive and of similar magnitude as the correlations in the entire meta-analytic set. If anything, the sensitivity analyses suggest that the meta-analytic correlations reported in this chapter are actually conservative estimates of the true relationships between CSP and CFP.

Corporate social and environmental performance. Table 4.1 also shows analyses for two different conceptualizations of CSP. When the entire meta-analytic set was divided into two sets, (a) those studies using a

Table 4.1 Overall Meta-Analytic Findings (Hypothesis 1)

Relationship between...	k[a]	Total sample size	Sample-size weighted mean observed r (r_{obs})	Observed variance	%Variance Explained[b]	Mean 'true-score' r (mean ρ)	Variance of $\rho[\sigma^2(\rho)]$	File Drawer Analysis[c]
1. CSP and CFP (entire meta-analytic set)	388	33,878	.1836	.0646	23.89%	.3648	.1896	1,037
2. CSP and CFP without CSP reputation and CFP survey measures	252	20,662	.0776	.0296	43.94%	.1543	.0641	139
3.a. CSP without corporate environmental performance and CFP	249	24,055	.2301	.0638	27.04%	.4671	.1891	897
3.b. Corporate environmental performance and CFP	139	9,823	.0562	.0383	40.33%	.1246	.1097	17

[a] k: number of correlation coefficients meta-analyzed;
[b] refers to percentage of cross-study observed variance explained by 3 study artifacts: sampling error, measurement error in CSP, meas. error in CFP;
[c] Hunter & Schmidt's (1990) effect size file drawer analysis: Number of missing studies averaging null findings needed to bring r_{obs} down to .05.

narrow definition of social performance only (thus excluding measures of environmental performance; $k = 249$; $N = 24,055$) and (b) those studies using a narrow definition of environmental performance only (thus excluding measures of social performance; $k = 139$; $N = 9,823$), the findings show that corporate environmental performance has a smaller relationship with CFP ($r_{obs} = .06$; $\rho = .12$) than do all other measures of CSP ($r_{obs} = .23$; $\rho = .47$), such as managerial principles and corporate reputations for minority hiring, for example. In the corporate environmental performance subset, the variances of observed and true-score correlations were also smaller than those in the purely social CSP subset. Furthermore, measurement error and sampling error explained more of the cross-study variance of r_{obs} in the corporate environmental performance subset than in the purely social CSP subset. Thus, the last two lines of Table 4.1 (entries 3.a and 3.b) demonstrate that the relatively lower correlation between corporate *environmental* performance and CFP is in fact much more consistent across industry and study contexts than the primary empirical studies would have us believe.

File drawer analysis. In the overall meta-analysis as in all subsequent meta-analyses, an effect size *file drawer analysis* was performed to address the possibility of availability bias. Availability bias is one of the most common criticisms leveled against meta-analysis, in that critics of meta-analysis often suspect that published studies will report larger effect sizes than unpublished studies. File drawer analysis addresses this issue by computing the number of additional unlocated (i.e., 'lost' or overlooked) studies needed to cause the correlation to decrease to a minimal critical level (r_{crit}), which is set at .05 in this study. Hunter and Schmidt (1990) present the underlying assumptions and techniques of file drawer analysis. For each correlation computed in Tables 4.1 through 4.4, the results of the file drawer analysis are presented in the last column. As shown in Table 4.1, a very large number of studies (1,037) would be needed to change the overall substantive conclusions of this meta-analysis (entry 1 in Table 4.1).

Temporal sequence

Tables 4.2a and 4.2b show the results relevant to Hypothesis 2, which proposed a virtuous cycle between CSP and CFP. Consistent with that hypothesis, there is about equal empirical support for the instrumental stakeholder and slack resources perspectives. Specifically, both the prior CFP and subsequent CFP subsets yielded observed correlations of .15, and corrected correlations of .29 (first two lines in Table 4.2a). Concurrent studies showed observed and corrected correlations with

Table 4.2a Good Management Theory and Slack Resources Theory (Hypothesis 2, All Measures of CSP, Incl. Environmental Performance)

Relationship between…	k^a	Total sample size	Sample-size weighted mean observed r (r_{obs})	Observed variance	%Variance Explained[b]	Mean 'true-score' r (mean ρ)	Variance of $\rho[\sigma^2(\rho)]$	File Drawer Analysis[c]
CSP and subsequent CFP	68	6,966	.1450	.0602	20.47%	.2881	.1847	129
CSP and prior CFP	111	9,929	.1481	.0578	23.90%	.2944	.1697	218
CSP and concurrent CFP (cross-sectional studies)	209	16,983	.2201	.0677	26.47%	.4375	.1919	711

Table 4.2b Hypothesis 2 'Purely Social' CSP Measures Only

Relationship between…	k^a	Total sample size	Sample-size weighted mean observed r (r_{obs})	Observed variance	%Variance Explained[b]	Mean 'true-score' r (mean ρ)	Variance of $\rho[\sigma^2(\rho)]$	File Drawer Analysis[c]
CSP and subsequent CFP	31	4,189	.2016	.0722	17.20%	.4005	.2306	94
CSP and prior CFP	54	6,800	.2262	.0443	32.07%	.4495	.1161	190
CSP and concurrent CFP (cross-sectional studies)	158	12,764	.2529	.0755	26.13%	.5027	.2151	641

[a] k: number of correlation coefficients meta-analyzed;

[b] refers to percentage of cross-study observed variance explained by 3 study artifacts: sampling error, measurement error in CSP, meas. error in CFP;

[c] Hunter & Schmidt's (1990) effect size file drawer analysis: Number of missing studies averaging null findings needed to bring r_{obs} down to .05.

CFP of .22 and .44, respectively (third line of Table 4.2a). Taken toge-ther, these findings suggest a virtuous cycle with quick cycle times or concurrent bi-directionality. However, the low percentages of observed cross-study variance explained by artifacts, ranging from 20% to 26%, and large true-score variances ranging from .17 to .19, indicate the presence of at least one moderator. As Table 4.2b shows, consistent with the overall analysis (Table 4.1; entries 3.a and 3.b), the results are stronger after corporate environmental measures were removed from CSP. Generally, though, the relationships reported in Table 4.2b con-firm the conclusions that can be drawn from Table 4.2a.

Mediator variables: learning and reputation

To investigate Hypothesis 3, studies were divided into two broad subsets: (1) studies that correlated both internal and external mea-sures of CSP with only accounting CFP measures (i.e., measures of *internal* resource utilization, such as ROA or return on equity ROE); and (2) studies that correlated only *externally visible measures of CSP*, such as CSP reputation or disclosures, with exclusively *external* (e.g., market return or sales growth) measures of CFP. The reputational argument is further subdivided into studies correlating external indi-cators of CFP with: (a) reputation indices of CSP; (b) CSP disclosures in annual reports and letters to shareholders, and (c) other exter-nally visible measures of CSP such as social audits and charitable contributions.

Based on the magnitude of the meta-analytic correlations, the find-ings support the reputation-effects viewpoint relatively more strongly than the internal viewpoint, as shown in Table 4.3 (compare the first two lines in Table 4.3, i.e., entry 1 with entry 2). In addition, a further hierarchical breakdown of the *reputation view* subset indi-cates that CSP disclosures appear to have a low reputational impact on CFP. This statistical conclusion is generalizable across study set-tings because a high proportion of variance (93%) is explained by study artifacts (entry 2.b in Table 4.3). Moreover, the timing of mea-surement (temporal sequence) is not an important moderator within the reputation view argument. As was the case in the overall meta-analysis, the correlations between CSP and subsequent CFP are almost identical to the ones found between CSP and prior CFP (ρ = .75 and .73, respectively; entries 2.a.1 and 2.a.2 in Table 3). Again, the correlations are highest when CSP and CFP were measured less than a year apart (ρ = .91, with 51% of cross-study variance explained by artifacts; entry 2.a.3).

Table 4.3 Subset Meta-Analysis: Reputation Theory and Internal Skills Theory of CSP (Hypothesis 3)

Type of relationship...	k[a,d]	Total sample size	Sample-size weighted mean observed r (r_{obs})	Observed variance	%Variance Explained[b]	Mean 'true-score' r (mean ρ)	Variance of ρ[$\sigma^2(\rho)$]	File Drawer Analysis[c]
1. Efficiency, skills, learning, and/or competence	130	12,957	.1630	.0280	49.66%	.3324	.0572	294
2. Reputation theory	177	14,274	.2484	.1024	19.59%	.4942	.3185	702
2.a. Reputation indexes	65	6,858	.4197	.0992	24.77%	.7593	.2386	481
2.a.1. Subsequent CFP	10	1,088	.3681	.1869	15.43%	.7504	.6420	64
2.a.2. Prior CFP	9	1,074	.3558	.1053	25.58%	.7254	.3182	55
2.a.3. Concurrent CFP	46	4,696	.4463	.0752	51.29%	.9099	.1488	365
2.b. Disclosure measures	75	4,351	.0586	.0192	93.49%	.1399	.0070	13
2.c. Other	37	3,065	.1356	.0978	14.75%	.2698	.3226	63

[a] k: number of correlation coefficients meta-analyzed;

[b] refers to percentage of cross-study observed variance explained by 3 study artifacts: sampling error, measurement error in CSP, meas. error in CFP;

[c] Hunter & Schmidt's (1990) effect size file drawer analysis: Number of missing studies averaging null findings needed to bring r_{obs} down to .05.

[d] Correlations in subsets 1 and 2 do not add up to 388 because assignment to type of relationship was questionable in certain cases.

Moderator analysis

The analyses of Hypothesis 3 alluded to an important feature of Hunter and Schmidt's (1990) meta-analytic technique; namely, the detection of cross-study moderators. Because this algorithm will be used extensively in the remaining meta-analyses, a brief explanation is in order. Hunter and Schmidt's (1990) moderator analysis consists of two distinct methods. First, the '75% rule' can be applied, stating that if 75% or more of the observed variance of correlations across studies is due to artifacts, then probably all of it is artifactual variance (on the grounds that the remaining 25% is likely due to artifacts not corrected for; Hunter & Schmidt, 1990). Thus, in cases where 75% or more of the variance is explained by study artifacts, including sampling error variance, moderators are unlikely to have caused a real variation in observed correlations (r_{obs}). This first method is able to detect the existence of unsuspected moderators.

The second method, which can detect discontinuous, theoretically predicted moderators, compares mean observed and true-score correlations across study domain subsets of the original entire set of studies aggregated in the meta-analysis. If in these meta-analytic subgroups a higher percentage of variance is accounted for by study artifacts relative to the entire meta-analytic set, then moderators are said to exist.

Measurement strategy as moderator. To examine Hypotheses 4a and 4b, the entire data set of 388 correlations was broken down hierarchically to investigate the presence of moderator effects based on the operationalizations of CSP and CFP (Table 4.4a). First, CFP and CSP operationalizations were disaggregated separately. Second, the four broad CSP operationalization subsets were broken down hierarchically into the two (or three, where available) CFP measurement categories. The lowest level in Table 4.4a is the only one that is not confounded by lack of standardized measurement and, thus, is the most informative.

In general, Table 4.4a indicates that the association between CSP and CFP depends on the firm's and / or researcher's operational definition of each construct. Accounting measures were more highly correlated with CSP than market-based measures (ρ = .42 vs. .15; entries 1.b vs. 1.a in Table 4.4a), and were particularly highly correlated with CSP reputation indices (ρ = .61; entry 2.b.2). In fact, overall the findings with respect to CSP operationalizations suggest that studies that used reputation indices as proxies for CSP showed the highest average correlation with CFP (ρ of .73 with a large variance of .19; entry 2.b in

Table 4.4a Subset Meta-Analysis of Operationalization Moderator Effects (Hypothesis 4b)

Operationalization	k[a]	Total sample size	Sample-size weighted mean observed r (r_{obs})	Observed variance	%Variance Explained[b]	Mean 'true-score' r (mean ρ)	Variance of ρ [$\sigma^2(\rho)$]	File Drawer Analysis[c]
1. CFP operationalizations	388	33,878						
1.a. Market-based	161	10,463	.0733	.0670	24.24%	.1459	.1965	75
1.b. Accounting-based	205	20,984	.2070	.0478	33.87%	.4215	.1282	644
1.c. Perceptual measures	22	2,431	.4471	.0727	45.64%	.8885	.1525	175
2. CSP operationalizations	388	33,878						
2.a. Disclosure	97	5,360	.0438	.0189	98.47%	.0871	.0011	NA
2.a.1. Market-based CFP	79	4,426	.0548	.0206	89.75%	.1090	.0081	8
2.a.2. Accounting CFP	18	934	-.0085	.0077	100.00%	-.0168	.0000	NA
2.b. Reputation indexes	123	12,252	.3657	.0745	34.77%	.7268	.1875	777
2.b.1. Market-based CFP	45	4,291	.3593	.0965	26.64%	.7141	.2730	278
2.b.2. Accounting CFP	69	6,494	.3059	.0546	39.61%	.6078	.1271	353
2.b.3. Perceptual CFP	9	1,467	.6495	.0019	100.00%	.9481	.0000	108
2.c. Social audits, corp. behaviours, processes, and outcomes	145	14,200	.0907	.0332	34.00%	.1803	.0844	118
2.c.1. Market-based CFP	60	4,858	.0207	.0556	22.58%	.0411	.1661	NA
2.c.2. Accounting CFP	82	8,652	.1312	.0188	61.79%	.2607	.0277	133
2.c.3. Perceptual CFP	3	690	.0767	.0004	100.00%	.1524	.0000	2
2.d. Corp.social responsibility values and attitudes	23	2,066	.1041	.0272	45.94%	.2068	.0567	25
2.d.1. Market-based CFP	0	0						
2.d.2. Accounting CFP	13	1,792	.0747	.0178	44.97%	.1484	.0377	6
2.d.3. Perceptual CFP	10	274	.2962	.0464	93.90%	.5886	.0109	49

[a] k: number of correlation coefficients meta-analyzed;
[b] refers to percentage of cross-study observed variance explained by 3 study artifacts: sampling error, measurement error in CSP, meas. error in CFP;
[c] Hunter & Schmidt's (1990) effect size file drawer analysis: Number of missing studies averaging null findings needed to bring r_{obs} down to .05.

Table 4.4a). Of course, this high correlation may partially be due to the halo effect (Brown & Perry, 1994).

Furthermore, repeating the pattern of results testing reputation-theory effects (Table 4.3), disclosure measures appear to be only minimally related to CFP (r_{obs} = .04; ρ = .09, as shown in entry 2.a). This finding is generalizable because almost all the observed variance is explained by artifacts. Social audits, CSP processes, and outcomes are only modestly correlated with CFP (r_{obs} = .09; ρ = .18; entry 2.c). Similar mean correlations were found for the relationship between corporate social responsibility values or attitudes and CFP (r_{obs} = .10; ρ = .21; entry 2.d).

The second level in the hierarchical breakdown supports the view that differences in previous findings resulted from study artifacts, stakeholder mismatching, other theoretical mis-specifications, or lack of theory (see also McWilliams & Siegel, 2000). As discussed above, the overall percentage of cross-study variance (in r_{obs}) explained is 24%. In general, this percentage tends to increase in the measurement sub-groups listed in Table 4.4a, which suggests that studies systematically differ with respect to the distortions caused by (previously uncorrected) statistical and methodological artifacts. The fact that artifacts account for 15% to 100% of cross-study variance (which indicates the notorious 'inconsistencies' of this research stream) provides support for Hypothesis 4a.

The support for *theoretical* inconsistencies (stakeholder mismatching) becomes apparent by looking at some second-level hierarchical subgroups. First, the correlation of CSP disclosure measures with accounting CFP measures is slightly negative (ρ = −.02; entry 2.a.2). This small correlation supports the stakeholder mismatching thesis because there is no theoretical causal mechanism between CSP disclosures and internal (i.e., accounting) CFP measures. Second, the observed and corrected correlations between (a) social audit and other observable or 'objective' (e.g., dollar amount of charitable contributions) measures of CSP processes and (b) market-based measures of CFP are close to zero (Table 4.4, entry 2.c.1), which again supports the stakeholder mismatching thesis. As Wood and Jones (1995, p. 242) argued earlier, 'There is no theory to explain why stockholders would or would not prefer a company that gives one percent of pre-tax earnings to charity, that hires and develops minority or women workers, or that ranks higher in pollution control indices'. In other words, the data suggest that capital market participants dismiss certain concrete behavioral measures of CSP (such as charitable donations), perhaps because they are perceived as direct attempts by firms to manage external impressions (see the discussion of impression management in Chapter 3).

To examine the measurement moderators within subgroup 2.c even more closely, Table 4.4b shows results for social audits disaggregated from other CSP behaviors, which are further broken down. Two findings are noteworthy. First, social audits were consistently, but only modestly, correlated with CFP ($\rho = .23$, 100% of cross-study variance explained). Second, across industry contexts, philanthropic donations were related with CFP at $\rho = .29$, which was higher than the respective correlation coefficients found for all other measures of CSP behaviors. However, the file drawer analyses (last column of Table 4.4b) suggest that some of the findings presented in Table 4.4b are not conclusive because a small number of additional studies could change these particular conclusions.

Discussion

Theoretical implications

Based on this meta-analysis, which integrated thirty years of research, the answer to the introductory question posed by *Business Week* is affirmative. The results of this meta-analysis show that there is indeed a positive association between CSP and CFP across industries and study contexts. In that sense, we can confirm Frooman's (1997) conclusions (based on event studies), which support the validity of enlightened self-interest or the view that socially responsible actions may, especially in the long run, serve the economic interests of the firm and its owners. On the other hand, the data accumulated over the last thirty years do not support contingency theories of CSR that suggest an overall null relationship, such as that proposed by McWilliams and Siegel (2001). Consistent with earlier research reviews, these authors took inconsistent findings in primary studies at face value (i.e., they ignored the possible impact of sampling and measurement errors) and explained the (apparent) inconsistency with a demand/supply model of CSR. In contrast, the temporal dissection of our meta-analysis shows that the positive association between CFP and lagged CSP (*à la* the slack resources argument) does not mask a weaker negative association between CSP and lagged CFP. Furthermore, our findings were generally confirmed by a later meta-analysis by French researchers (Allouche, 2006; Allouche & Laroche, 2005), which included more European data points and several additional statistical analyses.

Can CSP be motivated by an 'ecological selection process based on profit maximization or organizational survival' (Wholey & Brittain,

Table 4.4b Further Subset Analyses of CSP in Terms of Social Audits, Corp. Behavior, Processes, and Outcomes with CFP (Hypothesis 4b)

Type of CSP	k^a	Total sample size	Sample-size weighted mean observed r (r_{obs})	Observed variance	%Variance Explained[b]	Mean 'true-score' r (mean ρ)	Variance of $\rho[\sigma^2(\rho)]$	File Drawer Analysis[c]
Social audits	35	5,016	.1143	.0081	100.00%	.2272	.0000	45
CSP behaviors:								
Philanthropic donations	17	1,283	.1463	.0642	24.60%	.2907	.1867	33
Environmental Assessment/Forecasting	3	401	.0592	.0143	55.62%	.1177	.0245	1
Issues Management	3	690	.0767	.0004	100.00%	.1524	.0000	2
Stakeholder Management	7	513	.0717	.0105	100.00%	.1425	.0000	3
Environmental Management	80	6,297	.0657	.0517	25.83%	.1306	.1479	25

[a] k: number of correlation coefficients meta-analyzed;
[b] refers to percentage of cross-study observed variance explained by 3 study artifacts: sampling error, measurement error in CSP, meas. error in CFP;
[c] Hunter & Schmidt's (1990) effect size file drawer analysis: Number of missing studies averaging null findings needed to bring r_{obs}

1986 in Husted, 2000, p. 33)? Husted (2000, p. 34) agrees with the narrative reviews in this area, stating that it is 'premature' to conclude that adaptation to market and nonmarket environments might force organizations to consider social issues and CSP in their day-to-day strategizing. But our meta-analysis suggests just the opposite. In fact, some of our observed correlations are higher than the correlations typically found between strategy-structure fit and CFP (Amburgey & Dacin, 1994; Donaldson, 1987). Ironically, despite these lower correlations, the strategy-structure-performance paradigm is firmly grounded in the assumption of an economic survival mechanism (across industry contexts), analogous to the logic supporting Hypothesis 1. It should also be noted that, on the one hand, our meta-analysis contradicts Rowley and Berman's (2000) suggestion that there cannot be a consistently positive relationship between CSP and CFP. Yet, on the other hand, in agreement with Rowley and Berman (2000), we demonstrate that the *universally positive* relationship varies (from highly positive to modestly positive) because of contingencies, such as reputation effects, market measures of CFP, or CSP disclosures.

Traditionally, researchers have worried that any positive correlations are artifactual, due to halo effects (Brown & Perry, 1994, 1995; Wood, 1995). However, it is important to keep in mind that the only credible halo linkage would be from CFP to CSP; i.e., companies that perform better financially receive higher CSP ratings, regardless of their true underlying CSP. The meta-analytic breakdown has shown that the potential halo effect or CFP → lagged CSP correlation does not dominate a weaker CSP → lagged CFP correlation and distort results. In fact, the two correlations are identical at two digits (.29, Table 4.2a). Also, when all potentially problematic studies are removed (i.e., those that measure CSP reputations only and those that measure CFP with a survey instrument), the meta-analysis still shows a nontrivial positive 'true-score' correlation of .15 (Table 4.1). Furthermore, the halo argument would suggest a much higher correlation between external (market) CFP and CSP reputation than between internal (accounting) CFP and CSP reputation. In fact, however, the correlations in both subgroups were similar (entries 2.b.1 versus 2.b.2 in Table 4.4a).

When the CFP survey measures and CSP reputation measures are removed, the cross-study variation of r_{obs} can be shown to be increasingly a function of the artifacts of sampling and measurement error (44%; entry 2 in Table 4.1). Thus, many of the negative findings in individual studies are artifactual, so that the generalization of a positive CSP-CFP relationship applies more broadly than previously suggested (e.g., Jones & Wicks, 1999; Pava & Krausz, 1995; Ullmann 1985; Wood & Jones, 1995). We can therefore state with some confidence that the association between CSP and lagged CFP is not negative. Moreover, the causation seems to be that CSP and CFP mutually affect each other through a virtuous cycle: financially successful companies spend more because they can afford it, but CSP also helps them become a bit more financially successful. Moreover, the file drawer analysis indicates that the present findings cannot be dismissed by availability bias.

This meta-analysis both rejects and confirms notions developed by neoclassical economists. On the one hand, it rejects the idea that CSP is necessarily inconsistent with shareholder wealth maximization (see Friedman, 1970; Levitt, 1958). Instead, organizational effectiveness may be a broader concept that encompasses both financial and social performance (Andrews, 1987; Judge, 1994), the former serving the legitimate interests of owner-stakeholders (see Donaldson & Preston, 1995; Jones & Wicks, 1999). On the other hand, our findings point to a need to revisit government regulation in the area of CSP. For if the statistical relationship between CSP and CFP were negative, then bottom-line considerations might constitute barriers to pursuing desirable social outcomes. Logically, this might make government intervention on behalf of 'the public interest' a necessity. Yet, the current study suggests that the case for such regulation is not preordained because, in many cases, organizations, shareholders, and other constituents can all benefit from managers' prudent analysis, evaluation, and balancing of multiple constituent preferences. This recalls the importance of building a trustful dialogue with stakeholders, as discussed in Chapter 3. Along these lines, CSP actions would ideally be adopted by managers voluntarily over time, based on a robust knowledge of the costs and benefits of firm investments, including the reputational benefits of responding to and balancing multiple stakeholder interests.

In contrast, 'socially responsible' command-and-control regulation may prescribe inflexible policies and procedures that are less informed and therefore inappropriate for a particular firm's nonmarket and market environments (Majumdar & Marcus, 2001). That is, such regulation might actually discourage a virtuous cycle between CSP and CFP. This suggests that a complementary contingency theory of regulation needs to be developed, based on public policy aimed at encouraging continual business innovations in CSP while protecting important public interests when necessary, a point to which we shall return.

Implications for future research

The meta-analysis helps to identify areas in which there have been relatively few studies conducted, and which warrant more research (e.g., social responsibility values and market CFP; Table 4.4a). Additionally, the analysis shows areas in which the unexplained variance across studies remains relatively large, so that further inquiry is needed to identify moderators (e.g., CSP reputation measures and market-based CFP; CSP audits and market CFP; see Table 4.4a). However, since measurement errors were also relatively large, the field' scholars should make a concerted effort to improve the reliability of CSP and CFP measures. In several subgroups, the percentage of variance of r_{obs} explained by measurement error (i.e., low reliability) was substantial. In addition to psychometric refinements, these findings imply that CSP researchers must decide whether CSP *processes* should really be regarded as a social performance measure. Including processes is equivalent to acknowledging business *effort*. Moreover previous studies might have been overinclusive with respect to definitions of stakeholders and thus, overstate proxies for CSP (see Roman *et al.*, 1999).

Another concern that may be raised relates to the differences in CSP measurement. This issue, the subject of Chapter 8, definitely needs to be examined in future theoretical and empirical work. We believe that CSP, like CFP, is a valid theoretical construct – admittedly a meta-construct – which can be measured in a variety of ways. Consistent with Meyer and Gupta's (1994) view, the possible independence of the operationalizations might be a natural outcome of differences in organizational strategies, structures, and environments. Moreover, many meta-analysts (e.g., Cooper, 1989; Dalton, Daily, Johnson & Ellstrand, 1999; Hunter & Schmidt, 1990; Smith & Glass, 1977) think that broad constructs can – and should – be operationalized in a number of ways. As long as researchers' and organizations' choices of CSP (and CFP) measures are informed by prior judgments of their theoretical meaningfulness and subjected to peer review, then relatively low correlations across measurement categories do not present an obstacle to research integration. More important to the present case, however, is that our review of CSP generalizability coefficients shows that different CSP measures are in fact rather highly correlated ($r_{xx} = .71$). In other words, conceptual speculations about the impossibility of meaningful integration of prior research are not supported by empirical evidence (for a detailed review of this topic, see Orlitzky, 1998).

Implications for managers

Despite previous assumptions of inconclusive findings (e.g., Jones & Wicks, 1999; McWilliams & Siegel, 2001; Roman *et al.*, 1999; Ullmann, 1985; Wood & Jones, 1995), we can legitimately derive implications for corporate strategy from the our meta-analysis. First and foremost, we can infer that market forces generally do not penalize companies that are high in corporate social performance. Hence, managers can afford to be socially responsible. If managers believe that CSP is an antecedent of CFP, they may eventually pursue CSP actively because they think the market will reward them for doing so. The corollary is that top managers should learn to use CSP as a reputational lever ($\rho = .73$) and be attentive to perceptions of third parties, regardless of whether they are market analysts, public interest groups, or the media. Whereas social audits in and of themselves are only moderately beneficial ($\rho = .23$), a company that is high in CSP may especially benefit from receiving public endorsements from federal agencies such as the EPA or OSHA. As Fombrun (1996) suggests, the key to reaping benefits from CSP is a return from reputation (see also Roberts & Dowling, 2000).

As findings about the positive relationships between CSP and CFP become more widely known, managers may be more likely to pursue CSP as part of their strategy for attaining high CFP. These strategic management considerations would be consistent with Baron's (2006) managerial approach to the business-society interface. Baron argues that successful executives are able to integrate market strategies with nonmarket strategies in order to position their firm for optimal effectiveness, a view similar to the emphasis placed on receptive leadership in Chapter 2. Alternatively, social performance may increase through less deliberate decision processes, as firms emulate others that are experiencing high financial success (DiMaggio & Powell, 1983). Either evolutionary process would potentially reduce the importance of coercive control mechanisms (in the form of government regulations) for effecting public welfare and ecological sustainability. A caveat, however, is that some managers may not realize the possibility for gains through CSP because business schools have been slow to incorporate coursework in this area (Swanson & Fisher, in press). Without such coursework, the perception of a preordained tradeoff between profits and corporate social responsibility may persist in many circles.

Even so, our meta-analytic findings support the business case that many successful executives use to justify organizational investments in CSP. This meta-analysis is also consistent with the view held, among others, by Hart (2007) and Hawken, Lovins and Lovins (1999) that business, natural, and human interests can be aligned. Contrary to many doubters (especially in academia), CSP can represent a proactive response toward changing social and environmental conditions that yields many economic benefits (e.g., the avoidance of expensive litigation or government regulation). Even Milton Friedman (2005) came around to acknowledging the strategic benefits of corporate social responsibility, at least under some circumstances.

At this point a caveat is in order, so that our findings are not misunderstood. By emphasizing the positive reinforcing relationship between CSP and CFP, we do not suggest that CFP is the *only* or even *primary* justification for CSR. We do not advocate in any normative sense the view that CFP must be invoked to justify CSR. All we are doing is *describing* this empirical relationship in statistical (probabilistic) terms. Furthermore, we do not show that high CSP will *always* lead to high CFP at the organizational level of analysis. In fact, because of the large variability, in about 15% of all cases, it will not. The point is that this chapter describes the empirical relationship in statistical (probabilistic) terms in order to inform further research in this area.

That said, it is worth considering Husted and Salazar's (2006) proposition that CSP conveys the most benefits to business *and* society when it is chosen for strategic (i.e., business) purposes. This raises the possibility that social and economic benefits will be more limited if business is coerced to be socially responsible. But not all CSR experts agree. For example, Vogel (2005, p. 171) admonishes business that firms sometimes have a moral obligation to lobby government for imposing regulatory (compliance) control, which in some cases would hamper firms' profit-seeking. The danger of adopting this stance wholecloth is that a rush to create an equal-playing field for *all* firms or an entire industry may (a) dampen incentives to innovate in the area of stakeholder and environmental management and (b) decrease the economic reputational benefits for those who might have otherwise established a lead in CSP. The probability of establishing a lead will be particularly high when the entire industry has such a bad reputation that a good corporate citizen will be easily recognized by stakeholders, especially external ones. The point is that forcing firms to follow the same bureaucratic rule book may make it more difficult for any one firm to differentiate itself strategically from the others. As a result, CSP innovations could be dampened in the long run, leading to less social welfare over time (see B. M. Friedman, 2005; Greenspan, 2007). We will return to this possibility in our final chapter in terms of implications for regulation.

Conclusion

Portraying managers' choices with respect to CSP and CFP as an either/or tradeoff is not justified in light of 30 years of empirical data. Nor is it justified in terms of the theoretical frameworks developed in Chapters 1 and 2. This meta-analysis has shown that (1) across studies, CSP is positively correlated with CFP, (2) the relationship tends to be reciprocal and almost simultaneous, (3) reputation appears to be an important mediator of the relationship, and (4) stakeholder mismatching, sampling error, and measurement error can explain between 15% and 100% of the cross-study variation in various subsets of CSP-CFP correlations. The lesson is that corporate virtue in the form of social and, to a lesser extent, environmental responsibility can be rewarding both to the business sector and the general public.

References

References marked with an asterisk indicdjate studies included in the meta-analysis.

* Abbott, W. F. & Monsen, J. R. (1979). On the measurement of corporate social responsibility: Self-reported disclosure as a method of measuring corporate social involvement. *Academy of Management Journal, 22*, 501–515.

Aldag, R. J. & Bartol, K. M. (1978). Empirical studies of corporate social performance and policy: A survey of problems and results. In L. E. Preston (ed.), *Research in corporate social performance and policy, 1* (pp. 165–199). Greenwich, CT: JAI Press.

* Alexander, G. J. & Buchholz, R. A. (1978). Corporate social performance and stock market performance. *Academy of Management Journal, 21*, 479–486.

Allouche, J. (2006). *Corporate social responsibility, Vol. 2: Performances and stakeholders*. London: Palgrave Macmillan.

Allouche, J. & Laroche, P. (2005). A meta-analytical investigation of the relationship between corporate social and financial performance. *Revue de gestion des ressources humaines, 57*, 18–41.

Amburgey, T. L. & Dacin, T. (1994). As the left foot follows the right? The dynamics of strategic and structural change. *Academy of Management Journal, 37*, 1427–1452.

* Anderson, J. C. & Frankle, A. W. (1980). Voluntary social reporting: An iso-beta portfolio analysis. *Accounting Review, 55*, 467–479.

Andrews, K. R. (1987). *The concept of corporate strategy* 3rd ed. Homewood, IL: Irwin.

Aupperle, K. E. (1984). An empirical measure of corporate social orientation. In L. E. Preston (ed.), *Research in corporate social performance and policy, 6* (pp. 27–54). Greenwich, CT: JAI Press.

Aupperle, K. E. (1991). The use of forced-choice survey procedures in assessing corporate social orientation. In J. E. Post (ed.), *Research in corporate social performance and policy, 12* (pp. 269–279). Greenwich, CT: JAI Press.

* Aupperle, K. E., Carroll, A. B. & Hatfield, J. D. (1985). An empirical investigation of the relationship between corporate social responsibility and profitability. *Academy of Management Journal, 28*, 446–463.
Barnett, M. L. (2007). Stakeholder influence capacity and the variability of financial returns to corporate social responsibility. *Academy of Management Review, 32*(3), 794–816.
Barney, J. (1991). Firm resources and sustained competitive advantage. *Journal of Management, 17*, 771–792.
Baron, D. P. (2006). *Business and its environment* 5th ed. Upper Saddle River, NJ: Prentice Hall.
* Belkaoui, A. (1976). The impact of the disclosure of the environmental effects of organizational behavior on the market. *Financial Management, 5*, 26–31.
* Blackburn, V. L., Doran, M. & Shrader, C. B. (1994). Investigating the dimensions of social responsibility and the consequences for corporate financial performance. *Journal of Managerial Issues, 6*, 195–212.
* Bowman, E. H. (1976). Strategy and the weather. *Sloan Management Review, 17*, 49–58.
* Bowman, E. H. (1978). Strategy, annual reports, and alchemy. *California Management Review, 20*, 64–71.
* Bowman, E. H. & Haire, M. (1975). A strategic posture toward corporate social responsibility. *California Management Review, 18*, 49–58.
* Bragdon, J. H., Jr. & Marlin, J. A. T. (1972). Is pollution profitable? *Risk Management, 19*, 9–18.
* Brown, B. & Perry, S. (1994). Removing the financial performance halo from *Fortune*'s 'Most Admired Companies'. *Academy of Management Journal, 37*, 1346–1359.
* Brown, B. & Perry, S. (1995). Halo-removed residuals of *Fortune*'s 'responsibility to the community and environment': A decade of data. *Business & Society, 34*, 199–215.
Carroll, A. B. (1979). A three-dimensional conceptual model of corporate social performance. *Academy of Management Review, 4*, 497–506.
Carroll, A. B. (1991). Corporate social performance measurement: A commentary on methods for evaluating an elusive construct. In J. E. Post (ed.), *Research in corporate social performance and policy, 12* (pp. 385–401). Greenwich, CT: JAI Press.
* Chen, K. H. & Metcalf, R. W. (1980). The relationship between pollution control record and financial indicators revisited. *Accounting Review, 55*, 168–177.
Clarkson, M. B. E. (1991). Defining, evaluating, and managing corporate social performance: The stakeholder management model. In J. E. Post (ed.), *Research in corporate social performance and policy, 12* (pp. 331–358). Greenwich, CT: JAI Press.
Clarkson, M. B. E. (1995). A stakeholder framework for analyzing and evaluating corporate social performance. *Academy of Management Review, 20*, 92–117.
* Cochran, P. L. & Wood, R. A. (1984). Corporate social responsibility and financial performance. *Academy of Management Journal, 27*, 42–56.
* Conine, T. E. & Madden, G. P. (1987). Corporate social responsibility and investment value: The expectational relationship. In W. D. Guth (ed.), *Handbook of business strategy 1986/1987 yearbook* (pp. 18-1 to 18-9). Boston: Warren, Gorham & Lamont.

Cook, T. D. & Campbell, D. T. (1979). *Quasi-Experimentation: Design & analysis issues for field settings*. Boston, MA: Houghton Mifflin.

Cooper, H. M. (1989). *Integrating research: A guide for literature reviews* 2nd ed. Newbury Park, CA: Sage.

Cornell, B. & Shapiro, A. (1987). Corporate stakeholders and corporate finance. *Financial Management, 16*, 5–14.

* Cowen, S. S., Ferreri, L. B. & Parker, L. D. (1987). The impact of corporate characteristics on social responsibility disclosure: A typology and frequency-based analysis. *Accounting, Organizations and Society, 12*, 111–122.

Cronbach, L. J., Gleser, G. C., Nanda, H. & Rajaratnam, N. (1972). *The dependability of behavioral measurements: Theory of generalizability of scores and profiles*. New York: Wiley.

Dalton, D. R., Daily, C. M., Johnson, J. L. & Ellstrand, A. E. (1999). Number of directors and financial performance: A meta-analysis. *Academy of Management Journal, 42*, 674–686.

Damanpour, F. (1991). Organizational innovation: A meta-analysis of effects of determinants and moderators. *Academy of Management Journal, 34*, 555–590.

Datta, D. K., Pinches, G. E. & Narayanan, V. K. (1992). Factors influencing wealth creation from mergers and acquisitions: A meta-analysis. *Strategic Management Journal, 13*, 67–84.

* Davidson, W. N. III & Worrell, D. L. (1992). Research notes and communications: The effect of product recall announcements on shareholder wealth. *Strategic Management Journal, 13*, 467–473.

Davis, K. (1973). The case for and against business assumptions of social responsibilities. *Academy of Management Journal, 16*, 312–317.

DiMaggio, P. J. & Powell, W. W. (1983). The iron cage revisited: Institutional isomorphism and collective rationality in organizational fields. *American Sociological Review, 48*, 147–160.

Donaldson, L. (1987). Strategy and structural adjustment to regain fit and performance: In defense of contingency theory. *Journal of Management Studies, 24*, 1–24.

Donaldson, T. & Preston, L. E. (1995). The stakeholder theory of the corporation: Concepts, evidence, and implications. *Academy of Management Review, 20*, 65–91.

* Dooley, R. S. & Lerner, L. D. (1994). Pollution, profits, and stakeholders: The constraining effect of economic performance on CEO concern with stakeholder expectations. *Journal of Business Ethics, 13*, 701–711.

* Fogler, H. R. & Nutt, F. (1975). A note on social responsibility and stock valuation. *Academy of Management Journal, 18*, 155–160.

Fombrun, C. J. (1996). *Reputation: Realizing value from the corporate image*. Boston, MA: Harvard Business School Press.

Fombrun, C. J., Gardberg, N. A. & Barnett, M. L. (2000). Opportunity platforms and safety nets: Corporate citizenship and reputational risk. *Business and Society Review, 105*, 85–106.

* Fombrun, C. & Shanley, M. (1990). What's in a name? Reputation building and corporate strategy. *Academy of Management Journal, 33*, 233–258.

* Freedman, M. & Jaggi, B. (1982). Pollution disclosures, pollution performance and economic performance. *Omega: The International Journal of Management Science, 10*, 167–176.

* Freedman, M. & Jaggi, B. (1986). An analysis of the impact of corporate pollution disclosures included in annual financial statements on investors' decisions. *Advances in Public Interest Accounting, 1*, 192–212.

Freeman, R. E. (1984). *Strategic management: A stakeholder approach*. Marshfield, MA: Pitman.

Freeman, R. E. & Evan, W. M. (1990). Corporate governance: A stakeholder interpretation. *Journal of Behavioral Economics, 19*(4), 337–359.

Friedman, B. M. (2005). *The moral consequences of economic growth*. New York: Knopf.

Friedman, M. (1970, September 13). The social responsibility of business is to increase its profits. *New York Times Magazine*: 33+.

Friedman, M. (2005). Making philanthropy out of obscenity. *Reason, 37*(5), 32–33.

Frooman, J. (1997). Socially irresponsible and illegal behavior and shareholder wealth: A meta-analysis of event studies. *Business & Society, 36*, 221–249.

Gephardt, R. P., Jr. (1991). Multiple methods for tracking corporate social performance: Insights from a study of major industrial accidents. In J. E. Post (ed.), *Research in corporate social performance and policy, 12* (pp. 359–383). Greenwich, CT: JAI Press.

Godfrey, P. C. (2005). The relationship between corporate philanthropy and shareholder wealth: A risk management perspective. *Academy of Management Review, 30*(4), 777–798.

Gooding, R. Z. & Wagner, J. A. III. (1985). A meta-analytic review of the relationship between size and performance: The productivity and efficiency of organizations and their subunits. *Administrative Science Quarterly, 30*, 462–481.

* Graves, S. B. & Waddock, S. A. (1994). Institutional owners and corporate social performance. *Academy of Management Journal, 37*, 1034–1046.

* Greening, D. W. (1995). Conservation strategies, firm performance, and corporate reputation in the U.S. electric utility industry. *Research in Corporate Social Performance and Policy, Supplement 1* (pp. 345–368). Greenwich, CT: JAI Press.

Greening, D. W. & Turban, D. B. (2000). Corporate social performance as a competitive advantage in attracting a quality workforce. *Business & Society, 39*, 254–280.

Greenspan, A. (2007). *The age of turbulence: Adventures in a new world*. New York: Penguin.

* Griffin, J. J. & Mahon, J. F. (1997). The corporate social performance and corporate financial performance debate: Twenty-five years of incomparable research. *Business & Society, 36*, 5–31.

* Hansen, G. S. & Wernerfelt, B. (1989). Determinants of firm performance: The relative importance of economic and organizational factors. *Strategic Management Journal, 10*, 399–411.

Hart, S. L. (1995). A natural resource-based view of the firm. *Academy of Management Review, 20*, 986–1014.

Hart, S. L. (2007). *Capitalism at the crossroads: Aligning business, Earth, and humanity* (2nd ed.). Upper Saddle River, NJ: Wharton School Publishing.

Hawken, P., Lovins, A. B. & Lovins, L. H. (1999). *Natural capitalism: The next industrial revolution*. London: Earthscan.

Hedges, L. V. (1987). How hard is hard science, how soft is soft science? The empirical cumulativeness of research. *American Psychologist, 42*(2), 443–455.

Hedges, L. V. & Olkin, I. (1980). Vote counting methods in research synthesis. *Psychological Bulletin, 88,* 359–369.

* Heinze, D. C. (1976). Financial correlates of a social involvement measure. *Akron Business and Economic Review, 7,* 48–51.

* Herremans, I. M., Akathaporn, P. & McInnes, M. (1993). An investigation of corporate social responsibility reputation and economic performance. *Accounting, Organizations and Society, 18,* 587–604.

Hill, C. W. L. & Jones, T. M. (1992). Stakeholder-agency theory. *Journal of Management Studies, 29,* 131–154.

Hunt, M. (1997). *How science takes stock: The story of meta-analysis.* New York: Russell Sage Foundation.

Hunter, J. E. & Schmidt, F. L. (1990). *Methods of meta-analysis: Correcting errors and bias in research findings.* Newbury Park, CA: Sage.

Husted, B. W. (2000). A contingency theory of corporate social performance. *Business & Society, 39,* 24–48.

Husted, B. W. & Salazar, J. D. J. (2006). Taking Friedman seriously: Maximizing profits and social performance. *Journal of Management Studies, 43*(1), 75–91.

* Ingram, R. W. (1978). An investigation of the information content of (certain) social responsibility disclosures. *Journal of Accounting Research, 16,* 270–285.

* Ingram, R. W. & Frazier, K. B. (1980). Environmental performance and corporate disclosure. *Journal of Accounting Research, 18,* 614–622.

* Jacobson, R. (1987). The validity of ROI as a measure of business performance. *American Economic Review, 77,* 470–478.

Jones, T. M. (1995). Instrumental stakeholder theory: A synthesis of ethics and economics. *Academy of Management Review, 20,* 404–437.

Jones, T. M. & Wicks, A. C. (1999). Convergent stakeholder theory. *Academy of Management Review, 24,* 206–221.

Judge, W. Q., Jr. (1994). Correlates of organizational effectiveness: A multilevel analysis of a multidimensional outcome. *Journal of Business Ethics, 13*: 1–10.

* Kedia, B. L. & Kuntz, E. C. (1981). The context of social performance: An empirical study of Texas banks. In L. E. Preston (ed.), *Research in corporate social performance and policy, 3* (pp. 133–154). Greenwich, CT: JAI Press.

Ketchen, D. J., Jr., Combs, J. G., Russell, C. J., Shook, C., *et al.* (1997). Organizational configurations and performance. *Academy of Management Journal, 40,* 223–240.

Levitt, T. (1958, Sept./Oct.). The dangers of social responsibility. *Harvard Business Review, 36,* 38–44.

* Levy, F. K. & Shatto, G. M. (1980). Social responsibility in large electric utility firms: The case for philanthropy. In L. E. Preston (ed.), *Research in corporate social performance and policy, 2* (pp. 237–249). Greenwich, CT: JAI Press.

Light, R. J. & Smith, P. V. (1971). Accumulating evidence: Procedures for resolving contradictions among different research studies. *Harvard Educational Review, 41,* 429–471.

* Long, W. F. & Ravenscraft, D. J. (1984). The misuse of accounting rates of return: comment. *American Economic Review, 74,* 494–501.

Mackey, A., Mackey, T. B. & Barney, J. B. (2007). Corporate social responsibility and firm performance: Investor preferences and corporate strategies. *Academy of Management Review, 32*(3), 817–835.

Majumdar, S. K. & Marcus, A. A. (2001). Rules versus discretion: The productivity consequences of flexible regulations. *Academy of Management Journal, 44,* 170–179.

* Marcus, A. A. & Goodman, R. S. (1986). Compliance and performance: Toward a contingency theory. In L. E. Preston (ed.), *Research in corporate social performance and policy, 8* (pp. 193–221). Greenwich, CT: JAI Press.

McGuire, J. B., Schneeweis, T. & Branch, B. (1990). Perceptions of firm quality: A cause or result of firm performance. *Journal of Management, 16,* 167–180.

* McGuire, J. B., Sundgren, A. & Schneeweis, T. (1988). Corporate social responsibility and firm financial performance. *Academy of Management Journal, 31,* 854–872.

McWilliams, A. & Siegel, D. (2000). Corporate social responsibility and financial performance: Correlation or misspecification? *Strategic Management Journal, 21,* 603–609.

McWilliams, A. & Siegel, D. (2001). Corporate social responsibility: A theory of the firm perspective. *Academy of Management Review, 26,* 117–127.

Meyer, M. W. & Gupta, V. (1994). The performance paradox. *Research in Organizational Behavior, 16,* 309–369.

Mitchell, R. K., Agle, B. R. & Wood, D. J. (1997). Toward a theory of stakeholder identification and salience: Defining the principle of who and what really counts. *Academy of Management Review, 22,* 853–886.

Moskowitz, M. R. (1972). Choosing socially responsible stocks. *Business and Society Review, 1,* 71–75.

Moskowitz, M. R. (1975). Profiles in corporate social responsibility. *Business and Society Review, 13,* 29–42.

* Newgren, K. E., Rasher, A. A., LaRoe, M. E. & Szabo, M. R. (1985). Environmental assessment and corporate performance: A longitudinal analysis using a market-determined performance measure. In Lee E. Preston (ed.), *Research in corporate social performance and policy, 7* (pp. 153–164). Greenwich, CT: JAI Press.

The Next Bottom Line. (1999, May 3). *Business Week (Asian Edition)*: 45–96.

Nunnally, J. C. & Bernstein, I. H. (1994). *Psychometric theory* (3rd ed.). New York: McGraw-Hill.

* O'Neill, H. M., Saunders, C. B. & McCarthy, A. D. (1989). Board members, corporate social responsiveness and profitability: Are tradeoffs necessary? *Journal of Business Ethics, 8,* 353–357.

Orlitzky, M. (1998). *A meta-analysis of the relationship between corporate social performance and firm financial performance.* Dissertation thesis, University of Iowa, UMI.

* Parket, I. R. & Eilbirt, H. (1975). Social responsibility: The underlying factors. *Business Horizons, 18,* 5–10.

* Patten, D. M. (1990). The market reaction to social responsibility disclosures: The case of the Sullivan Principles signings. *Accounting, Organizations and Society, 15,* 575–587.

* Pava, M. L. & Krausz, J. (1995). *Corporate responsibility and financial performance: The paradox of social cost.* Westport, CT: Quorum.

Post, J. E. (ed.). (1991). *Research in corporate social performance and policy, vol. 12.* Greenwich, CT: JAI Press.

Preston, L. E. (1978a). Corporate social performance and policy: A synthetic framework for research and analysis. In L. E. Preston (ed.), *Research in corporate social performance and policy, 1* (pp. 1–25). Greenwich, CT: JAI Press.

* Preston, L. E. (1978b). Analyzing corporate social performance: Methods and results. *Journal of Contemporary Business, 7*, 135–150.

Price, J. L. & Mueller, C. W. (1986). *Handbook of organizational measurement* 2nd ed. Marshfield, MA: Pitman.

* Reimann, B. C. (1975). Organizational effectiveness and management's public values: A canonical analysis. *Academy of Management Journal, 18*, 224–241.

* Riahi-Belkaoui, A. (1991). Organizational effectiveness, social performance and economic performance. In J. E. Post (ed.), *Research in corporate social performance and policy, 12* (pp. 143–153). Greenwich, CT: JAI Press.

Roberts, P. W. & Dowling, G. R. (2000, August). *Reputation and sustained superior financial performance.* Academy of Management Best Paper Proceedings, BPS M1-M6.

* Roberts, R. W. (1992). Determinants of corporate social responsibility disclosure: An application of stakeholder theory. *Accounting, Organizations and Society, 17*, 595–612.

Roman, R. M., Hayibor, S. & Agle, B. R. (1999). The relationship between social and financial performance: Repainting a portrait. *Business & Society, 38*, 109–125.

Rosenthal, R. (1995). Writing meta-analytic reviews. *Psychological Bulletin, 118*, 183–192.

Rosenthal, R. & DiMatteo, M. R. (2001). Meta-analysis: Recent developments in quantitative methods for literature reviews. *Annual Review of Psychology, 52*, 59–82.

Roth, P. L., BeVier, C. A., Switzer, F. S. III. & Schippmann, J. S. (1996). Meta-analyzing the relationship between grades and job performance. *Journal of Applied Psychology, 81*, 548–557.

Rowley, T. J. (1997). Moving beyond dyadic ties: A network theory of stakeholder influences. *Academy of Management Review, 22*, 887–910.

Rowley, T. J. & Berman, S. (2000). A brand new brand of corporate social performance. *Business & Society, 39*, 397–418.

* Russo, M. V. & Fouts, P. A. (1997). A resource-based perspective on corporate environmental performance and profitability. *Academy of Management Journal, 40*, 534–559.

Schmidt, F. L. (1992). What do data really mean? Research findings, meta-analysis, and cumulative knowledge in psychology. *American Psychologist, 47*, 1173–1181.

Schmidt, F. L. & Hunter, J. E. (1977). Development of a general solution to the problem of validity generalization. *Journal of Applied Psychology, 62*, 529–540.

Schuler, D. A. & Cording, M. (2006). A corporate social performance-corporate financial performance behavioral model for consumers. *Academy of Management Review, 31*(3), 540–558.

Schwenk, C. (1989). A meta-analysis on the comparative effectiveness of devil's advocacy and dialectical inquiry. *Strategic Management Journal, 10*: 303–306.

* Shane, P. B. & Spicer, B. H. (1983). Market response to environmental information produced outside the firm. *Accounting Review, 58*, 521–538.

* Sharfman, M. (1996). A concurrent validity study of the KLD social performance ratings data. *Journal of Business Ethics, 15*, 287–296.

Shavelson, R. J., Webb, N. M. & Rowley, G. L. (1989). Generalizability theory. *American Psychologist, 44*, 922–932.

Shrivastava, P. (1995). Ecocentric management for a risk society. *Academy of Management Review, 20*, 118–137.

* Simerly, R. L. (1994). Corporate social performance and firms' financial performance: An alternative perspective. *Psychological Reports, 75*, 1091–1103.

* Simerly, R. L. (1995). Institutional ownership, corporate social performance, and firms' financial performance. *Psychological Reports, 77*, 515–525.

Smith, M. L. & Glass, G. V. (1977). Meta-analysis of psychotherapy outcome studies. *American Psychologist, 32*, 752–760.

* Spencer, B. A. & Taylor, S. G. (1987). A within and between analysis of the relationship between corporate social responsibility and financial performance. *Akron Business and Economic Review, 18*, 7–18.

* Spicer, B. H. (1978). Investors, corporate social performance and information disclosure: An empirical study. *Accounting Review, 53*, 94–111.

* Starik, M. (1990). *Stakeholder management and firm performance: Reputation and financial relationships to U.S. electric utility consumer-related strategies.* Unpublished doctoral dissertation, University of Georgia, Athens, GA.

Starik, M. (1995). Should trees have managerial standing? Toward stakeholder status for non-human nature. *Journal of Business Ethics, 14*, 207–217.

* Sturdivant, F. D. & Ginter, J. L. (1977). Corporate social responsiveness: Management attitudes and economic performance. *California Management Review, 19*, 30–39.

Swanson, D. L. (1995). Addressing a theoretical problem by reorienting the corporate social performance model. *Academy of Management Review, 20*, 43–64.

Swanson, D. L. (1999). Toward an integrative theory of business and society: A research strategy for corporate social performance. *Academy of Management Review, 24*, 506–521.

Swanson, D. L. & Fisher, D. (in press). Business ethics education: If we don't know where we are going, any road will take us there. In Swanson, D. L & Fisher, D. (eds), *Advancing Business Ethics Education,* Information Age Publishing.

Traub, R. E. (1994). *Reliability for the social sciences: Theory and applications* Vol. 3. Thousand Oaks, CA: Sage.

* Turban, D. B. & Greening, D. W. (1997). Corporate social performance and organizational attractiveness to prospective employees. *Academy of Management Journal, 40*, 658–672.

Ullmann, A. (1985). Data in search of a theory: A critical examination of the relationship among social performance, social disclosure, and economic performance. *Academy of Management Review, 10*, 540–577.

* Vance, S. (1975). Are socially responsible firms good investment risks? *Management Review, 64*, 18–24.

Venkatraman, N. & Ramanujam, V. (1986). Measurement of business performance in strategy research: A comparison of approaches. *Academy of Management Review, 11*, 801–814.

* Venkatraman, N. & Ramanujam, V. (1987). Measurement of business economic performance: An examination of method convergence. *Journal of Management, 13*, 109–122.

Vogel, D. (2005). *The market for virtue: The potential and limits of corporate social responsibility.* Washington, DC: Brookings Institution Press.

* Waddock, S. A. & Graves, S. B. (1997). The corporate social performance-financial performance link. *Strategic Management Journal, 18*, 303–319.

Waddock, S. A. & Mahon, J. F. (1991). Corporate social performance revisited: Dimensions of efficacy, effectiveness, and efficiency. In J. E. Post (ed.), *Research in corporate social performance and policy, 12* (pp. 231–262). Greenwich, CT: JAI Press.

Wagner, J. A., II. & Gooding, R. Z. (1987). Effects of societal trends on participation research. *Administrative Science Quarterly, 32*, 241–262.

* Wartick, S. L. (1988). How issues management contributes to corporate performance. *Business Forum, 13*, 16–22.

Wartick, S. L. & Cochran, P. L. (1985). The evolution of the corporate social performance model. *Academy of Management Review, 10*, 758–769.

Webb, E. J., Campbell, D., Schwartz, R., Sechrest, L. & Grove, J. (1981). *Nonreactive measures in the social sciences*. Boston: Houghton Mifflin.

Wernerfelt, B. (1984). A resource-based view of the firm. *Strategic Management Journal, 5*, 171–180.

Wholey, D. R. & Brittain, J. W. (1986). Organizational ecology: Findings and implications. *Academy of Management Review, 11*, 513–533.

Willums, J.-O. (1999, May 3). Social responsibility and shareholder value. *Business Week* (Asian Edition), 85.

* Wiseman, J. (1982). An evaluation of environmental disclosures made in corporate annual reports. *Accounting, Organizations and Society, 7*, 53–63.

Wokutch, R. E. & McKinney, E. W. (1991). Behavioral and perceptual measures of corporate social performance. In J. E. Post (ed.), *Research in corporate social performance and policy, 12* (pp. 309–330). Greenwich, CT: JAI Press.

* Wokutch, R. E. & Spencer, B. A. (1987). Corporate sinners and saints: The effects of philanthropic and illegal activity on organizational performance. *California Management Review, 29*, 62–77.

* Wolfe, R. (1991). The use of content analysis to assess corporate social responsibility. In J. E. Post (ed.), *Research in corporate social performance and policy, 12* (pp. 281–307). Greenwich, CT: JAI Press.

Wolfe, R. & Aupperle, K. A. (1991). Introduction. In J. E. Post (ed.), *Research in corporate social performance and policy, 12* (pp. 265–268). Greenwich, CT: JAI Press.

Wood, D. J. (1991a). Corporate social performance revisited. *Academy of Management Review, 16*, 691–718.

Wood, D. J. (1991b). Social issues in management: Theory and research in corporate social performance. *Journal of Management, 17*, 383–406.

Wood, D. J. (1995). The *Fortune* database as a CSP measure. *Business & Society, 34*, 197–198.

Wood, D. J. & Jones, R. E. (1995). Stakeholder mismatching: A theoretical problem in empirical research on corporate social performance. *International Journal of Organizational Analysis, 3*, 229–267.

5
Corporate Social Performance and Business Risk

The previous chapter suggested that measures of corporate social performance (CSP), such as charitable donations, responsibility to environment, and fair treatment of employees, may be positively correlated with return measures of firm financial performance, such as return on assets (ROA) or stock appreciation. However, true economic performance manifests itself in both high financial return and low financial risk. The possibility that CSP might heighten financial *variability* and, thus, negate its positive implications for a firm's level of economic performance has not been explored empirically in any breadth or depth. For example, Frooman (1997) meta-analyzed event studies to show how cases of irresponsible and illicit behaviors impact share price performance. Thus, Frooman's (1997) study did not focus on risk, used one specific market indicator of corporate financial performance, and approached CSP from the perspective of its absence (and not various degrees of presence).

The following quantitative cross-study and cross-industry integration of empirical findings builds on previous research by expanding the scope of measurement of CSP and focusing on business risk. In the context of CSP, firm risk has typically been considered to be an adjustment factor of return measures of financial performance. For example,

This chapter was originally published in 2001 as Orlitzky, M. & Benjamin, J. D., 'Corporate social performance and firm risk: A meta-analytic review', *Business & Society* 40(4), 369–396. It was revised for publication in this book, and the material from the original chapter was used with permission of SAGE Publications. This study was selected for the 2001 Best Article Award by the International Association for Business & Society in association with *California Management Review*.

Aupperle, Carroll & Hatfield (1985) adjusted ROA figures for a firm's general risk characteristics by using Value Line's safety index. This safety index is generally considered the most comprehensive measure of total risk confronting a firm because 'safety' is defined as price stability, adjusted for trend factors as well as factors such as company size, market penetration, product market volatility, degree of financial leverage, earnings quality, and the overall condition of the balance sheet (*Value Line Investment Survey*, 1981, cited in Aupperle, Carroll & Hatfield, 1985, pp. 458–459). Correction of financial return measures for total risk has been argued to be necessary to ensure cross-firm and cross-industry comparisons (Aupperle, Carroll & Hatfield, 1985). Nevertheless, reviews of the social-financial performance literature usually do not correct for any potentially confounding CSP-risk effects. Instead, many of these previous reviews and studies relating CSP to corporate financial outcomes have focused almost exclusively on performance level instead of performance variability (e.g. Griffin & Mahon, 1997; Ullmann, 1985; Wood & Jones, 1995). This meta-analysis starts with the assumption that, in the context of corporate social responsibility, risk must also be considered in and of itself, and not only as an adjustment factor. Therein lies the original, unique contribution of this follow-up analysis to the previous chapter.

Risk is defined as uncertainty about outcomes or events, especially with respect to the future (Bloom & Milkovich, 1998; Brigham & Gapenski, 1996; Miller & Bromiley, 1990). Firm risk measures the amount of financial performance fluctuations over time (Donaldson, 1999). These fluctuations may occur in share prices (market risk) or in internal accounting returns (accounting risk; e.g., SD_{ROA} and SD_{ROE}). Because firm risk impairs forecasting and planning activities (Bettis & Thomas, 1990; Brigham & Gapenski, 1996; Sharpe, 1990), it indicates not only increased variability in organizational returns, but also an increased chance of corporate decline and mortality (Baird & Thomas, 1985; Fiegenbaum & Thomas, 1988; Miller & Bromiley, 1990). From a practical perspective, both principals and agents are likely to be concerned about the degree of risk incurred by their firm (Bloom & Milkovich, 1998). From an organization theory perspective, the increasing importance of firm risk is illustrated by portfolio theory (Donaldson, 1999), a model of performance-driven organizational change, in which risk plays a central role. As Donaldson (1999, p. 18) states, 'To understand whether an organization is likely to make adaptive changes or not, and whether it is likely to grow or not, we need to understand its degree of risk'.

In the wake of the stock market downturns of 2000 and 2001, investors increasingly realize that it is not only the level of firm financial performance that counts, but also the underlying risk of the companies in their investment portfolios. Finding the relationship between CSP and the level of financial performance has been a very long project in our field, dating as far back as the early 1970s. However, past research has often presented CSP-risk analyses as a tangential side issue only. From a managerial, practical perspective, today's managers will not only be concerned with possible predictors (and consequences) of financial performance levels, but also of their variability (i.e., firm risk), especially at a time when various economic forecasters predict the coming of harsh times for stock market investors (e.g., Shiller, 2005). Executives' ability to manage firm risk can make the difference between future bankruptcy (or at least drastic downsizing) and organizational health. Over the long run, the market and other events in the organization's environment are going to penalize behavior that increases firm risk. Many managers and financial analysts (as well as researchers in finance, accounting, and economics) are still convinced that CSP increases firm risk and is therefore an activity penalized by market forces. Conversely, the question becomes: if managers know that their company currently experiences high levels of risk, should they then decide to increase or decrease CSP?

From a theoretical perspective, this meta-analysis is also warranted because risk and return measures of organizational performance are not correlated in a straightforward way, as had been assumed for a long time by conventional economic wisdom (Chatterjee, Lubatkin & Schulze, 1999; McNamara & Bromiley, 1999; Wiseman & Catanach, 1997; see also Bowman, 1980, 1982, 1984; Brealey & Myers, 1981; Fiegenbaum & Thomas, 1988). If risk and return were perfectly negatively correlated, then all we would have to do would be to find the true relationship between CSP and a firm's level of performance (and could safely ignore risk as a variable in the equation). However, this is not the case. So given the integrative review presented in the previous chapter (on the positive relationships between CSP and business financial return), its correlation with financial risk would not follow automatically.

These practical and theoretical issues could, of course, have been examined in a primary empirical study. However, we are more interested in the sign and magnitude of the *context-independent* association between CSP and firm risk, and in the likely temporal / causal order of any effects. We think that, given its benefits, the statistical technique of meta-analysis, which is concerned with parameters, or more specifically, true-score correlation coefficients (ρ), is best suited to answer our questions. First, meta-analysis can shed light on the empirical generalizability of previous findings – regardless of the specific study (e.g., industry) context. Furthermore, unlike primary studies, meta-analysis can determine the extent to which different measures of CSP and firm risk affect the associations found and, thus, provide evidence for measurement as a moderator of the risk-CSP relationship. Finally, meta-analysis can correct for study artifacts such as sampling error and measurement error (i.e., lack of reliability), which is not always possible in primary studies.

In the following section, we develop six hypotheses linking CSP to firm risk. Not all existing studies, which have examined the relationship between social and financial performance, are included in this meta-analysis because only a minority measured risk. However, those that were integrated quantitatively can be separated according to the temporal order of measures taken: (1) prior CSP → subsequent risk; (2) prior risk → subsequent CSP; and (3) contemporaneous (cross-sectional) measures.

CSP as an antecedent of risk

From the perspective of instrumental stakeholder theory (Donaldson & Preston, 1995; Jones, 1995) or 'good management' theory (Waddock & Graves, 1997), CSP is expected to decrease a firm's financial risk. A particular firm's disregard of implicit stakeholder claims, i.e., claims by those persons or organizations with a relationship to the firm or its products, may lead to expensive explicit claims. In today's litigious business environment, such disregard will lead to higher risk than if stakeholder claims were considered in the firm's strategic decision-making process from the beginning (McGuire, Sundgren & Schneeweis, 1988). Recent examples of relatively high financial risk that has arguably been caused by low CSP are the lawsuits against various air and water polluters, cigarette manufacturers, harvesters of old-growth redwoods, and wetlands developers. Firm risk may not only increase because of increasing probability of civil and/or criminal legal proceedings, but also because of the increasing likelihood of regulatory intervention by state or federal governments if firms do not proactively engage in socially responsible actions.

On the other hand, firms with high CSP may be characterized as having good relations with a variety of primary and secondary stakeholders. Primary stakeholders (for instance, the firm's employees, customers, suppliers, and shareholders) are those groups, organizations, or persons without whose continuing participation the corporation cannot survive as a going concern. Secondary stakeholders (for instance, local

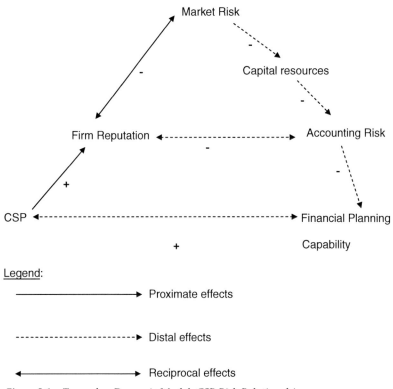

Figure 5.1   Towards a Dynamic Model: CSP-Risk Relationships

communities and the legislative branch of the government) are those groups or individuals who influence or affect, or are influenced or affected by the corporation, but are not engaged in transactions with the corporation and are not essential for its survival (Clarkson, 1995). In modern capitalist society, managerial actions in the best interests of shareholders increasingly require the fair treatment and support of all stakeholders (Berman, Wicks, Kotha & Jones, 1999). CSP includes environmental assessment (Wood, 1991a; see also Chapters 1 and 2), which allows firms to anticipate and address stakeholder concerns. By addressing these actions proactively, firms may be in a better position to decrease the variability of their business returns. Socially and ecologically responsible organizations may have incorporated organizing principles that are surprise-avoiding (King, 1995; see also Frederick, 1995). In sum, based on this set of arguments derived from the stakeholder approach, financial risk is anticipated to decrease with increasing CSP.

Hypothesis 1a: Overall, corporate social performance is negatively correlated with firm risk.
Hypothesis 1b: Prior corporate social performance is negatively correlated with subsequent firm risk.

The effects of CSP as the temporal, negative antecedent of financial risk will be either proximate or distal, depending on the risk measure that is considered. Figure 5.1 depicts these proposed relationships. Market reactions to CSP investments, the proximate effects of CSP, will be more immediate and stronger than internal accounting return fluctuations. In other words, market investors will have a more marked response to CSP than accounting measures of capital use, for two main reasons. First, corporations with stable stakeholder group relations probably encounter fewer difficulties attracting new equity investment to the firm (Burgstahler & Dichev, 1997; Clarkson, 1988; Waddock & Graves, 1997). Moreover, low investment in CSP may be interpreted as a lack of management skills because the firm has not acquired a 'progressive' reputation. Therefore, potential investors and lenders would perceive a low-CSP firm's future and stock as riskier than the future and shares of a high-CSP firm (Alexander & Buchholz, 1978; McGuire, Sundgren & Schneeweis, 1988; Spicer, 1978a). Second, because lenders and investors increasingly use social responsibility investment screens, low CSP may restrict a firm's access to market capital, which in turn contributes to greater financial risk (McGuire, Sundgren & Schneeweis, 1988).

The distal effects of CSP investments are the tenuous, long-term learning processes in interorganizational cooperation, which enable a firm to lower transaction costs (Coase, 1937; Hill, 1990; Williamson, 1975, 1985). Trust in a contracting relationship can decrease monitoring and coordination costs (Hosmer, 1995; Milgrom & Roberts, 1992). To the extent that trusting stakeholder relations are manifested in socially responsible policies and outcomes, as proposed in Chapter 3, CSP can sow the seeds for more efficient contracting with customers and other external stakeholders, such as government agencies (Jones, 1995). Simultaneously, CSP can create an organizational expectation of altruism, in which opportunistic politicking has no place – and, thus, no costs associated with it. Recruitment processes can reinforce the anti-shirking climate of social responsibility (Turban & Greening, 1997). Yet, these processes are not as closely linked as the relationship between CSP reputations and investors' positive perceptions, and between CSP and market risk. For instance, consumers' preference for products of socially responsible companies over those of irresponsible companies is tenuous (Auger, Devinney & Louviere, 1999). Seasonal forces or pricing may overshadow the ethical attributes and determine fluctuations in net income and assets (numerator and denominator, respectively, of ROA, an accounting return measure) more readily than CSP. Hence, we propose the following moderator effect:

Hypothesis 2: Measurement of firm risk moderates the relationship between corporate social performance and risk, so that the negative correlation between corporate social performance and market risk will be larger than the negative correlation between corporate social performance and accounting risk.

As a corollary to the aforementioned arguments, CSP must be visible to have an effect on financial risk. One of the assumptions of instrumental stakeholder theory is that the ability to satisfy multiple stakeholder groups decreases the risk of financial decline. Without visibility of CSP, stakeholders cannot use CSP as an informational signal of a firm's successful attempts at satisfying stakeholder groups (Fombrun & Shanley, 1990). Reflecting different degrees of visibility, CSP can be measured in a variety of ways: (1) CSP disclosures, (2) CSP reputation ratings, (3) social audits, CSP processes, and observable outcomes (such as charitable contributions), and (4) CSR, which refers to the principles and values of corporate social responsibility (see chapters 1, 2, and 4 and Post, 1991). Of those four broad categories, CSP reputation ratings are expected to show the largest negative correlation with risk because CSP reputations are visible. Furthermore, investors may regard ratings by a third party (e.g., *Fortune* magazine rankings or KLD ratings) as more trustworthy than firms' own disclosures in annual reports or letters to shareholders. Therefore, assuming that the CSP database is separated into broad measurement moderator subgroups, the following hypothesis is proposed:

Hypothesis 3: Of the four different categories of corporate social performance measures, reputation indices will show the largest negative correlation with financial risk.

The extent to which an issue is institutionalized can determine its impact on firm policies (Hoffman, 1999). In comparison to other social issues, such as race or gender discrimination, the green movement cannot be demarcated by its high degree of institutionalization, especially in the United States where most of the data have been collected.

For example, the relationship between expressed environmental concern and active consumer action has been shown to be weak (Auger, Devinney & Louviere, 1999; Roberts, 1996). Yet, in such areas as diversity and human resource management in general, the business community is much more aware that public responsibility can lead to financial benefits (Pfeffer, 1998; Turban & Greening, 1997). Moreover, environmental policies (e.g., strict compliance with environmental regulations) are probably much less visible to investors and consumers than other CSP actions (e.g., community involvement and maternity/paternity leave), since nowadays the latter are often an integral aspect of a corporation's public relations efforts to attract and retain talent. For example, specific instances of CSP are often featured on firms' Internet web sites frequented by job applicants preparing for interviews.

Hypothesis 4: Of all the measures of corporate social performance, corporate environmental performance will have the smallest (negative) relationship with firm risk.

Risk as an antecedent of CSP

In their particular sample, Waddock and Graves (1997) found some evidence for a virtuous cycle between CSP and firm return. That is, CSP was not only an antecedent of the level of financial performance, but also a consequence of a given level of performance. As stated in Chapter 4, financially successful companies may spend more on CSP because they can afford it and, in turn, CSP may help them become a bit more successful financially. According to this perspective, good financial performance can provide the slack resources necessary for discretionary CSP expenses. An analogous slack-resources argument can be made for firm risk. Low risk may allow for better planning because low firm risk makes projections of a firm's future cash flows more certain (Bettis & Thomas, 1990; Sharpe, 1990). Therefore, managers in low-risk firms face less uncertainty with respect to future opportunities – and opportunity costs – concerning social responsibility. Given a sufficient level of slack resources, when financial planning and cash-flow projections are more precise and reliable, more capital can be committed to social issues that are not directly related to the economic survival of the firm. Thus, in the context of instrumental stakeholder theory, the temporal order could also be reversed.

Hypothesis 5: A negative true-score correlation is observed between prior risk and subsequent corporate social performance.

Contemporaneous correlations (reciprocal causality)

The virtuous cycle argument implies reciprocal effects between CSP and risk, which means that CSP and financial risk codetermine each other in the same time period (i.e., CSP ↔ risk). Arguably, current Western business environments foster a virtuous cycle (Berman, Wicks, Kotha & Jones, 1999). Notably, media cycles are becoming shorter and shorter (Sennett, 1999). Especially in the expanding Internet environment, good news and bad news travel fast (Kirsner, 1998). Reputations of firms can change quickly and affect firm performance, as The Body Shop stock price decline showed so strikingly after Jon Entine's (1994) article 'Shattered Image' (Kelly, 1994). For this reason, the financial risk consequences may not lag far behind changes in stakeholder assessments of CSP, and *vice versa*. From the perspective of the efficient markets hypothesis, the assumption that changes in stakeholder perceptions are immediately reflected in changes in financial performance can be taken as valid.

Hypothesis 6: The contemporaneous (cross-sectional) true-score correlation between corporate social performance and risk is negative.

Methods

As already noted in the previous chapter, and in keeping with the title of this book, meta-analysis is a quantitative method of research *integration* (Cooper, 1989). Increasingly, it has replaced the narrative literature review as a technique of summarizing a research area. This study of CSP and risk relied on the meta-analytic guidelines provided by Hunter and Schmidt (1990). Their meta-analytic techniques correct the observed sample statistics (the observed correlation *r* in primary studies) for methodological distortions due to *sampling error* and *measurement error*. These distortions are called *study artifacts*.

Each observed correlation must be weighted by the sample size of the primary study in order to calculate the *observed mean weighted correlation* (r_{obs}) across all of the studies involved in the analysis. The standard deviation of the observed correlations (SD_r) can then be computed to estimate the variability in the relationship between the variables of interest. The total variability across studies includes several components, such as the true variation in the population, variation due to sampling error, and variation due to other artifacts (e.g., lack of reliability in measures). Acknowledging and controlling for these artifacts allows for a better estimate of the true variability around the population correlation. Thus, the most important outcome of the meta-analysis is the population parameter (i.e., the estimated *corrected or true score correlation ρ*) between any two variables.

Literature search

Computer searches of *ABI/Informs Global (ProQuest), PsycINFO,* and *EconLit* were conducted. *ABI/Informs* provides access to the full text and images of over 1,200 U.S. and international business and trade journal articles (1970–1999), while *PsycINFO* indexes abstracts of journal articles and book chapters in psychology starting in 1974. The computer searches cover the years 1982–1999 (*ABII*), 1967–1999 (*PsychLit*), 1987–1999 (*Psyc-INFO*), and 1969–1999 (*EconLit*). To make the search more comprehensive, cross-citations from previous narrative reviews were explored as well (e.g., Aldag & Bartol, 1978; Arlow & Gannon, 1982; Aupperle, Carroll & Hatfield, 1985; Frooman, 1997; Griffin & Mahon, 1997; McGuire, Sundgren & Schneeweis, 1988, pp. 857–860; Pava & Krausz, 1995; Starik & Carroll, 1991; Ullmann, 1985; Waddock & Mahon, 1991; Wartick & Cochran, 1985; Wood 1991a, 1991b; Wood & Jones, 1995).

Criteria for relevance

The studies deemed relevant for the meta-analysis have the following characteristics. First, the studies quantitatively examined the relationship between CSP and firm risk. The reported effect size does not have to be a Pearson's product-moment correlation *r*, but can also be a *t*-test statistic or effect size *d* (both *t* and *d* can be transformed to *r*; see Hunter & Schmidt, 1990). Second, the studies were concerned with at least one aspect of a firm's general risk characteristics, be they accounting- or market-related. Third, all retrieved measures of CSP were checked against Wood's (1991a) definition of CSP. If the dependent or independent variable could not be classified as one of the three categories of Wood's (1991a) model, as outlined below, the study was excluded.

Operational definitions of constructs

CSP is a multidimensional construct, and thus can be measured in a variety of ways. Wood (1991a) conceptualized CSP as a tripartite model consisting of (1) principles of social responsibility, (2) processes of social responsiveness, and (3) policies, programs, and observable outcomes as they relate to the firm's societal relationships. For our purposes, Wood's conceptual model, roughly an input-process-output systems model of CSP, was supplemented with a four-part typology of CSP centered around the four *measurement* categories: (1) CSP disclosures, (2) CSP reputation ratings, (3) social audits, CSP processes, and observable outcomes (such as charitable contributions), and (4) CSR, which consists of managerial CSP principles and values (see previous chapter and Post, 1991). Although there is no consensus on the relative quality of measures of CSP, we regard measurement diversity as beneficial at this early stage of empirical research (see also Harrison & Freeman, 1999). *Multiple operationism* is an advantage because it helps determine whether a true relationship exists in different industry contexts with different operationalizations of the two focal constructs (Cook & Campbell, 1979; Cooper, 1989; Webb, Campbell, Schwartz, Sechrest & Grove, 1981). However, the use of any *particular* measure in any given study is subject to measurement error. A meta-analysis can circumvent this downside of primary studies through the correction for relative lack of reliability, in addition to the correction of aggregated observed correlations for sampling error (i.e., deviation of primary-study sample size from infinity).

Studies of environmental management are included as a dimension of CSP for several reasons. First, several studies, especially earlier ones, use environmental performance as a proxy for social responsibility. Second, stakeholder proxies, such as environmental interest groups and government agencies, may in fact claim a social 'stake' for, or give voice to, the natural environment (Starik, 1995). Finally, the business community tends to regard social responsibility as a concept comprising both social performance (in its narrow sense) and environmental performance (see Willums, 1999). However, the argument can be made that the literature on CSP differs from that on corporate environmental performance in many respects. To investigate differences in the relationship of corporate environmental performance to firm risk and, thus, to examine Hypothesis 4, a separate meta-analysis was performed using only environmental performance measures.

Business risk can be subdivided into measures of accounting risk and market risk. It is important to note that accounting risk and market risk are not so much two different conceptual components of risk, but different operationalizations of the same underlying construct. *Accounting risk* can be estimated by the coefficient of variation (the ratio of the standard deviation to the mean) of return on invested capital (ROIC), a measure used by Fombrun and Shanley (1990), for instance. Other examples of measures of accounting risk are the percentage of a firm's total or long-term debt relative to assets (see Graves & Waddock, 1994; McGuire, Sundgren & Schneeweis, 1988; Miller & Bromiley, 1990) or the standard deviation of a firm's long-term ROA or ROE (see, O'Neill, Saunders & McCarthy, 1989).

Total market risk is defined as the degree to which stock returns for a particular company vary over time. It is typically measured as the standard deviation *(SD)* of R_{it} in Sharpe's (1964) original model: $R_{it} = \alpha i + \beta_i R_{mt} + \varepsilon_{it}$, where R_{it} is the estimated return on security *i* in period *t*; R_{mt} is the aggregate return on all securities in the market in period *t* (i.e., the market factor); and ε_{it} is a random disturbance term which reflects that portion of a security's return in time period *t* that is not a linear function of R_{mt} (Spicer, 1978a, p. 103 and Spicer, 1978b, p. 73). This equation is known as the Sharpe-Lintner capital asset pricing model (CAPM; Lintner, 1965; Modigliani & Pogue, 1993; Sharpe, 1964).

Within the category of external market risk measures, total market risk is distinguished from systematic (or nondiversifiable) risk. In contrast to *SDR(it)*, *systematic market risk* represents the contribution of an individual security to a completely diversified portfolio's risk (Spicer, 1978a, b) and is represented by β_i (beta coefficient) from Sharpe's (1964) aforementioned equation. A completely diversified portfolio would mean that all risk unique to individual stock returns had been diversified away. Therefore, systematic market risk is also known as 'nondiversifiable risk'. Sharpe's beta regression coefficient measures the relative volatility of a given stock versus the market. Thus, beta is a market sensitivity index that assesses a stock's volatility relative to the market. For this reason, systematic risk is typically considered the appropriate risk measure for shareholders of diversified portfolios.

Characteristics of primary studies

Reliability (1 – measurement error) is traditionally defined as the ratio of true-score variance to observed-score variance (Traub, 1994). The present study occasionally estimates measurement error with the coefficient of generalizability (e.g., as contained in the statistical analyses by Sharfman, 1996). The technical appendix to this chapter presents more information on this particular coefficient of reliability. A total of 60 (= *k*) correlation coefficients were meta-analyzed, with a total sample size *(N)* of 6,186 observations. The ratio of studies using internal accounting risk relative to external market risk measures is 1:2. Thirty-nine of the 60 correlation coefficients that were meta-analyzed were obtained in cross-sectional studies. However, the studies that use lagged measures of CSP and firm risk contain more observations than the integrated cross-sectional studies (*N* = 3,480 observations versus 2,706 observations). The cross-sectional data, while arguably less meaningful than lagged data, are still useful in the context of our overall meta-analysis (see Hypothesis 6).

Several studies did not report coefficients of reliability for this construct. Therefore, correlations could not be corrected individually for measurement error. Instead, results obtained from primary empirical studies were meta-analyzed using artifact distributions. Artifact-distribution meta-analysis involves first computing the means and variances of reported correlations and of the considered artifacts (e.g., reliability of independent variable, reliability of dependent variable, and range variation). Then, the distribution of observed correlations is corrected for sampling error. Finally, the distribution corrected for sampling error is corrected for error of measurement (Hunter & Schmidt, 1990). Hunter and Schmidt (1990, pp. 160–173) present further technical details regarding the correction factors used for reported correlations and their variances.

Results

As Table 5.1 shows, the overall mean observed (r_{obs}) and true score (ρ) correlations between firm risk and CSP were negative ($r_{obs} = -.15$; $\rho = -.21$). This holds for all the different measures of firm risk and all the different measures of CSP. In addition, the temporal sequence consistent with the causal chain from prior CSP to subsequent risk (CSP → risk) shows an even stronger relationship ($r_{obs} = -.20$; $\rho = -.28$) than the overall correlation. (Following the computational procedures suggested by Kleinbaum, Kupper, and Muller, 1988 for testing for the equality of two correlations, the difference between the two correlations is significant at $\rho < .05$.) The overall and temporally subdivided studies provide evidence that supports Hypotheses 1a and 1b. Hence, the data collected and analyzed between 1976 and 1999 do not show that CSP initiatives heighten risk. At the same time, the variance accounted for by study artifacts (sampling error and measurement error in CSP) was 24%. If this variance had been 75% or more, we could have safely concluded that all cross-study and cross-industry variance was due to artifacts and that no real moderators exist (see Hunter & Schmidt, 1990). However, since the variance explained by artifacts is below the 75% threshold and, thus, the variance (σ^2) of the true-score correlation r is fairly large ($\sigma_\rho^2 = .07$ in overall meta-analytic set; $\sigma_\rho^2 = .05$ in CSP → risk subset), the moderator breakdown suggested by Hypotheses 2 through 6 must be pursued. With few exceptions (see Table 5.1), the cross-study variance in r_{obs} explained by artifacts increases when the moderator breakdown analysis is applied.

Table 5.1 Relationship between CSP and Firm Risk

Relationship between...	k[a]	Total sample size (N)	Sample-size weighted mean observed r	Observed variance	%Variance Explained[b]	Mean 'true-score' r (mean ρ)	Variance of ρ(σ_ρ^2)	File Drawer Analysis[c]
CSP and firm risk (overall) (H1a)	60	6,186	-.1487	.0476	23.58%	-.2087	.0700	118
Temporal Subdivisions:								
CSP → subsequent risk (H1b)	7	1,172	-.2030	.0349	25.78%	-.2849	.0498	21
Prior risk → CSP (H5)	14	2,308	-.1054	.0319	21.62%	-.1480	.0482	16
Cross-sectional studies (H6)	39	2,706	-.1620	.0635	25.30%	-.2273	.0913	87
Operationalizations:								
1. CSP correlated with...								
(a) Accounting risk (H2)	20	3,350	-.0940	.0334	19.90%	-.1319	.0515	18
(b) Market risk (H2)	40	2,836	-.2132	.0568	29.70%	-.2993	.0768	131
(b.1.) Total market risk	20	1,070	-.4064	.0282	96.16%	-.5704	.0021	143
(b.2.) Systematic market risk (beta)	20	1,766	-.0965	.0377	31.93%	-.1354	.0494	19
2. Firm risk correlated with...								
(a) CSP disclosures	2	213	-.0741	.0381	25.85%	-.1041	.0543	1
(b) CSP reputation ratings (H3)	35	2,816	-.2292	.0722	21.76%	-.3217	.1088	125
(c) Social audits, processes, and outcomes	19	2,465	-.0910	.0166	50.19%	-.1277	.0159	16
(d) CSR managerial values (H4)	4	692	-.0490	.0111	53.71%	-.0688	.0099	NA
Corp. environmental performance (H4)	8	136	-.0168	.1552	40.27%	-.0235	.1784	NA

[a] k: number of correlation coefficients meta-analyzed; [b] refers to percentage of observed variance explained by sampling error and measurement error in CSP; [c] Hunter & Schmidt's (1990) effect size file drawer analysis: Number of missing studies needed to bring t_{obs} up to -.05.

Risk subdivisions

Hypothesis 2 postulated that market risk would show a larger negative correlation with CSP than accounting risk. This hypothesis is supported by the data analysis. The true-score correlation (ρ) between CSP and market risk is –.21, while the correlation between CSP and accounting risk is only –.09. The meta-analytic comparison of these two moderator subgroups supports Hypothesis 2 in that the difference between these two correlations (using statistical significance tests recommended by Kleinbaum, Kupper & Muller, 1988; computed $Z = 4.78$) reaches statistical significance at $p < .0001$. Hence, the type of risk measure acts as a moderator of the CSP-risk relationship.

Furthermore, market risk measures are further subdivided into total market risk and systematic market risk (beta) measures. Here, the results suggest that CSP tends to reduce the diversifiable total market risk (i.e., the general risk characteristics) relatively more ($r_{obs} = -.41$ and $\rho = -.57$) than it reduces the nondiversifiable risk characteristics (between CSP and systematic risk [beta]: $r_{obs} = -.10$ and $\rho = -.14$). This difference is again statistically significant at $p < .0001$. In addition, virtually all (96%) of the observed variance in the CSP-total market risk correlation (from study to study) can be explained by the study artifacts of (a) sampling error and (b) measurement error (i.e., lack of reliability) in CSP. This large percentage of variance explained by study artifacts implies that the meta-analytic mean corrected correlation represents an accurate estimate of parameter ρ and that no additional variables moderate the CSP-risk relationship in this subset.

CSP subdivisions

The CSP measures are also subdivided into distinct measurement categories to examine Hypotheses 3 and 4. As Table 5.1 shows, CSP reputation ratings are the most highly negative correlations with firm risk ($r_{obs} = -.23$; $\rho = -.32$), which is consistent with Hypothesis 3. Social audit measures, CSP processes and outcomes ($\rho = -.13$), CSP disclosures and content analysis ($\rho = -.10$), and social value (or CSR) measures ($\rho = -.07$) all show smaller true-score correlations with firm risk than CSP reputations. Also, in both the social audits and the values measures subgroups of CSP, the two study artifacts considered explain more than 50% of the observed cross-study variance in the correlation between CSP and firm risk.

In addition, corporate environmental performance shows a very small negative correlation with firm risk ($r_{obs} = -.02 = \rho$). The correlation coming closest to this one is between risk and values and principles of social responsibility (CSR; $ro_{bs} = -.05$; $\rho = -.07$). This difference ($Z = .337$) is not statistically significant, nor is the difference between the correlation linking corporate environmental performance with risk ($r_{obs} = -.02 = \rho$) and the overall correlation ($r_{obs} = -.15$; $\rho = -.21$; $Z = 1.519$). Moreover, in a subsequent analysis, when the two extreme outliers (Pava & Krausz, 1995) are deleted from the meta-analytic set, the true-score correlation between environmental performance and firm risk becomes $-.21$, with all of the cross-study variance accounted for by artifacts (not shown in Table 5.1). The decision to delete this outlier study, which reported suspiciously large (positive) correlations, was based on recommendations of statisticians including Tukey (1960, 1977), Huber (1980), and Hedges (1987). The data analysis excluding the outlier casts some doubt on the empirical support for Hypothesis 4, as the result may have been unduly influenced by one outlier study.

Temporal sequence subdivisions

The meta-analytic data set was further subdivided to examine the temporal sequences consistent with the causal chains suggested by Hypotheses 5 (risk → CSP) and 6 (CSP ↔ risk contemporaneously). This subdivision indicates that risk is also a negative temporal antecedent of CSP ($r_{obs} = -.11$; $\rho = -.15$) and that risk and CSP are also correlated when measured in the same time period ($r_{obs} = -.16$; $\rho = -.23$). The temporal subdivisions show that while the correlation is highest when CSP precedes risk ($r_{obs} = -.20$; $\rho = -.28$; Hypothesis 1b), the causality between the two constructs is likely to be reciprocal. Risk also appears to precede CSP, and this correlation is negative as well. Overall, the findings of the temporal subgroups lend support to Hypotheses 5 and 6 and the virtuous-cycle argument. It is important to note, though, that the negative correlation between prior CSP and subsequent risk is about twice as large as the correlation between prior risk and subsequent CSP.

For all analyses, a file drawer analysis was performed to check the meta-analytic data set for publication bias (see Hunter & Schmidt, 1990). File drawer analysis computes the number of unlocated (i.e., 'lost' or 'missing') studies needed to cause a change in the empirical conclusions. File drawer analysis is a way of addressing the criticism that the studies available for any given meta-analysis are a biased sample of all available studies. For example, critical readers may argue that if the meta-analyst had greater access to some unpublished studies, the empirical conclusions would change dramatically. Hunter and Schmidt (1990) recommend an effect-size file drawer analysis, establishing a critical level (r_c) and computing the number of unlocated studies that would bring the absolute value of the meta-analytic, observed *r* down to that level (e.g., $|r_c| = .05$). The formula for the file drawer computation is: $x = k(\bar{r}_k / \bar{r}_c - 1)$, where $\bar{r}_k = \frac{\Sigma r_k}{k}$ and $r_k = $ the r_{obs} reported in the primary study. In the case of this meta-analysis, it is unlikely that we overlooked as many studies as computed and presented in the last column of Table 5.1, given the multiple ways in which studies were located. As one exception, publication bias may be a problem for our conclusions about CSP disclosures.

In sum, not a single mean correlation between CSP and firm risk was positive. Although a number of primary studies found positive correlations, these positive correlations are most likely due to sampling error. Still, in most cases, sampling error and measurement error in CSP cannot explain the entire observed cross-study variance of correlations, so that true contingencies, or moderator variables, are likely to exist. In the CSP and risk measurement subsets, the percentage of variance explained by study artifacts tends to be higher than in the entire meta-analytic set, indicating that the operationalization (or type) of each variable is in fact a moderator. Testing the statistical significance of the difference between various moderator subgroup correlations, we found empirical support for all hypotheses except Hypothesis 4.

Discussion

This meta-analysis suggests that the higher a firm's corporate social performance, the lower the financial risk incurred by the firm. That is, being a good corporate citizen tends to reduce firm risk. Investment in CSP appears to lower external market-based risk relatively more than internal accounting-based risk. The image of the firm has a greater impact on measures of market risk than measures of accounting risk. While some of the relationships depicted in Figure 5.1 could not be examined with our meta-analytic data set, the relatively greater true-score correlation between CSP and market risk suggests that CSP has both proximate and distal effects. The correlation of CSP with accounting risk may be lower because the risk-reducing (distal) effects of CSP are mediated by reputation, market risk, and further provision of new capital resources.

The CSP subset with the largest negative correlation with risk was social performance reputation. It might be argued that this negative correlation is due to halo effects between CSP and financial *return* measures of firm performance (Brown & Perry, 1994, 1995; Wood, 1995). This argument would be more plausible if return and risk measures of financial performance were highly positively or negatively correlated.

Yet, the empirical evidence on the risk-return relationship is not definitive in either direction (McNamara & Bromiley, 1999). Therefore, we believe that this finding reiterates one of Waddock and Graves' (1997) conclusions that firms that even appear to be doing good things benefit from a virtuous cycle between corporate financial performance (CFP) and CSP. It is possible that opportunistic managers use CSP as a smoke-and-mirrors public relations stunt to appease investors' concerns about future firm risk (see our discussion of impression management in chapter 3). This possibility warrants further research.

Other aspects of CSP are related to firm risk to a much smaller extent. Social audits and managerial values (CSR) may have a smaller impact on risk because they are not as visible as CSP reputations. Indeed, Clarkson (1995, p. 105) argues that 'whether a corporation and its management are motivated by enlightened self-interest, common sense, or high standards of ethical behavior cannot be determined by the empirical methodologies available today'. Waddock and Smith (2000) regard writing of the final report for company managers and the audit steering committee as the tenth and final step in a social audit. This may be insufficient for a company whose CSP exceeds that of its competitors. Instead, the final step must be the wider circulation of the audit. Typically, external auditors or consultants conduct social audits. CSP disclosures, on the other hand, result from internal data collection. This may explain why CSP disclosures have a smaller impact on financial risk of the firm. The broader organizational community simply does not trust these internal data. At any rate, the message in Chapter 2 that the value orientation of the top executive highly influences a firm's CSP orientation is not disputed by this study, which focuses on the relationships between CSP and risk, and not the impact of executive values or decision making on CSP (addressed in Chapter 9).

In fact, practicing managers can derive some comfort from the conclusions of this study. Companies with high financial risk (e.g., those with high long-term debt or wide share price fluctuations) should be able to increase their investments in CSP without negative financial repercussions down the road. According to the evidence, markets will not punish them in the form of making their risk exposure even greater. Quite to the contrary, CSP reduces business risk. And low-risk companies in turn are the most likely to initiate CSP activities. At the same time, managers of high-risk firms can no longer argue that social responsibility 'simply costs too much, given the current financially threatening circumstances of the firm'. If the argument that CSP is only an expense and not a risk-reducing contribution to the bottom line were true, the need for government regulation would certainly be higher than the results of this meta-analysis warrant, similar to our conclusions in the previous chapter.

In the short run, the risk-reducing tendencies of CSP should probably be interpreted as a beneficial factor for firm survival. However, Donaldson (1999) argues that, over time, lower risk may also reduce corporate adaptation to external environments. Low exposure to market- and accounting-return fluctuations can insulate the firm from the therapeutic effects of financial performance crises. Thus, in the long run, low risk may be a mixed blessing because, on the one hand, it makes financial performance more predictable and stable, but, on the other, may also decrease the probability of organizational change (Donaldson, 1999). Alternatively, a firm may incur low risk because it constantly monitors its environment and makes continuous small incremental changes proactively, consistent with the typification of the normatively receptive executive who leads his or her firm to be attuned to the external environment, *à la* Chapter 2.

While the meta-analysis has answered some questions from the literature, there is plenty of room for further study of mediating factors and a wider nomological net. McWilliams and Siegel (2001) introduce a number of variables that may not only affect the relationship between financial performance *level* and CSP, but also performance *variability* and CSP. Many of the variables that they propose could be correlated with the provision of social responsibility attributes and with firm risk. For instance, if research and development (R&D) expenditures are high relative to sales, a firm may not only have higher CSP, but also incur greater risk because many of these R&D expenditures may never pay off financially. Many other variables that, according to McWilliams and Siegel (2001), affect the demand and supply of CSP may also affect risk and, thus, influence the relationships analyzed in our study.

Two possible weaknesses of our meta-analytic review must be acknowledged. First, a potential concern with our meta-analytic review may be the small number of aggregated correlation coefficients in a number of subanalyses. There is no rule of thumb that can be used to justify rejection of a meta-analysis if its overall or subgroup k is below a certain number (Frank Schmidt, personal communication). That is, even a meta-analysis of three studies is better than evidence from a single primary study because the total sample size N goes up and often corrections for study artifacts can be made. Despite small ks in some of the subgroups, the majority of our statistical significance tests (testing for the equality of two correlations) reached significance.

Second, the assumption of statistical independence was violated in a minority of cases. However, many meta-analyses have reported multiple correlations from the same study for different measures. This lack of independence in the form of replicated measurement may only affect (i.e., inflate) the observed variance of correlations across studies. Violations of the assumption of independence do not have a systematic effect on the mean r_{obs} or r values in a meta-analysis (Hunter & Schmidt, 1990). In fact, Monte Carlo simulations have shown the mean effect sizes and estimates of variance are unaffected by nonindependence (Tracz, 1985). Because nonindependence is argued to have minor effects on statistical precision (Hedges, 1986), use of nonindependent data should be acknowledged, but not necessarily avoided in meta-analysis (Preiss & Allen, 1990).

Conclusion

In the early 1980s, the assumption that social-responsibility screens reduced stock portfolio performance was widespread (Rudd, 1981). Now, evidence has accumulated suggesting that CSP screens may not adversely impact investment performance (Sauer, 1997). The present meta-analysis contributes to the growing literature that shows the positive financial effects of responsible stakeholder management (Harrison & Freeman, 1999), which may be manifested as high CSP. Another meta-analysis has shown that corporate social responsibility may enhance shareholder wealth (Frooman, 1997). Notably, if the return-inducing effects of CSP also increased financial risk, then managers would face a strategic dilemma in the form of a risk-return tradeoff. This chapter has shown that this does not seem to be the case. Instead, drawing on this meta-analytic data set covering the last two decades, we found that risk is negatively correlated with CSP. In fact, among all risk measures, high CSP appears to be most highly negatively correlated with total market risk. Furthermore, the better a firm's CSP reputation, the lower its risk. In the final analysis, it appears that a firm that is socially responsible and responsive may be able to increase interpersonal trust between and among internal and external stakeholders, build social capital, lower transaction costs, and therefore ultimately reduce uncertainty regarding its financial performance.

References

References marked with an asterisk indicate studies included in the meta-analysis.

Aldag, R. J. & Bartol, K. M. (1978). Empirical studies of corporate social performance and policy: A survey of problems and results. In L. E. Preston (ed.), *Research in corporate social performance and policy, 1* (pp. 165–199). Greenwich, CT: JAI Press.

* Alexander, G. J. & Buchholz, R. A. (1978). Corporate social performance and stock market performance. *Academy of Management Journal, 21*, 479–486.

Arlow, P. & Gannon, M. J. (1982). Social responsiveness, corporate structure, and economic performance. *Academy of Management Review, 7*, 235–241.

Auger, P., Devinney, T. M. & Louviere, J. J. (1999). *Wither ethical consumerism: Do consumers value ethical attributes?* AGSM Working Paper 99-006. Sydney, Australia: AGSM.

* Aupperle, K. E., Carroll, A. B. & Hatfield, J. D. (1985). An empirical investigation of the relationship between corporate social responsibility and profitability. *Academy of Management Journal, 28*, 446–463.

Baird, I. S. & Thomas, H. (1985). Toward a contingency model of strategic risk taking. *Academy of Management Review, 10*, 230–243.

* Baldwin, S. A., Tower, J. W., Litvak, L., Karpen, J. F., Jackson, H. F. & McTigue, B. (1986). *Pension funds and ethical investment.* New York: Council on Economic Priorities.

Berman, S. L., Wicks, A. C., Kotha, S. & Jones, T. M. (1999). Does stakeholder orientation matter? The relationship between stakeholder management models and firm financial performance. *Academy of Management Journal, 42*, 488–506.

Bettis, R. A. & Thomas, H. (1990). *Risk, strategy, and management.* Greenwich, CT: JAI Press.

Bloom, M. & Milkovich, G. T. (1998). Relationships among risk, incentive pay, and organizational performance. *Academy of Management Journal, 41*, 283–297.

Bowman, E. H. (1980). A risk/return paradox for strategic management. *Sloan Management Review, 21*(3), 17–31.

Bowman, E. H. (1982). Risk seeking by troubled firms. *Sloan Management Review, 23*(4), 33–42.

Bowman, E. H. (1984). Content analysis of annual reports for corporate strategy and risk. *Interfaces, 14*, 61–72.

Brealey, R. & Myers, S. (1981). *Principles of corporate finance.* New York: McGraw-Hill.

Brigham, E. F. & Gapenski, L. C. (1996). *Intermediate Financial Management* 5th ed. Orlando, FL: Dryden.

Brown, B. & Perry, S. (1994). Removing the financial performance halo from *Fortune*'s 'Most Admired Companies.' *Academy of Management Journal, 37*, 1346–1359.

Brown, B. & Perry, S. (1995). Halo-removed residuals of *Fortune*'s 'responsibility to the community and environment': A decade of data. *Business & Society, 34*(2), 199–215.

Burgstahler, D. & Dichev, I. (1997). Earnings management to avoid earnings decreases and losses. *Journal of Accounting and Economics, 24*(1), 99–126.

Chatterjee, S., Lubatkin, M. H. & Schulze, W. S. (1999). Toward a strategic theory of risk premium: Moving beyond CAPM. *Academy of Management Review, 24,* 556–567.

* Chen, K. H. & Metcalf, R. W. (1980). The relationship between pollution control record and financial indicators revisited. *Accounting Review, 55*(1), 168–177.

Clarkson, M. B. E. (1988). Corporate social performance in Canada, 1976–86. In L. E. Preston (ed.), *Research in corporate social performance and policy, vol. 10* (pp. 241–265). Greenwich, CT: JAI Press.

Clarkson, M. B. E. (1995). A stakeholder framework for analyzing and evaluating corporate social performance. *Academy of Management Review, 20,* 92–117.

Coase, R. H. (1937). The nature of the firm. *Economica, 4,* 386–405.

Cook, T. D. & Campbell, D. T. (1979). *Quasi-Experimentation: Design & analysis issues for field settings.* Boston, MA: Houghton Mifflin.

Cooper, H. M. (1989). *Integrating research: A guide for literature reviews* 2nd ed. Newbury Park, CA: Sage.

Cronbach, L. J., Gleser, G. C., Nanda, H. & Rajaratnam, N. (1972). *The dependability of behavioral measurements: Theory of generalizability of scores and profiles.* New York: Wiley.

Donaldson, L. (1999). *Performance-driven organizational change: The organizational portfolio.* Thousand Oaks, CA: Sage.

Donaldson, T. & Preston, L. E. (1995). The stakeholder theory of the corporation: Concepts, evidence, and implications. *Academy of Management Review, 20,* 65–91.

Entine, J. (1994, Sept./Oct.). Shattered image: Is The Body Shop too good to be true? *Business Ethics,* 23–28.

Fiegenbaum, A. & Thomas, H. (1988). Attitudes toward risk and the risk-return paradox. *Academy of Management Journal, 31,* 85–106.

* Fombrun, C. & Shanley, M. (1990). What's in a name? Reputation building and corporate strategy. *Academy of Management Journal, 33,* 233–258.

Frederick, W. C. (1995). *Values, nature, and culture in the American corporation.* New York: Oxford University Press.

Frooman, J. (1997). Socially irresponsible and illegal behavior and shareholder wealth: A meta-analysis of event studies. *Business & Society, 36,* 221–249.

* Graves, S. B. & Waddock, S. A. (1994). Institutional owners and corporate social performance. *Academy of Management Journal, 37,* 1034–1046.

Griffin, J. J. & Mahon, J. F. (1997). The corporate social performance and corporate financial performance debate: Twenty-five years of incomparable research. *Business & Society, 36,* 5–31.

Harrison, J. S. & Freeman, R. E. (1999). Stakeholders, social responsibility, and performance: Empirical evidence and theoretical perspectives. *Academy of Management Journal, 42,* 479–487.

Hedges, L. (1986). Issues in meta-analysis. In E. Rothkopf (ed.), *Review of research in education, vol. 13* (pp. 353–398). Washington, DC: American Research Association.

Hedges, L. V. (1987). How hard is hard science, how soft is soft science: The empirical cumulativeness of research. *American Psychologist, 42,* 443–455.

* Heinze, D. C. (1976). Financial correlates of a social involvement measure. *Akron Business and Economic Review, 7*(1), 48–51.

* Herremans, I. M., Akathaporn, P. & McInnes, M. (1993). An investigation of corporate social responsibility reputation and economic performance. *Accounting, Organizations and Society, 18,* 587–604.

Hill, C. W. L. (1990). Cooperation, opportunism, and the invisible hand: Implications for transaction cost theory. *Academy of Management Review, 15*, 500–513.

Hoffman, A. J. (1999). Institutional evolution and change: Environmentalism and the U.S. chemical industry. *Academy of Management Journal, 42*, 351–371.

Hosmer, L. T. (1995). Trust: The connecting link between organizational theory and philosophical ethics. *Academy of Management Review, 20*, 379–403.

Huber, P. J. (1980). *Robust statistics.* New York: John Wiley.

Hunter, J. E. & Schmidt, F. L. (1990). *Methods of meta-analysis: Correcting errors and bias in research findings.* Newbury Park, CA: Sage.

Jones, T. M. (1995). Instrumental stakeholder theory: A synthesis of ethics and economics. *Academy of Management Review, 20*, 404–437.

Kelly, M. (1994, Sept./Oct.). To tell the truth. *Business Ethics*, 6–8.

King, A. (1995). Avoiding ecological surprise: Lessons from long-standing communities. *Academy of Management Review, 20*, 961–985.

Kirsner, S. (1998, March). Inside the WSJ interactive edition: A day in the life of a world famous Web site. *Editor & Publisher*, 4–9.

Kleinbaum, D. G., Kupper, L. L. & Muller, K. E. (1988). *Applied regression analysis and other multivariate methods.* Belmont, CA: Duxbury.

Lintner, J. (1965). The valuation of risk assets and the selection of risky investments in stock portfolios and capital budgets. *Review of Economics and Statistics, 47*, 13–37.

* McGuire, J. B., Sundgren, A. & Schneeweis, T. (1988). Corporate social responsibility and firm financial performance. *Academy of Management Journal, 31*, 854–872.

McNamara, G. & Bromiley, P. (1999). Risk and return in organizational decision making. *Academy of Management Journal, 42*, 330–339.

McWilliams, A. & Siegel, D. (2001). Corporate social responsibility: A theory of the firm perspective. *Academy of Management Review, 26*, 117–127.

Milgrom, P. & Roberts, J. (1992). *Economics, organizations, and management.* Englewood Cliffs, NJ: Prentice-Hall.

Miller, K. & Bromiley, P. (1990). Strategic risk and corporate performance: An analysis of alternative risk measures. *Academy of Management Journal, 33*, 759–779.

Modigliani, F. & Pogue, G. A. (1993). An introduction to risk and return: Concepts and evidence. In S. Levine (ed.), *Financial analysts' handbook*, (pp. 183–200). Homewood, IL: Dow Jones-Irwin.

* O'Neill, H. M., Saunders, O. B. & McCarthy, A. D. (1989). Board members, corporate social responsiveness and profitability: Are tradeoffs necessary? *Journal of Business Ethics, 8*, 353–357.

* Pava, M. L. & Krausz, J. (1995). *Corporate responsibility and financial performance: The paradox of social cost.* Westport, CT: Quorum.

Pfeffer, J. (1998). *The human equation: Building profits by putting people first.* Boston, MA: Harvard Business School Press.

Post, J. E. (ed.). (1991). *Research in corporate social performance and policy, vol. 12.* Greenwich, CT: JAI Press.

Preiss, R. & Allen, M. (1990, June). *Precautions and prospects for using meta-analysis.* Paper presented at the meeting of International Communication Association Convention, Dublin, Ireland.

Roberts, J. A. (1996). Will the socially responsible consumer please step forward? *Business Horizons, 39*(1), 79–83.

* Roberts, R. W. (1992). Determinants of corporate social responsibility disclosure: An application of stakeholder theory. *Accounting, Organizations and Society, 17*(6), 595–612.

Rudd, A. (1981). Social responsibility and portfolio performance. *California Management Review, 23*(4), 55–62.

Sauer, D. A. (1997). The impact of social-responsibility screens on investment performance: Evidence from the Domini 400 Social Index and Domini Equity Mutual Fund. *Review of Financial Economics, 6*(2), 137–149.

Sennett, F. (1999, April). Coming clean on corrections. *Editor & Publisher,* 38.

Sharfman, M. (1996). A concurrent validity study of the KLD social performance ratings data. *Journal of Business Ethics, 15*(3), 287–296.

Sharpe, W. F. (1964). Capital asset prices: A theory of market equilibrium under conditions of risk. *Journal of Finance, 19,* 425–442.

Sharpe, W. F. (1990). *Quantifying the market risk premium phenomenon for investment decision making.* Charlottesville, VA: Institute for Chartered Financial Analysts.

Shavelson, R. J., Webb, N. M. & Rowley, G. L. (1989). Generalizability theory. *American Psychologist, 44,* 922–932.

Shiller, R. J. (2005). *Irrational exuberance* (2nd ed.). Princeton, NJ: Princeton University Press.

* Simerly, R. L. (1995). Institutional ownership, corporate social performance, and firms' financial performance. *Psychological Reports, 77,* 515–525.

* Spicer, B. H. (1978a). Investors, corporate social performance and information disclosure: An empirical study. *Accounting Review, 53,* 94–111.

* Spicer, B. H. (1978b). Market risk, accounting data and companies' pollution control records. *Journal of Business, Finance, & Accounting, 5,* 67–83.

* Starik, M. (1990). *Stakeholder management and firm performance: Reputation and financial relationships to U.S. electric utility consumer-related strategies.* University of Georgia, Athens. Unpublished doctoral dissertation.

Starik, M. (1995). Should trees have managerial standing? Toward stakeholder status for non-human nature. *Journal of Business Ethics, 14,* 207–217.

Starik, M. & Carroll, A. B. (1991). In search of beneficence: Reflections on the connection between firm social and financial performance. In K. Paul (ed.), *Contemporary issues in business and society in the United States and abroad,* (pp. 79–108). New York: Edwin Mellen Press.

Tracz, S. (1985). The effect of the violation of the assumption of independence when combining correlation coefficients in a meta-analysis (Doctoral dissertation, Southern Illinois University at Carbondale, 1985). *Dissertation Abstracts International, 46,* 688A.

Traub, R. E. (1994). *Reliability for the social sciences: Theory and application, vol. 3.* Thousand Oaks, CA: Sage.

* Trotman, K. T. & Bradley, G. W. (1981). Associations between social responsibility disclosure and characteristics of companies. *Accounting, Organizations and Society, 6*(4), 355–362.

Tukey, J. W. (1960). A survey of sampling from contaminated distributions. In I. Olkin, J. G. Ghurye, W. Hoffding, W. G. Madoo & H. Mann (eds), *Contributions to probability and statistics.* Stanford, CA: Stanford University Press.

Tukey, J. (1977). *Exploratory data analysis.* Reading, MA: Addison-Wesley.

Turban, D. B. & Greening, D. W. (1997). Corporate social performance and organizational attractiveness to prospective employees. *Academy of Management Journal, 40*, 658–672.

Ullmann, A. (1985). Data in search of a theory: A critical examination of the relationship among social performance, social disclosure, and economic performance. *Academy of Management Review, 10*, 540–577.

* Waddock, S. A. & Graves, S. B. (1997). The corporate social performance-financial performance link. *Strategic Management Journal, 18*, 303–319.

Waddock, S. A. & Mahon, J. F. (1991). Corporate social performance revisited: Dimensions of efficacy, effectiveness, and efficiency. In J. E. Post (ed.), *Research in corporate social performance and policy, 12* (pp. 231–262). Greenwich, CT: JAI Press.

Waddock, S. & Smith, N. (2000, Winter). Corporate responsibility audits: Doing well by doing good. *Sloan Management Review, 41*(2), 75–83.

Wartick, S. L. & Cochran, P. L. (1985). The evolution of the corporate social performance model. *Academy of Management Review, 10*, 758–769.

Webb, E. J., Campbell, D., Schwartz, R., Sechrest, L. & Grove, J. (1981). *Nonreactive measures in the social sciences*. Boston: Houghton Mifflin.

Williamson, O. E. (1975). *Markets and hierarchies: Analysis and antitrust implications*. New York: Free Press.

Williamson, O. E. (1985). *The economic institutions of capitalism: Firms, markets, relational contracting*. New York: Free Press.

Willums, J.-O. (1999, May 3). Social responsibility and shareholder value. *Business Week (Asian Edition)*, 85.

Wiseman, R. & Catanach, A. (1997). A longitudinal disaggregation of operational risk under changing regulations: Evidence from the savings and loan industry. *Academy of Management Journal, 40*, 799–830.

Wood, D. J. (1991a). Corporate social performance revisited. *Academy of Management Review, 16*, 691–718.

Wood, D. J. (1991b). Social issues in management: Theory and research in corporate social performance. *Journal of Management, 17*, 383–406.

Wood, D. J. (1995). The *Fortune* database as a CSP measure. *Business & Society, 34*, 197–198.

Wood, D. J. & Jones, R. E. (1995). Stakeholder mismatching: A theoretical problem in empirical research on corporate social performance. *The International Journal of Organizational Analysis, 3*, 229–267.

Technical Appendix

Reliability

Classical measurement theory is concerned with the correspondence between observed scores and true scores. Some of the reliability coefficients used in this study are in the tradition of classical measurement theory, such as coefficient alpha reliabilities. Sometimes it becomes necessary, though, to count not only variation due to item sampling, but also day-to-day variation in scores as measurement error. In classical theory, one can accomplish this task by using an alternate-forms coefficient of reliability, with the different forms being administered on different days. Generalizability theory is less restrictive in its assumptions than classical theory (Cronbach, Gleser, Nanda & Rajaratnam, 1972).

Therefore, the present study occasionally estimates measurement error with the coefficient of generalizability, which reflects the degree to which observed scores allow for generalization about a firm's behavior in a defined universe of situations (Cronbach, Gleser, Nanda & Rajaratnam, 1972; Shavelson, Webb & Rowley, 1989). According to psychometric theory, all coefficients of reliability used in the meta-analysis provide conservative estimates of, that is, a lower bound to, the reliability of the CSP measurement instrument.

6
Organizational Size, Corporate Social Performance, and Business Performance

In the previous two chapters, we presented meta-analytic evidence which suggests that corporate social performance (CSP) is positively related to company financial performance (Chapter 4) and inversely related to business risk (Chapter 5). Even so, Stanwick and Stanwick's (1998) study raises the suspicion that organizational size may be an exogenous determinant of both CSP and corporate financial performance (CFP). That is, it is possible that the significantly positive path coefficient between CSP and CFP is spurious and disappears when firm size is entered as a third variable (Chen & Metcalf, 1980). However, Stanwick and Stanwick's (1998) conclusions are limited to their specific sample (*Fortune* 500 companies) and operationalizations of CSP (*Fortune* Corporate Reputation Index). The study presented in this chapter takes a broader, more representative perspective.

The present study integrates, in a meta-analysis, 41 different CSP-size correlations and combines this quantitative review with Gooding and Wagner's (1985) meta-analysis of the empirical relationship between firm size and CFP. Through the addition of the meta-analytic data set of the previous two chapters, a three-variable path diagram is developed. Figure 6.1 presents the theoretical model upon which this empirical study is based, the proposition that there may be positive paths between firm size and CSP, on the one hand, and firm size and CFP, on the other. In other words, firm size may be the real determinant of *both*

This chapter was originally published in 2001 as Orlitzky, M., 'Does organizational size confound the relationship between corporate social performance and firm financial performance?', *Journal of Business Ethics, 33*(2), 167–180. It was revised for publication in this book. The material of the original chapter was reproduced with permission of Springer Verlag.

CSP *and* CFP and, therefore, may cause the positive bivariate relationship between CSP and CFP to be spurious.

Instead of conducting a primary study of this potentially confounding effect of firm size, the decision was made to undertake a meta-analysis for several reasons. First, unlike a primary study, a meta-analysis can correct for at least two study artifacts, sampling error and measurement error (i.e., lack of reliability). Second, meta-analytic results may form the basis of path analyses (Hunter & Schmidt, 2004), which can, unlike multiple regression results, depict collinear relationships among two independent variables. Third, and most importantly, meta-analysis does not rely on a limited sample of firms (such as that represented by *Fortune 500* companies) and particular operationalizations of CSP, CFP, and firm size (see, for instance, Wood, 1995 on the dubious nature of the *Fortune* Reputation Index for operationalizations of CSP). In other words, meta-analysis acknowledges the conceptual multidimensionality and 'multiple operationism' of CSP (Cook & Campbell, 1979; Cooper, 1989; Webb, Campbell, Schwartz, Sechrest & Grove, 1981).

It should be noted that this study is not concerned with firm size as a *moderator* of the CSP-CFP relationship. The moderator hypothesis would state that the CSP-CFP relationship would systematically vary with a given level of firm size, but not that the CSP-CFP relationship would vanish once size is added to the equation. Undoubtedly, the moderator hypothesis would be valuable to pursue, but it requires a very different approach from the one chosen in this study. The moderator hypothesis would have to be examined by dividing the (primary-study or meta-analytic) sample into distinct size subgroups, which is what Pinkston and Carroll (1993) had done in their primary study on the extent to which social responsibility orientations, organizational stakeholders, and social issues varied among firms of different sizes. From a practical standpoint, this analysis is difficult to conduct because all primary-study authors would have to provide size subgroup correlation results between CSP and CFP. These data may either not exist anymore or be statistically unstable because relatively small sample sizes would decrease even further in those subgroup analyses. At any rate, the method used below presumes that the moderator hypothesis is less important than the question of the potential spuriousness of the CSP-CFP relationship due to firm size.

The path model's causal relations

Modern stakeholder theory, transaction cost economics, agency theory, and the resource-based view of the firm can all be used as theoretical explanations for a positive relationship between CSP and CFP. Chapters 4 and 5 provided an overview of these theoretical explanations (succinct summaries are also provided in Orlitzky, 2006, 2008). The key findings were twofold. First, the generally positive relationship between CSP and CFP tends to vary, depending on, for instance, how CSP and CFP are measured, what business strategies are pursued, and what stakeholders are considered (see Chapter 4 and Hillman & Keim, 2001). Second, when sampling error and measurement error are corrected statistically, the CSP-CFP correlation becomes stronger and more predictably positive (see Chapter 4).

Although the theoretical explanations (with CSP as a predictor of CFP) will not be reviewed here, it should be noted that CFP might also predict CSP positively (*à la* the 'slack resources theory', discussed in previous chapters; see also Waddock & Graves, 1997). The theoretically possible, and empirically supported, reciprocal causality between CSP and CFP (see Chapter 4) explains the two arrows between CSP and CFP in Figure 6.1. This chapter will focus on the other two causal arrows depicted in Figure 6.1, namely those between (a) CSP and firm size and (b) firm size and CFP.

CSP, defined as 'a business organization's configuration of principles of social responsibility, processes of social responsiveness, and policies, programs, and observable outcomes as they relate to the firm's societal relationships' (Wood, 1991, p. 693), and firm size, defined as the 'scale

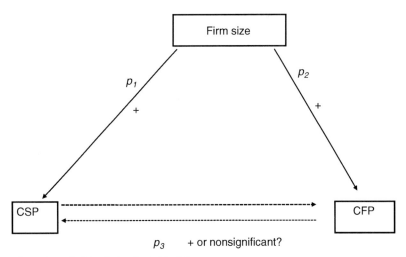

Figure 6.1   Full Path-Analytic Model

of operations in an organization' (Price & Mueller, 1986, p. 233; see also Kimberly, 1976), may be positively related because larger firms have greater visibility and, thus, engage in more and better social performance initiatives than smaller firms with relatively lower visibility (Chen & Metcalf, 1980). This may occur because a growing or large firm attracts more attention from various stakeholder groups, to whose demands the large firm needs to respond more attentively (Burke, Logsdon, Mitchell, Reiner & Vogel, 1986; Waddock & Graves, 1997). Additionally, small firms need an entrepreneurial spirit at the helm in order to grow. Often, those entrepreneurial strategies in early stages of firm growth demand an emphasis on economic factors rather than on the legal, ethical, and philanthropic pursuits defined by Carroll (1979) as also comprising corporate social responsibility (Aupperle, Simmons & Acar, 1990; Pinkston & Carroll, 1993). Because of these external and internal reasons, firm size would be expected to be a positive predictor of CSP (see Figure 6.1).

At the same time, firm size could also be positively related to CFP because it may lead to economies of scale in manufacturing operations (Thompson, 1967), greater control over external stakeholders and resources (Aldrich & Pfeffer, 1976; Pfeffer & Salancik, 1978), and increased promotional opportunities resulting in the attraction and retention of better employees (Mueller, 1969; Stanford, 1980; Williamson, 1975). For all these reasons, firm size may be a positive predictor of CFP (Gooding & Wagner, 1985).

Depicting these theoretical linkages, Figure 6.1 presents a model in which firm size confounds the relationship between CSP and CFP. In other words, the positive bivariate correlation between CSP and CFP might become statistically nonsignificant after the addition of firm size as a third, confounding variable, one that Chen and Metcalf (1980) would call a 'background factor'. To conclude that size, in fact, confounds the CSP-CFP relationship, the following three conditions would have to be met. First, CSP would have to be shown to be positively related to size (path coefficient p_1). Second, CSP would have to be positively correlated with CFP. And finally, the previously significant path coefficient p_3 between CSP and CFP without size would have to decrease to statistical nonsignificance after size is correlated with CFP (path coefficient p_2). The results from these three regression equations (the first two conditions are bivariate correlations, the third one is a multiple regression) can be combined with those from the path model to provide empirical answers to the following research question under investigation here.

Research Question: Does firm size confound the positive relationship between CSP and CFP?

Methods

Literature search

To investigate the path-analytic model shown in Figure 6.1, three different bivariate relationships were examined meta-analytically. First, previous studies on the relationship between CSP and firm size were meta-analyzed (see Table 1 in Orlitzky, 2001). Second, for the CSP-CFP relationships, Orlitzky's meta-analytic data set and analyses (presented in Chapter 4) were used. (The studies comprising the CSP-CFP meta-analytic data set are identified in the Reference section.) Third, for the firm size-CFP relationship, the results from Gooding and Wagner's (1985) meta-analysis were inserted into the model. Any objection to integrating our data set with the other, more recent studies is tantamount to arguing that the size-CFP relationship has changed over time. In this case, though, there is no theoretical reason why this association would have become larger or smaller since the mid-1980s. Furthermore, Kayande and Bhargava (1994) show that the performance-organizational size relationship is stable over time (see also Capon, Farley & Hoenig, 1990; Gooding & Wagner, 1985). Additionally, of all studies examining general temporal effects in meta-analyses, only one by Datta and Narayanan (1989) on the concentration-performance relationship showed significant temporal patterns (in the form of a weakening of the concentration-performance relationship between 1936 and 1972; see Kayande & Bhargava, 1994).

Criteria for relevance

The studies that were deemed relevant for the meta-analysis of firm size and CSP had the following characteristics. First, the studies quantitatively examined the relationship between CSP and firm size. The reported effect size did not have to be a Pearson's product-moment correlation r, but could also be a t-test statistic or effect size d (both t and d can be transformed to r; see Hunter & Schmidt, 1990). Second, the studies were concerned with at least one operationalization of firm size, whether it be annual sales, total amount of assets in dollars, or number of employees (see, for example, Gooding & Wagner, 1985; Kimberly, 1976; Price & Mueller, 1986). Third, all retrieved studies were double-checked for conforming to Wood's (1991) definition of CSP, given previously. The relevance criteria for the other two meta-analyses can be found in Chapter 4 and Gooding and Wagner (1985).

Operationalizations of firm size, CSP, and CFP differed from one study to the next. This 'multiple operationism', however, is not a study weakness, but rather a strength (Cook & Campbell, 1979; Cooper, 1989; Webb, Campbell, Schwartz, Sechrest & Grove, 1981). Positive correlations between different operationalizations (e.g., amount of sales revenue and number of employees in the case of firm size) indicate the measurement of the same underlying construct. In other words, the external validity of the meta-analysis is helped rather than hampered by 'multiple operationism'.

While the literature on CSP differs in many respects from that on corporate environmental performance, studies of environmental management are included in the meta-analysis as a subcategory of CSP. Our reasoning is that constituents who act on behalf of environmental issues, such as environmental activists and government agencies, may in fact give voice to nonhuman nature, which is in and of itself an important stakeholder (Starik, 1995). More pointedly, as discussed in Chapter 1, a firm's ability to ecologize or forge integrative linkages with the environment that function adaptively to sustain life is an important aspect of CSP (see Frederick, 1995; Swanson, 1995).

Characteristics of primary studies

In this study, reliability, which is defined as the ratio of true-score variance to observed-score variance (Traub, 1994), was often estimated by the coefficient of generalizability (Cronbach, Gleser & Rajaratnam, 1963). The corrections for measurement error are based on Orlitzky's (1998) tabulation of CSP and CFP reliability coefficients. The reliability of size is based on correlations between different operationalizations of size. The average of these correlations was calculated to be .67. The meta- and path-analytic results correct for this relatively low level of inter-measure reliability and the other, relatively low levels of reliability. In other words, low reliability does not artificially attenuate study results.

Statistical conventions used in the meta-analysis

Like the two previous chapters, this meta-analysis used Hunter and Schmidt's (1990) methods for integrating correlations and correcting for various study artifacts. According to psychometric theory, artifacts, including sampling and measurement errors, affect observed correlations in certain specifiable ways. These include sampling error, defined as $\sigma_e = (1 - \rho^2) / (\sqrt{N - 1})$, and measurement error, which refers to lack of reliability. Through the use of Hunter and Schmidt's meta-analytic techniques, corrections can be made to obtain a 'true-score' correlation (*r*) between CSP and firm size.

Since not all measurement error data points were available for each study, correlations could not be corrected individually for measurement error. Instead, correlations were meta-analyzed using artifact distributions. Artifact distribution meta-analysis first computes the means and variances of observed correlations and the measurement error in CSP, CFP, and firm size. Then the distribution of observed correlations is corrected for sampling error. Finally, the distribution corrected for sampling error is corrected for measurement error (Hunter & Schmidt, 1990).

Schmidt's computer program INTNL, using artifact distributions, was used to perform the meta-analysis. INTNL uses an interactive formula for the simultaneous, rather than sequential, computation of true score variance (s^2_r), which is given by Hunter and Schmidt (1990, p. 186). Based on the results of computer simulations, interactive formulas are most accurate (Schmidt, Law, Hunter & Rothstein, 1993). The percentage of observed-score variance explained by sampling and measurement errors provides an estimate of the generalizability of the meta-analytic results to the respective population parameters.

Path analysis

The overall results of the CSP-CFP meta-analysis and the observed correlations of firm size with CSP and CFP were entered into Hunter and Hamilton's least-squares path-analysis program, first using the full path-analysis model (i.e., including all three possible links). The complete path model (Figure 6.1) specifies that firm size has a direct and an indirect impact on CFP *vis-à-vis* CSP. The full path model is then compared to reduced models with different paths alternately dropped. All coefficients in the path model are corrected for study artifacts, namely primary-study sampling and measurement errors of CSP and CFP (the former embodying variations in sample sizes *n* smaller than infinity that may lead to erroneous conclusions in primary studies and the latter involving unreliable measures that systematically attenuate effect size estimates in primary studies).

Results

The path analysis is based on the results reported in Table 6.1, the meta-analytic database presented in Chapter 4, and Gooding and Wagner's (1985) meta-analysis of the relationship between organizational size and

Table 6.1 Meta-Analysis of CSP-Size Correlations

k[a]	Total sample size	Sample-size weighted mean observed r	Observed variance	%Variance Explained[b]	Corrected r (mean ρ)	Variance of corrected r	SD_ρ	80% Credibility Interval	File Drawer Analysis[c]
41	6,889	.0611	.0197	31.90%	.1050	.0388	.1969	[−.0608; .2708]	9

[a] k: number of correlation coefficients meta-analyzed;

[b] refers to percentage of observed variance explained by three study artifacts: sampling error, measurement error in CSP, meas. error in CFP;

[c] FDA Hunter & Schmidt's (1990) effect size file drawer analysis: Number of missing studies averaging null findings needed to bring r_{obs} down to .05.

organizational financial performance. As Table 6.1 shows, the 41 studies aggregated for the size-CSP meta-analysis had a mean observed correlation of .06 and a corrected mean correlation (ρ) of .11. The considered study artifacts accounted for 32% of observed variance, suggesting that at least one other variable, so far unknown, might moderate the relationship between firm size and CSP. Further examination of the meta-analytic data set for moderators may be unproductive, however, because in general the present meta-analysis of firm size and CSP does not support an empirical link between the two constructs.

Effect-size file drawer analysis was performed to check the meta-analytic data sets for availability bias (Hunter & Schmidt, 1990). File drawer analysis computes the number of unlocated (i.e., 'lost' or 'missing') studies needed to cause a change in the empirical conclusions (see also the last column of Table 6.1). In most cases, it is unlikely that so many (unpublished or unknown) studies were overlooked, given the multiple ways in which studies were located. The file drawer analyses of all three meta-analyses suggest that availability bias was not a serious problem for the remaining analyses.

The three meta-analyses formed the foundation for the path analyses. The path p_1 between size and CSP is based on the present CSP-size findings (presented in Table 6.1). Path p_2 (size-CFP) is based on Gooding and Wagner's (1985) mean observed correlation of .027 (with an observed variance of .0684). Finally, path p_3 between CSP and CFP is based on the meta-analysis presented in Chapter 4.

Individual-link and fit analyses suggest that organizational size has no significant paths to CSP or CFP (Figure 6.2). The only path that cannot be dropped in this three-variable model is from CSP to CFP (or *vice versa*). Furthermore, the corrected path coefficient p_3 of .37 between CSP and CFP (i.e., p_3 corrected for sampling error and unreliability) remained stable across all possible modifications of the path model, with alternate paths (p_1 and p_2) dropped (but not shown in Figure 6.2).

Moreover, the path-analytic results are supported by the analysis of the three statistical conditions that have to exist to answer the research question in the affirmative. First, across 41 studies with a total N of 6,889, firm size and CSP are correlated to only a minor extent (r_{obs} = .06; t = .38; *ns.*). Second, CSP and CFP are significantly positively correlated (r_{obs} = .18; t = 3.58; significant at α = .0005). Also, the *beta* coefficient between CSP and CFP, as the only two variables in the model, is statistically significant (t = 3.515; p = .005). And finally, the corrected path coefficient p_3 remains significant (at a probability level of α = .01) after the nonsignificant relationship (multiple-regression

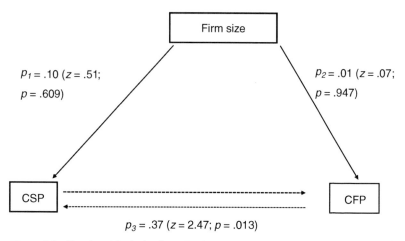

Figure 6.2 Empirical Path-Analytic Findings

beta = .0162; p = .83) between firm size and CFP is added (and controlled for). Because of these results, based on an average total sample size of N = 15,241 (average k of 166 correlations meta-analyzed), we fail to conclude that firm size confounds the relationship between CSP and CFP. This finding is reassuring in that the positive CSP-CFP relationship appears to be generalizable regardless of firm size.

Discussion

Criteria for demonstrating causality are (1) temporal order (2) covariation, and (3) nonspuriousness. Chapter 4 addressed the first two criteria and showed that high CSP is both a predictor and consequence of high CFP. Hence, this previous meta-analysis provided broad, externally valid empirical support for Waddock and Graves' (1997) earlier finding of a virtuous cycle in their more limited sample. The present study addressed one of the most frequently proposed variables that could potentially confound the relationship between CSP and CFP, namely firm size. The empirical analysis, based on the integration of meta-analytic results of over two decades of research in path modeling demonstrated that when firm size is controlled for, the positive correlation between CSP and CFP still holds. In other words, the observed covariation between CSP and CFP is not due to the influence of this specific third factor that has been postulated to cause both high CSP and high CFP.

Of course, the question remains whether other potential variables may make the positive relationship spurious. For example, both CSP and CFP might be the consequence of rigorous strategic planning and, once quality or content of 'strategic management' is controlled for, the positive relationship may disappear. Future research should control not only for sampling error, measurement error, and firm size but also for other possible predictors of both high CSP and high CFP, such as managerial talent, organizational learning, research and development, and organizational knowledge. Providing further empirical evidence regarding causality between CSP and CFP will depend on expanding the bi- and trivariate meta-analysis to a multivariate causal model based on a multitude of prior empirical work. Moreover, other potential moderators could be explored empirically, including population- or industry-level effects such as population density, environmental characteristics such as complexity, munificence, and dynamism, stage in the industry life-cycle, and, perhaps most importantly, the amount and type of industry regulation.

Some readers may argue that a large overlap of meta-analytic data sets, especially the data sets covering paths p_1 and p_3, may be problematic. This would ignore the fact that most path analyses published in the organization studies and psychology literature overlap 100% because the researchers only examined *one* sample in *one* primary study. Overlap in and of itself, while admittedly 68% in the CSP-size and CSP-CFP meta-analyses, is not problematic. The inclusion of firm size in a path model is an advance relative to primary studies, which cannot correct for study artifacts and, thus, often produce erroneous conclusions (e.g., Chen & Metcalf, 1980). In addition, weighting for sample size does not exacerbate the overlaps. Instead, weighting allows for a statistically correct computation and correction for sampling error. Larger samples (e.g., Waddock & Graves, 1997) are more meaningful than smaller samples in terms of their empirical content.

Overall, this meta-analysis can be considered a second step toward proving causality in that it builds on other studies (such as those presented in Chapters 4 and 5) showing covariation and temporal precedence of CSP (before CFP). Importantly, the present path analysis controls for an internal organizational factor which has been one the most frequently cited potentially confounding 'suspects' in the CSP-CFP literature. The fact that it is based on more than 15,000 observations casts doubt on the arguments of skeptics like Chen and Metcalf (1980), who proposed that firm size was the real cause of both CSP and CFP by relying on a single-sample study. In contrast, the present study indicates that their finding was largely due to sampling error because across samples there is neither a significantly positive correlation between firm size and CSP nor between firm size and CFP. Notably, the meta- and path-analyses described herein show that control for firm size in primary studies cannot be considered a *generalizable* answer to this chapter's central question. The hypothesis that large firms are more likely to engage in socially responsive activities and, at the same time, are more likely to perform well financially has failed to garner empirical support. Therefore, the failure to find firm size as a confounding variable in the positive relationship between CSP and CFP is reassuring, since the evidence presented in this chapter suggests that both large *and* small firms can benefit financially from CSP.

References

References marked with an asterisk indicate studies included in the CSP-size and CSP-CFP meta-analyses.

* Abbott, W. F. & Monsen, J. R. (1979). On the measurement of corporate social responsibility: Self-reported disclosure as a method of measuring corporate social involvement. *Academy of Management Journal, 22*, 501–515.

Aldrich, H. E. & Pfeffer, J. (1976). Environments of organizations. In A. Inkeles (ed.), *Annual Review of Sociology, 2* (pp. 79–105). Palo Alto, CA: Annual Reviews.

* Alexander, G. J. & Buchholz, R. A. (1978). Corporate social performance and stock market performance. *Academy of Management Journal, 21*, 479–486.

* Anderson, J. C. & Frankle, A. W. (1980). Voluntary social reporting: An iso-beta portfolio analysis. *Accounting Review, 55*, 467–479.

Aupperle, K. E., Simmons, F. B. & Acar, W. (1990, August). *An empirical investigation into how entrepreneurs view their social responsibilities.* Paper presented at the Academy of Management meetings, San Francisco, CA.

* Belkaoui, A. (1976). The impact of the disclosure of the environmental effects of organizational behavior on the market. *Financial Management, 5*, 26–31.

* Blackburn, V. L., Doran, M. & Shrader, C. B. (1994). Investigating the dimensions of social responsibility and the consequences for corporate financial performance. *Journal of Managerial Issues, 6*(2), 195–212.

* Bowman, E. H. (1976). Strategy and the weather. *Sloan Management Review, 17*, 49–58.

* Bowman, E. H. (1978). Strategy, annual reports, and alchemy. *California Management Review, 20*, 64–71.

* Bowman, E. H. & Haire, M. (1975). A strategic posture toward corporate social responsibility. *California Management Review, 18*, 49–58.

* Bragdon, J. H., Jr. & Marlin, J. A. T. (1972). Is pollution profitable? *Risk Management, 19*, 9–18.

* Brown, B. & Perry, S. (1994). Removing the financial performance halo from *Fortune*'s 'Most Admired Companies.' *Academy of Management Journal, 37*, 1346–1359.

Burke, L., Logsdon, J. M., Mitchell, W., Reiner, M. & Vogel, D. (1986). Corporate community involvement in the San Francisco Bay Area. *California Management Review, 28*(3), 122–141.

Capon, N., Farley, J. U. & Hoenig, S. (1990, Oct.). Determinants of financial performance: A meta-analysis. *Management Science, 36,* 1143–1159.

Carroll, A. B. (1979). A three-dimensional model of corporate performance. *Academy of Management Review, 4,* 497–505.

* Chen, K. H. & Metcalf, R. W. (1980). The relationship between pollution control record and financial indicators revisited. *Accounting Review, 55*(1), 168–177.

* Cochran, P. L. & Wood, R. A. (1984). Corporate social responsibility and financial performance. *Academy of Management Journal, 27,* 42–56.

* Conine, T. E. & Madden, G. P. (1987). Corporate social responsibility and investment value: The expectational relationship. In W. D. Guth (ed.), *Handbook of business strategy 1986/1987 yearbook* (pp. 18-1 to 18-9). Boston: Warren, Gorham & Lamont.

Cook, T. D. & Campbell, D. T. (1979). *Quasi-Experimentation: Design & analysis issues for field settings.* Boston, MA: Houghton Mifflin.

Cooper, H. M. (1989). *Integrating research: A guide for literature reviews* 2nd ed. Newbury Park, CA: Sage.

* Cowen, S. S., Ferreri, L. B. & Parker, L. D. (1987). The impact of corporate characteristics on social responsibility disclosure: A typology and frequency-based analysis. *Accounting, Organizations and Society, 12*(2), 111–122.

Cronbach, L. J., Gleser, G. C. & Rajaratnam, N. (1963). Theory of generalizability: A liberalization of reliability theory. *British Journal of Mathematical and Statistical Psychology, 16,* 137–173.

Datta, D. & Narayanan, V. K. (1989). A meta-analytic review of the concentration-performance relationship: Aggregating findings in Strategic Management. *Journal of Management, 15*(3), 469–483.

* Davidson, W. N. III & Worrell, D. L. (1992). Research notes and communications: The effect of product recall announcements on shareholder wealth. *Strategic Management Journal, 13,* 467–473.

* Dooley, R. S. & Lerner, L. D. (1994). Pollution, profits, and stakeholders: The constraining effect of economic performance on CEO concern with stakeholder expectations. *Journal of Business Ethics, 13,* 701–711.

* Fogler, H. R. & Nutt, F. (1975). A note on social responsibility and stock valuation. *Academy of Management Journal, 18,* 155–160.

* Fombrun, C. & Shanley, M. (1990). What's in a name? Reputation building and corporate strategy. *Academy of Management Journal, 33,* 233–258.

Frederick, W. C. (1995). *Values, nature, and culture in the American corporation.* New York: Oxford University Press.

* Freedman, M. & Jaggi, B. (1982). Pollution disclosures, pollution performance and economic performance. *Omega: The International Journal of Management Science, 10,* 167–176.

* Freedman, M. & Jaggi, B. (1986). An analysis of the impact of corporate pollution disclosures included in annual financial statements on investors' decisions. *Advances in Public Interest Accounting, 1,* 192–212.

Gooding, R. Z. & Wagner, J. A., III. (1985). A meta-analytic review of the relationship between size and performance: The productivity and efficiency of organizations and their subunits. *Administrative Science Quarterly, 30,* 462–481.

* Goodstein, J. D. (1992). Small business and corporate social performance: An empirical exploration of small business involvement in employer supported child care. In J. E. Post (ed.), *Research in corporate social performance and policy: Markets, politics, and social performance, 13* (pp. 141–158). Greenwich, CT: JAI Press.

* Graves, S. B. & Waddock, S. A. (1994). Institutional owners and corporate social performance. *Academy of Management Journal, 37,* 1034–1046.

* Greening, D. W. (1995). Conservation strategies, firm performance, and corporate reputation in the U.S. electric utility industry. *Research in Corporate Social Performance and Policy, Supplement 1* (pp. 345–368). Greenwich, CT: JAI Press.

* Griffin, J. J. & Mahon, J. F. (1997). The corporate social performance and corporate financial performance debate: Twenty-five years of incomparable research. *Business & Society, 36,* 5–31.

* Hansen, G. S. & Wernerfelt, B. (1989). Determinants of firm performance: The relative importance of economic and organizational factors. *Strategic Management Journal, 10,* 399–411.

* Heinze, D. C. (1976). Financial correlates of a social involvement measure. *Akron Business and Economic Review, 7,* 48–51.

* Herremans, I. M., Akathaporn, P. & McInnes, M. (1993). An investigation of corporate social responsibility reputation and economic performance. *Accounting, Organizations and Society, 18,* 587–604.

Hillman, A. J. & Keim, G. D. (2001). Shareholder value, stakeholder management, and social issues: What's the bottom line? *Strategic Management Journal, 22,* 125–139.

Hunter, J. E. & Schmidt, F. L. (1990). *Methods of meta-analysis: Correcting errors and bias in research findings.* Newbury Park, CA: Sage.

Hunter, J. E. & Schmidt, F. L. (2004). *Methods of meta-analysis: Correcting error and bias in research findings* (2nd ed.). Thousand Oaks, CA: Sage.

* Ingram, R. W. (1978). An investigation of the information content of (certain) social responsibility disclosures. *Journal of Accounting Research, 16,* 270–285.

* Ingram, R. W. & Frazier, K. B. (1980). Environmental performance and corporate disclosure. *Journal of Accounting Research, 18,* 614–622.

* Jacobson, R. (1987). The validity of ROI as a measure of business performance. *American Economic Review, 77,* 470–478.

Kayande, U. & Bhargava, M. (1994). An examination of temporal patterns in meta-analysis. *Marketing Letters, 5*(2), 141–151.

* Kedia, B. L. & Kuntz, E. C. (1981). The context of social performance: An empirical study of Texas banks. In L. E. Preston (ed.), *Research in corporate social performance and policy, 3* (pp. 133–154). Greenwich, CT: JAI Press.

Kimberly, J. R. (1976). Organizational size and the structuralist perspective: A review, critique, and proposal. *Administrative Science Quarterly, 21,* 571–597.

* Levy, F. K. & Shatto, G. M. (1980). Social responsibility in large electric utility firms: The case for philanthropy. In L. E. Preston (ed.), *Research in corporate social performance and policy, 2* (pp. 237–249). Greenwich, CT: JAI Press.

* Long, W. F. & Ravenscraft, D. J. (1984). The misuse of accounting rates of return: comment. *American Economic Review, 74,* 494–501.

* Marcus, A. A. & Goodman, R. S. (1986). Compliance and performance: Toward a contingency theory. In L. E. Preston (ed.), *Research in corporate social performance and policy, 8* (pp. 193–221). Greenwich, CT: JAI Press.
* McGuire, J. B., Sundgren, A. & Schneeweis, T. (1988). Corporate social responsibility and firm financial performance. *Academy of Management Journal, 31*, 854–872.
Mueller, H. (1969, Summer). The policy of the European coal and steel community toward mergers and agreements by steel companies. *Antitrust Bulletin, 14*, 413–448.
* Newgren, K. E., Rasher, A. A., LaRoe, M. E. & Szabo, M. R. (1985). Environmental assessment and corporate performance: A longitudinal analysis using a market-determined performance measure. In L. E. Preston (ed.), *Research in corporate social performance and policy, 7* (pp. 153–164). Greenwich, CT: JAI Press.
* O'Neill, H. M., Saunders, C. B. & McCarthy, A. D. (1989). Board members, corporate social responsiveness and profitability: Are tradeoffs necessary? *Journal of Business Ethics, 8*, 353–357.
Orlitzky, M. (1998). *A meta-analysis of the relationship between corporate social performance and firm financial performance.* Unpublished dissertation thesis, The University of Iowa, Iowa City, IA.
Orlitzky, M. (2001). Does organizational size confound the relationship between corporate social performance and firm financial performance? *Journal of Business Ethics, 33*(2), 167–180.
Orlitzky, M. (2006). Links between corporate social responsibility and corporate financial performance: Theoretical and empirical determinants. In J. Allouche (ed.), *Corporate social responsibility, Vol. 2: Performances and stakeholders* (pp. 41–64). London: Palgrave Macmillan.
Orlitzky, M. (2008). Corporate social performance and financial performance: A research synthesis. In A. Crane, A. McWilliams, D. Matten, J. Moon & D. Siegel (eds), *The Oxford Handbook of CSR*. Oxford, UK: Oxford University Press.
* Patten, D. M. (1990). The market reaction to social responsibility disclosures: The case of the Sullivan Principles signings. *Accounting, Organizations and Society, 15*, 575–587.
* Pava, M. L. & Krausz, J. (1995). *Corporate responsibility and financial performance: The paradox of social cost.* Westport, CT: Quorum.
Pfeffer, J. & Salancik, G. R. (1978). *The external control of organizations.* New York: Harper & Row.
* Pinkston, T. S. & Carroll, A. B. (1993). An investigation of the relationship between organizational size and corporate social performance. *IABS Proceedings*, 109–114.
* Preston, L. E. (1978). Analyzing corporate social performance: Methods and results. *Journal of Contemporary Business, 7*, 135–150.
Price, J. L. & Mueller, C. W. (1986). *Handbook of organizational measurement* 2nd ed. Marshfield, MA: Pitman.
* Reimann, B. C. (1975). Organizational effectiveness and management's public values: A canonical analysis. *Academy of Management Journal, 18*, 224–241.
* Riahi-Belkaoui, A. (1991). Organizational effectiveness, social performance and economic performance. In J. E. Post (ed.), *Research in corporate social performance and policy, 12* (pp. 143–153). Greenwich, CT: JAI Press.

* Roberts, R. W. (1992). Determinants of corporate social responsibility disclosure: An application of stakeholder theory. *Accounting, Organizations and Society, 17*(6), 595–612.
* Russo, M. V. & Fouts, P. A. (1997). A resource-based perspective on corporate environmental performance and profitability. *Academy of Management Journal, 40*, 534–559.
Schmidt, F. L., Law, K., Hunter, J. E. & Rothstein, H. R. (1993). Refinements in validity generalization methods: Implications for the situational specificity hypothesis. *Journal of Applied Psychology, 78*, 3–12.
* Shane, P. B. & Spicer, B. H. (1983). Market response to environmental information produced outside the firm. *Accounting Review, 58*, 521–538.
* Sharfman, M. (1996). A concurrent validity study of the KLD social performance ratings data. *Journal of Business Ethics, 15*, 287–296.
Stanford, R. E. (1980). The effects of promotion by seniority in growth-constrained organizations. *Management Science, 26*, 680–693.
* Simerly, R. L. (1994). Corporate social performance and firms' financial performance: An alternative perspective. *Psychological Reports, 75*, 1091–1103.
* Simerly, R. L. (1995). Institutional ownership, corporate social performance, and firms' financial performance. *Psychological Reports, 77*, 515–525.
* Spencer, B. A. & Taylor, S. G. (1987). A within and between analysis of the relationship between corporate social responsibility and financial performance. *Akron Business and Economic Review, 18*, 7–18.
* Spicer, B. H. (1978). Investors, corporate social performance and information disclosure: An empirical study. *Accounting Review, 53*, 94–111.
Stanwick, P. A. & Stanwick, S. D. (1998). The relationship between corporate social performance, and organizational size, financial performance, and environmental performance: An empirical examination. *Journal of Business Ethics, 17*, 195–204.
* Starik, M. (1990). *Stakeholder management and firm performance: Reputation and financial relationships to U.S. electric utility consumer-related strategies.* Unpublished dissertation thesis, University of Georgia, Athens, GA.
Starik, M. (1995). Should trees have managerial standing? Toward stakeholder status for non-human nature. *Journal of Business Ethics, 14*, 207–217.
* Sturdivant, F. D. & Ginter, J. L. (1977). Corporate social responsiveness: Management attitudes and economic performance. *California Management Review, 19*, 30–39.
Swanson, D. L. (1995). Addressing a theoretical problem by reorienting the corporate social performance model. *Academy of Management Review, 20*, 43–64.
Thompson, J. D. (1967). *Organizations in action.* New York: McGraw-Hill.
Traub, R. E. (1994). *Reliability for the social sciences: Theory and applications.* Thousand Oaks, CA: Sage.
* Trotman, K. T. & Bradley, G. W. (1981). Associations between social responsibility disclosure and characteristics of companies. *Accounting, Organizations and Society, 6*(4), 355–362.
* Turban, D. B. & Greening, D. W. (1997). Corporate social performance and organizational attractiveness to prospective employees. *Academy of Management Review, 40*, 658–672.

* Useem, M. (1991). Organizational and managerial factors in the shaping of corporate social and political action. In J. E. Post (ed.), *Research in corporate social performance and policy, 12* (pp. 63–92). Greenwich, CT: JAI Press.

* Vance, S. (1975). Are socially responsible firms good investment risks? *Management Review, 64,* 18–24.

* Venkatraman, N. & Ramanujam, V. (1987). Measurement of business economic performance: An examination of method convergence. *Journal of Management, 13,* 109–122.

* Waddock, S. A. & Graves, S. B. (1997). The corporate social performance-financial performance link. *Strategic Management Journal, 18,* 303–319.

* Wartick, S. L. (1988). How issues management contributes to corporate performance. *Business Forum, 13,* 16–22.

Webb, E. J., Campbell, D., Schwartz, R., Sechrest, L. & Grove, J. (1981). *Nonreactive measures in the social sciences.* Boston: Houghton Mifflin.

Williamson, O. E. (1975). *Markets and hierarchies: Analysis and antitrust implications.* New York: Free Press.

* Wiseman, J. (1982). An evaluation of environmental disclosures made in corporate annual reports. *Accounting, Organizations and Society, 7,* 53–63.

* Wokutch, R. E. & Spencer, B. A. (1987). Corporate sinners and saints: The effects of philanthropic and illegal activity on organizational performance. *California Management Review, 29,* 62–77.

* Wolfe, R. (1991). The use of content analysis to assess corporate social responsibility. In J. E. Post (ed.), *Research in corporate social performance and policy, 12* (pp. 281 307). Greenwich, CT: JAI Press.

Wood, D. J. (1991). Corporate social performance revisited. *Academy of Management Review, 16,* 691–718.

Wood, D. J. (1995). The *Fortune* database as a CSP measure. *Business & Society, 34,* 197–198.

7
Doing Well by Doing Good: Objective Findings, Subjective Assumptions, or Selective Amplification?

As the integrative research reviews in the previous three chapters showed, the relationship between corporate social performance (CSP) and corporate financial performance (CFP) has been investigated for over three decades. A meta-analysis (see Chapter 4) shows that the average corrected correlation between CSP and CFP is positive (Orlitzky, Schmidt & Rynes, 2003). However, what previous research reviews failed to examine in depth is the considerable amount of *cross-study variability* (Ullmann, 1985; Wood & Jones, 1995). In other words, researchers have not conclusively determined why some studies might find economic benefits from CSP while others do not.

Prior research suggests a number of causes for this cross-study variability in findings. Theoretical reasons, such as executives' varying value orientations, decision-making discretion, and interest group pressures, might account for some of the unexplained variation in the CSP-CFP relationships (Agle, Mitchell & Sonnenfeld, 1999; Godfrey, 2005; Orlitzky & Swanson, 2002; Orlitzky, Swanson & Quartermaine, 2006). Business reputation and risk have also been implicated in causal explanations (e.g., Godfrey, 2005; Logsdon & Wood, 2002; Orlitzky & Benjamin, 2001). In addition, methodological factors may explain some cross-study variability. For example, variable measurement and research strategies could have affected findings to a great extent. As summarized in Chapter 4, Orlitzky *et al.* (2003) found that sampling errors and measurement errors in CSP and CFP explained between 15% and 100% of the cross-study variability in this research area.

This chapter is a major revision of Orlitzky, M., 'Doing well by doing good: Objective findings, subjective assumptions, or selective amplification?' *Best Paper Proceedings* of the Academy of Management (CD), ISSN 1543–8643, 2007.

The primary objective of this study is to investigate unexamined contingency factors – described below in terms of the social construction of knowledge – that may shed further light on the CSP-CFP cross-study variability. Specifically, this study attempts to answer the following closely related questions: Do journals vary in the empirical CSP-CFP links reported? If so, *how* do journals vary? Do editor, reviewer, and researcher backgrounds affect the variance? If so, why? A secondary aim is to show how prior meta-analytic conclusions, such as those of Orlitzky *et al.* (2003), have failed to consider this social construction of knowledge in summaries of empirical research. The problem is that overemphasis on average associations may fail to shed light on the variability and, thus, the contingent nature of these conclusions. The next section describes how the review process in general may lead to differences in conclusions and, then, how CSP-CFP research may be affected by these contingencies more specifically.

How journal editors and reviewers shape published research

Paradigmatic diversity is a fundamental characteristic of the current state of organizational sciences (Burrell, 1996; Burrell & Morgan, 1979; Pfeffer, 1993; Van Maanen, 1995). Compared to the natural sciences, the business disciplines in general have relatively low degrees of paradigm development, which makes particularism more likely (Beyer, Chanove & Fox, 1995; Kuhn, 1996; Lodahl & Gordon, 1972; Pfeffer, Leong & Strehl, 1977). Particularism, the opposite of universalism, may induce journal reviewers and editors to base their judgments about the acceptance or rejection of submitted manuscripts on personal relations or social status (Salancik & Pfeffer, 1974; Zuckerman, 1988). For example, Peters and Ceci (1982) showed how, in the absence of universalistic scientific norms, publication decisions are often nonreplicable. In contrast, universalistic norms would make publication decisions more reliable across reviewers and, thus, more predictable.

Paradigmatic differences in business disciplines, however, do not *have to* lead automatically to particularism and decisions tinted by political considerations. Instead, more innocuous forces may be at play in that paradigmatic diversity may manifest itself as different worldviews and perspectives (Burrell, 1996; Burrell & Morgan, 1979; Morgan, 1997). Over time, paradigmatic assumptions and perspectives may become more homogeneous in a given subdiscipline, due to the editors' gatekeeping function (Gans & Shepherd, 1994; Orum, 1990; Peters & Ceci, 1982). *Selective retention*, a process in which reviewers advise the authors what study content they should retain in the published article, is one such homogenizing force (Staw, 1985). Moreover, the review process can *selectively amplify* particular definitions of perceived manuscript quality by scholars from a particular field (Beyer *et al.*, 1995). In the context of paradigmatic diversity, different researchers are likely to use different definitions of 'research quality'. For example, what is perceived by one group of scholars as a sign of analytical rigor and clarity may strike scholars with different academic backgrounds as over-simplifications of constructs and causal relationships (see Windsor, 2001). Generally, reviewers and editors will advise the authors to shape the submitted manuscripts in ways that they, the reviewers and editors, consider most desirable. Beyer *et al.* (1995) refer to this process of selective retention combined with reviewer/editor coaching as *selective amplification*.

Unless journal editors deliberately encourage substantive and methodological diversity, the disciplinary convergence of selection criteria tends to lead to a considerable amount of homogeneity in the content or format of articles published in a particular journal – or a particular type of journal. Cross-disciplinary differences in the content, style, and format of articles give some credence to the argument that the aforementioned processes occur, at least to some extent, in the social sciences. For example, sociologists and economists studying the same subject (e.g., free market forces as determinants of income distributions) often reach very different conclusions based on their differences in paradigmatic assumptions. Because researchers are not only producers but also consumers of knowledge published in the different journals, certain publication norms are further reinforced in researchers' minds. These standards and norms are often accepted uncritically, especially by junior academics striving to advance professionally or gain tenure, because any fundamental paradigmatic disagreement would decrease the probability of publication, which is, after all, the major currency of academic success.

Given these contingencies, it is not difficult to realize that scholars from different business subdisciplines who examine the relationships between CSP and CFP may differ in their findings and conclusions. When they do, it raises the question of whether diverse subdisciplines conceptualize the subject differently and how selective amplification applies.

This is particularly important to understand in the case of economic research on the CSP-CFP link, especially because economists have, for decades, regarded corporate social responsibility (CSR) as a cost. Famously, Friedman (1970) insisted that CSR by definition is, and must be, an organizational expenditure without any financial return. Moreover, he considered opposing views, which interpreted CSR as investments in an organization's reputation and, thus, enlightened self-interest, to be analytically loose or, even worse, bordering on fraud. Specifically, Friedman (1970: 33) defines a 'socially responsible' act as an act that is 'not in the interest of employers'. Although he acknowledges that some actions that benefit the community may also attract better employees or reduce sabotage, calling these actions 'corporate social responsibility' could be considered 'hypocritical window-dressing' in his view. According to Friedman's stance toward CSR, there is no room for simultaneous (short-term or long-term) payoffs for both the firm and its environment and, hence, no enlightened self-interest possible at the organizational level of analysis. Although some hold that there is not necessarily a tradeoff between self-interest and other-interest (Dalai Lama, 1999; Locke, 2006; Solomon, 1985), many neoclassical economists have opposed conceptualizations of CSP and CFP as equally valid organizational performance dimensions that may, in some instances, pull in the same direction, namely toward more sustainable organizational success. This thinking only reinforces the epistemological orthodoxy that considers economic and duty-based conceptualizations of 'good' organizational performance to be contradictory or incompatible (see Chapter 1). The dilemma is that this *a priori* assumption may get in the way of a valid assessment of the empirical evidence.

Reinforcing this dilemma, Friedman and other economists and strategists (e.g., Levitt, 1958) voice skepticism about the financial benefits of CSP because they assume that it represents a distraction from an executive's primary mandate to maximize shareholder wealth (Davis, 1973). This theoretical perspective assumes that executives tend to have low competence (or considerable bias) with respect to the handling of social and environmental issues and, thus, often waste shareholder funds in their quest to be socially responsible and responsive (Anderson & Frankle, 1980; Simon, Powers & Gunnemann, 1972). When managers' decision making is artificially limited to such narrow economic thinking, then it is easily interpreted as amoral (Donaldson, 1990; Swanson, 1996), a stance that can be expected and rewarded in organizations (Carr, 1968). Besides reinforcing a dichotomy between 'the normative' and 'the descriptive', as discussed in Chapter 2, this premise leads to an interesting division of labor at the societal level of analysis. According to Friedman's early writings,[1] social concerns are exclusively governmental mandates. To the extent that the law and ethical customs institutionalize these concerns, a baseline for 'good' action is set. However, for firms to voluntarily go beyond this baseline is problematic in terms of economic orthodoxy.

Therefore, by default, the area is easily relegated to government mandate in the form of the law or social mandate in the form of ethical customs. This simplistic view can detract from research aimed at examining the CSP-CFP relationship in more detail and putting the empirical evidence in perspective.

For all the above reasons, economists would be expected to be more skeptical about a positive CSP-CFP relationship than researchers in Social Issues in Management (SIM), Business and Society, and Business Ethics. That is, in journals with an economics orientation, findings of a positive (and especially highly positive) relationship between CSP and CFP are likely to be regarded as poor research (McWilliams & Siegel, 2000). Studies that do not pass the economists' test of a properly specified model would be treated with suspicion by reviewers with a standard economics orientation – and are likely to be rejected by economics journals. In this way, conclusions drawn from research reviews by economists typically differ from those of ethicists. For instance, the first group, represented by McWilliams and her colleagues (McWilliams & Siegel, 1997; McWilliams, Siegel & Teoh, 1999), doubt the applicability and validity of event studies, while Frooman (1997), as part of the second group, (implicitly) affirms them.

In contrast to the skepticism of many economists, researchers in Social Issues in Management (SIM), business and society, or business ethics often – though not always – set out to test for a positive, theoretically-supported CSP-CFP link. Notably, instrumental stakeholder theory postulates a positive relationship between CSP and CFP (Jones, 1995), despite debates about which CSP measures and theories are appropriate to use (Ullmann, 1985; Wood, 1991, 1995; Wood & Jones, 1995). One line of reasoning is that CSP may translate into high CFP because socially responsible and responsive organizations can more effectively navigate the complex webs of stakeholder relations (Waddock & Graves, 1997a, 1997b). By engaging with different stakeholders in meaningful ways (Rahman, Waddock, Andriof & Husted, 2002), an organization can increase its legitimacy, develop a positive reputation, and thus enhance its financial viability as well, at least in the long run (Mahon, 2002; Suchman, 1995). All these paradigmatic assumptions are common views in the areas of SIM, business and society, and business ethics. Of course, scholars realize that the case for social and environmental responsibility becomes stronger if CSP results not only in social progress or environmental improvements but also in increased financial benefits (Holliday, Schmidheiny & Watts, 2002). This simply raises the stakes for understanding the true nature of the CSP-CFP relationship.

To investigate publication outlets as potential moderators of revealed empirical CSP-CFP relationships, a third area of scholarship can be considered in addition to the two groups discussed previously (i.e., economics on the one hand and SIM/business and society/business ethics on the other). This third set is constituted of general management journals. Based on the assumption that general management journals, such as the *Academy of Management Journal,* tend to publish research from all academic backgrounds, the findings reported in them are expected to fall in between those of the other two types of publication outlets. However, because much of general management research is dominated by economics assumptions and thinking (Bazerman, 2005; Ferraro, Pfeffer & Sutton, 2005; Ghoshal, 2005), conclusions published in general management journals are expected to be closer to those in the economics outlets. Furthermore, it is reasonable to propose that editors and scholars from non-SIM/non-ethics disciplines might discriminate against SIM and ethics researchers not only at their home institutions (Hosmer, 1999) but also in publication decisions – at least more so than against economics scholars. This may be a second reason for the numerical proximity of general management CSP-CFP findings to those reported in economics outlets, which for our purposes include finance and accounting publications as well.[2] The following three research hypotheses summarize the ideas introduced above:

Hypothesis 1 (H1): Publication outlet effects can be considered moderators of the previously found, highly variable corporate social–financial performance relationships.
Hypothesis 2 (H2): Corporate social–financial performance relationships reported in business ethics/business & society/SIM journals are larger in magnitude than findings in general management journals, which in turn are larger than findings reported in economics, finance, and accounting journals.
Hypothesis 3 (H3): Corporate social–financial performance relationships reported in general management journals are closer to findings reported in economics, finance, and accounting journals than to findings reported in business ethics/business & society/SIM journals.

Methods

To investigate the aforementioned hypotheses, this study uses meta-analysis, which is a quantitative method of research integration (Cooper, 1989). More specifically, this study relies on the meta-analytic guidelines provided by Hunter and Schmidt (2004). Their meta-analytic techniques correct the observed sample statistics (e.g., the observed correlation r in primary studies) for methodological distortions due to *sampling error* and *measurement error*. Because meta-analysis is able to correct for these distortions, or *study artifacts*, it has increasingly replaced the narrative literature review as a technique for summarizing a research area in many different scientific disciplines (Cooper & Hedges, 1994; Hunt, 1997).

In meta-analysis, each observed correlation is weighted by the sample size of the primary study in order to calculate the *observed mean weighted correlation* ($\bar{r}_{obs}$) across all of the collected studies. The standard deviation of the observed correlations can then be computed to estimate the variability in the relationship between the variables of interest. The total variability across studies includes several components, such as the true variation in the population, variation due to sampling error, and variation due to other artifacts (e.g., lack of reliability in measures). Recognition and statistical control of these artifacts allow for a more accurate estimate of the true variability around the population correlation. Thus, the most important outcome of the meta-analysis is the population parameter (i.e., the estimated *corrected* or *true-score correlation* ρ) between any two variables.

Literature search

This study reexamined the findings of two previous award-winning meta-analyses of the CSP-CFP empirical literature (Orlitzky & Benjamin, 2001; Orlitzky *et al.*, 2003).[3] If this moderator meta-analysis were based on a different data set, we would compare apples and oranges and, thus, would reach invalid conclusions about those earlier meta-analyses. As mentioned in the introduction, a secondary aim of this study is to show how the prior meta-analysis by Orlitzky, Schmidt, and Rynes (2003) might have failed to consider the issues related to the social construction of knowledge. Without identical meta-analytic data sets, we would not accomplish this second objective.

Criteria for relevance

The studies deemed relevant for this moderator meta-analysis have the following characteristics. First, the studies quantitatively examined the relationship between CSP and CFP. The reported effect size did not have to be a Pearson's product-moment correlation *r*, but could also be a *t*-test statistic or effect size *d* (both *t* and *d* can be transformed to *r*, according to Hunter and Schmidt, 2004). Second, the meta-analyzed studies were concerned with performance measures based on either accounting metrics (e.g., return on assets, return on equity) or market metrics (e.g., changes in share prices). Third, all retrieved measures of CSP were checked against Wood's (1991) definition of CSP. If the dependent or independent variable cannot be classified as one of the three broad categories of Wood's (1991) model, the study was excluded from analysis. Wood's model is briefly described next.

Different operational definitions of CSP

CSP is a multidimensional construct and can be measured in a variety of ways. Wood (1991) conceptualized CSP as a tripartite model consisting of (1) principles of social responsibility (2) processes of social responsiveness, and (3) policies, programs, and observable outcomes as they relate to the firm's societal relationships. For our purposes, Wood's conceptual model, roughly an input-process-output systems model of CSP, was supplemented with a four-part typology of CSP centered around the four *measurement* categories: (1) CSP disclosures (2) CSP reputation ratings (3) social audits, CSP processes, and observable outcomes (such as charitable contributions), and (4) CSR, which consists of managerial principles and values (see also Post, 1991). Although there is no consensus on the quality of specific measures of CSP (Chatterji & Levine, 2006; Entine, 2003; Sharfman, 1996; Waddock, 2003), measurement diversity arguably is beneficial at this relatively early stage of empirical research. Such 'multiple operationism' is an advantage because it helps determine whether a 'true' relationship exists in different industry contexts with different operationalizations of the two focal constructs (Cook & Campbell, 1979; Cooper, 1989; Webb, Campbell, Schwartz, Sechrest & Grove, 1981). However, the use of any *particular* measure in any given primary study is subject to measurement error. A meta-analysis can circumvent this downside of primary studies through the correction for relative lack of reliability (measurement error) – in addition to the correction of aggregated observed correlations for sampling error (the deviation of sample size n from infinity in primary studies).

Studies of corporate environmental performance (CEP) are included as a dimension of CSP for several reasons. First, meta-analyses have shown that several studies, especially earlier ones, use environmental performance as a proxy for CSP (Orlitzky & Benjamin, 2001; Orlitzky *et al.*, 2003). Second, stakeholder proxies, such as environmental interest groups and government agencies, may in fact claim a social 'stake' for, or give voice to, nature (Starik, 1995). Finally, many in the business community tend to regard social responsibility as a concept pertaining to social issues, such as employee rights, *and* environmental issues (e.g., Anderson, 1998; Willums, 1999). Because a comprehensive definition of CSP refers to environmental performance as well, a more descriptive term for the construct under consideration might be *corporate citizenship,* as suggested by the title of this book.

Characteristics of primary studies

The most important study characteristics tabulated in Orlitzky *et al.* (2003) are authors, date of study, sample size *n*, observed correlation *r* or a transformed and/or partially corrected *r* (i.e., *r* corrected for dichotomization and unequal sample sizes in the two groups compared in a *t* test), number of correlations per study, operationalization of CSP and firm performance, and estimates of reliability for CSP and CFP. Reliability is traditionally defined as the ratio of true-score variance to observed-score variance (Traub, 1994). The present study occasionally estimates reliability with the coefficient of generalizability (e.g., as contained in the statistical analyses by Sharfman, 1996). The technical appendix of Chapter 5 presents further details on this particular coefficient of reliability. A total of 388 (= *k*) correlation coefficients were meta-analyzed, with a total sample size (*N*) of 33,878 observations. Two-hundred and nine of the 388 correlation coefficients that were meta-analyzed were obtained in cross-sectional studies – with CSP and CFP measured concurrently. However, the studies that explicitly examined lagged effects contain only slightly fewer observations than the cross-sectional studies (*N* = 16,895 lagged observations versus 16,983 concurrent observations). The cross-sectional data, though less informative than lagged data about the underlying causal relationships, are still useful in the context of this moderator meta-analysis investigating differences in publication outlets.

Results

To study the possible influence of publication outlet effects, the meta-analytic data set was first examined for the statistical likelihood of unexamined moderators. One rule of thumb that can be used for this purpose is the 75% rule: If 75% or more of the variance is due to artifacts, we can conclude that all of it is, on grounds that the remaining 25% is likely to be due to artifacts for which no correction has been made (Hunter & Schmidt, 2004). When all cross-study variance is due to artifacts, then no true cross-study variability remains after the meta-analytic corrections. Hence, the standard deviation (SD_ρ) and variance (σ_ρ^2) of the true score correlation is zero. The first row of Table 7.1 shows the proportion of cross-study variance explained by the artifacts of sampling error, measurement error of CSP and CFP, and dichotom-ization of these variables (in some studies). This proportion is 24% and, therefore, far below the 75% threshold. This suggests the influence of one or more moderator variables. The omnibus chi-square test, which tests the null hypothesis (H1) that there is no variation in group mean correlations, is consistent with the conclusions drawn from the 75% rule of thumb. Hedges and Olkin's (1985) heterogeneity Q-test, dis-tributed as a chi-square statistic, was 3,211.96 and statistically sig-nificant at $p < .001$. Hunter and Schmidt prefer the 75% rule of thumb to Hedges and Olkin's chi-square test for heterogeneity because of the former technique's greater statistical power to detect moderators (Sackett, Harris & Orr, 1986). In the present meta-analysis, though, both heuristics point in the same direction: publication outlet may be one of several moderators because most cross-study variance is not explained by methodological artifacts.

This conclusion implies that the subdivision of the meta-analytic data set into the three distinct types of publication outlets mentioned in the theory section is a sensible next step in the analysis. The subgroup ana-lysis in Table 7.1 shows that business ethics/business & society/SIM jour-nals report a higher average correlation between CSP and CFP than do economics, finance, and accounting journals. Although statistical sig-nificance tests are often misleading (Cohen, 1994; McCloskey, 1998; Schmidt, 1996), including in meta-analysis, this statistical tool can be applied to the comparison of observed meta-analytic correlations. After application of Fisher's (1932) transformation formula for the comparison of two correlation coefficients, this difference ($\bar{r}_{obs} = .25$ versus .11) is highly significant ($p < .001$). The difference between the corrected correlation coefficients ($\rho = .49$ versus $\rho = .22$, respectively) confirms that this differ-ence is non-trivial: the average corrected correlation reported by SIM, business and society, and ethics researchers is more than twice as large as the one reported by economics, finance, and accounting researchers. This finding is consistent with Hypothesis 2.

Two findings reported in Table 7.1 are particularly noteworthy. First, the average observed ($\bar{r}_{obs}$) and true-score correlations (ρ) reported by economics, finance, and accounting journals are *not* negative, as some 'Friedmanites' might expect. At $r_{obs} = .11$, they are also considerably higher than zero or the conventional .05 threshold value in so-called 'file drawer analysis' (see last column of Table 7.1). File drawer analysis calculates the number of null findings needed to bring the observed meta-analytic correlation down to a predetermined level. Second, the average correlations reported in general management journals are only

Table 7.1   Meta-Analysis of Publication Outlet Moderator Effects

Publication Outlet	k^a	Total sample size	Sample-size weighted mean observed r ($\bar{r}_{Obs}$)	Observed variance	% Variance Explained[b]	Mean 'true-score' r ($\bar{\rho}$)	Variance of ρ [$=\sigma^2_\rho$]	File Drawer Analysis[c]
Overall meta–analysis	388	33,878	.1836	.0646	23.89%	.3648	.1896	1,037
Business ethics/ Business & Society/ SIM journals	100	7,794	.2488	.0578	34.46%	.4944	.1460	398
Economics, finance, and accounting journals	141	9,534	.1072	.0606	30.25%	.2186	.1718	161
General management journals	147	16,550	.2085	.0659	21.47%	.4143	.1995	466

[a] k: number of correlation coefficients meta-analyzed.
[b] refers to percentage of cross-study observed variance explained by three study artifacts: sampling error, measurement error in CSP, and measurement error in CFP.
[c] Number of missing studies averaging null findings needed to bring $\bar{r}_{obs}$ down to .05.

slightly lower than those reported in business ethics/business & society/ SIM journals ($\bar{r}_{obs}$ =.21 vs. 25 and ρ =.41 vs..49, respectively). So, on the one hand, general management studies fall in between the other two groups, which is consistent with Hypothesis 2. On the other hand, though, the findings in general management outlets are, in fact, closer to SIM scholars'/ethicists' findings than those reported by economics, finance, and accounting researchers. This contradicts Hypothesis 3 and will be interpreted in greater detail in the Discussion section below.

In sum, the meta-analysis reported in this study provides support for Hypotheses 1 and 2, but not Hypothesis 3. Albeit, this meta-analysis does not point to publication outlet as a *key* moderator because the cross-study variance explained in the three publication outlet subgroups is only marginally higher than in the overall meta-analytic set. If publication outlet were the *primary* moderator, the values reported in the '% Variance Explained' column of Table 7.1 would be over 75% in the three publication outlet subgroups (bottom three rows of Table 7.1).

Discussion

The findings reported in this moderator meta-analysis spanning over three decades of studies suggest that observations about the relationship between CSP and CFP depend on the nature of the publication outlet and background of the researcher. In studies published by economics, finance, or accounting researchers/journals, the average correlations found are only about half the magnitude of the values reported by business ethics/business & society/SIM journals (mean observed correlation coefficient $\bar{r}_{obs}$ =.11 vs. 25, respectively; mean corrected correlation coefficient ρ =.22 vs..49, respectively). It is still remarkable that, on average (1) economists generally did not find null or negative CSP-CFP correlations and (2) findings reported in general management outlets ($\bar{r}_{obs}$ =.21; ρ =.41) were closer to business ethics/business & society/ SIM results than those reported by economics, finance, and accounting researchers. Because researcher values and psychological and social forces affect almost all research domains (Barnes, Bloor & Henry, 1996; Latour & Woolgar, 1986), any meta-analysis that does not examine and report in detail on these research contexts is incomplete. Arguably, earlier meta-analyses, which concluded that companies can 'do well by doing good' (e.g., Orlitzky, 2001; Orlitzky & Benjamin, 2001; Orlitzky *et al.*, 2003), did not pay enough attention to the CSP-CFP paradigm as a values-impregnated enterprise. In contrast, this study qualifies these meta-analytic conclusions by pointing to the type of publication outlet as moderating the CSP-CFP relationship.

Implications for producers and consumers of organizational knowledge

These differences have important implications for producers and consumers of organizational knowledge. First, researchers of the CSP-CFP relationship can use the meta-analytic findings of this study to decide which journals to target. Due to journal reviewers' and editors' assumptions, business ethics/business & society/SIM outlets seem to be more open to arguments that suggest socially responsible activities can positively affect competitive advantage (Solomon, 1985, 1992, 1999). In contrast, economics, finance, and accounting researchers are more likely to consider nonmarket forces as threats rather than opportunities in corporate strategizing. This perspective is reflected, for example, in the overall tenor of Baron's (2006) textbook, which relies on political science and economics perspectives. Still, economics-oriented outlets might report positive CSP-CFP associations because better financial performance could conceivably provide the slack resources that allow for discretionary spending on CSR activities. In addition, according to this study, general management outlets seem most receptive to middle-of-the-road arguments that emphasize the influence of a variety of situational contingencies, moderators, or interactions (McWilliams & Siegel, 2001; Paine, 2003). Interestingly, however, these stipulated contingency variables can be shown to moderate generally positive CSP-CFP correlations, not null correlations, as a baseline assumption (see also Chapter 4).

Another implication of this study in terms of the social construction of knowledge is that journal readers, students, and other consumers of organizational research should not only consider researchers' values, but also critically and independently analyze the assumptions of the scientific community. Yet, the conclusion that *all* knowledge reported is, in the end, the outcome of subjective judgments may be too radical (Nola, 2003). Indeed, the numerical proximity of findings reported in business ethics/business & society/SIM journals to those in general management journals, in which economic assumptions tend to predominate (Bazerman, 2005; Ferraro *et al.*, 2005; Ghoshal, 2005), seems to suggest that positive CSP-CFP correlations are objectively true. Even so, because meta-analyses and narrative research reviews may be affected at least as much by researcher values as primary studies, consumers of knowledge also need to develop critical attitudes toward meta-analysts' and other research reviewers' values, predilections, and assumptions about business-and-society relationships. Without considering publication outlet as a moderator, as well as other possible contingencies pertaining to the research context, scholars cannot have complete confidence in any research review, whether narrative or statistical.

Study limitations

Like all studies, this moderator meta-analysis has its own set of limitations. First, the differences between different academic communities are, to some extent, cognitive and descriptive simplifications. The assumption of homogeneous and stable values among economists might not capture reality accurately. For example, Hilton Friedman (2005) recently acknowledged that some social responsibility initiatives could, in fact, lead to improved business reputation and greater profitability. Similarly, some economists have recently abandoned Friedman's (1970) original conceptualization of CSR which, by definition, made it opposed to business self-interest. Often, these economists now argue that CSR, as a normal good, might be positively related to profitability under certain conditions of demand and supply (McWilliams & Siegel, 2001). However, the assumption of a general null relationship between CSP and CFP still seems to predominate among economists, including McWilliams and Siegel (2001). Strategy experts, on the other hand, have moved closer to a promotion of CSR as an element of competitive advantage (Porter & Kramer, 2006). However, these cognitive shifts among strategists have been so recent that, arguably, they have not yet had time to inform study assumptions of empirical research in economics, finance, or accounting.

Similarly, business ethics/business & society/SIM researchers do not all share the same values. Those who do not have much faith in the morality of free markets may presume that often some sort of government intervention is necessary (see B. M. Friedman, 2005; McCloskey, 2006). In their view, free markets may lead to exploitation of employees, deception of consumers, and ecological damage instead of social progress. Thus, the finding that CSP and CFP are generally positively correlated may disturb those researchers that assume a 'natural' opposition of the market and morality. On the other hand, others in this group may welcome the positive findings. The point is that the disciplinary distinctions expressed in Hypothesis 2 simplify paradigmatic differences and, thus, refer to *average* moderator effects. There are varying viewpoints within each camp, each with their own risks of blind spots.

Second, the statistical research reported in this study does not really answer the question of *why* such differences exist. Ethnographic or other types of qualitative studies (similar to Barnes *et al.*, 1996; Shapin &

Schaffer, 1985) could shed light on the generative mechanisms that account for these paradigmatic differences. In addition, because these research context contingencies are unlikely to be limited to the CSP-CFP research domain, the questions about researcher values raised by this study could be expanded to other research programs (e.g., studies of diversity or income inequality).

Conclusion

The broader conclusions from this moderator meta-analysis may have far-reaching consequences. For one group of scholars, who are positivists or at least subscribe to an objectivist epistemology, this study raises the question of which conclusions come closest to the truth. This study would suggest that average positive effects between CSP and CFP – findings which strike some scholars as Pollyannish oversimplifications of theory or reality – may in fact be true. To other researchers, the comparison reported by this study may suggest that, consistent with Rorty's (1997) philosophical musings, truth may, in fact, be made rather than found. Therefore, the presumption that researchers and scientists can be value-neutral might be an illusion (Barnes *et al.*, 1996; Latour & Woolgar, 1986). After all, values and a wide range of conceptual, theoretical, and methodological assumptions tend to influence the construction of knowledge in scientific communities (Burrell & Morgan, 1979; Kuhn, 1996). From this perspective, quantitative researchers, like their phenomenological counterparts, have a responsibility to 'bracket' (set aside) their presuppositions (Moustakas, 1994). Without such healthy self-reflection, organizational scholars might ignore the assumptions and social forces that affect their research and become as ensnared by unexamined heuristics as nonscientific communities (Feyerabend, 1978; Kahneman, Slovic & Tversky, 1982).

Because social-scientific theories and research assumptions can become self-fulfilling prophecies (Ferraro *et al.*, 2005), journal editors and reviewers must become aware of the special responsibilities they exercise in the CSP-CFP research domain. Articles in academic journals, even those in the business disciplines, often question the morality of the dynamics of supply and demand (McCloskey, 2006). When a tradeoff between market-determined and human-centered worldviews is presumed *a priori*, the danger is that one worldview is elevated over the other without detailed investigation. For example, resistance to free markets can morph into a promotion of interventionist government and other nonmarket policies that favor conformity and collectivism over market mechanisms based on individualism and voluntary unanimity (Friedman, 1962, 1970; Nozick, 1974; Rothbard, 1998). The evidence on the nature of the relationship between CSP and CFP suggests that this tradeoff is artificially conceived in cases where high market performance and social performance go hand in hand. Several human resource scholars have reached similar conclusions, namely that human-centered organizational actions correlate positively with CFP (e.g., Huselid, 1995; Pfeffer, 1998), a view we will revisit in our final chapter on implementation.

In the final analysis, thirty years of CSP-CFP research suggest that the satisfaction of economic objectives might be a precondition for improved societal conditions and moral consequences in many instances. Journal editors and reviewers must be aware of the wide-ranging policy implications of these findings and alert consumers and producers of knowledge in order to avoid the prioritization of one set of (unquestioned) values over another set of (unquestioned) values.

Notes

1. Post-1970, Friedman's position evolved slightly, as discussed in a later section of this chapter.
2. For the purpose of this study, journals in finance and accounting will be assumed to publish studies that are more applied than the basic research of economics. However, in general, they are assumed to be based on the same paradigmatic assumptions as economic research (Swanson, 1996) and, thus, will be combined with economics journals into one set of journals (which could also be called 'economics-based' journals).
3. See Chapters 4 and 5. Arguably, the fact that these two meta-analyses won two different research awards makes the search and aggregation procedures of this study more credible. Orlitzky and Benjamin (2001) won the 2001 Best Article Award given by the International Association for Business and Society (IABS) in association with *California Management Review*. Orlitzky, Schmidt, and Rynes (2003) won the 2004 Moskowitz award for outstanding quantitative research relevant to the social investment field. The Moskowitz Prize is awarded annually to the research paper that best meets the following criteria: (1) practical significance to practitioners of socially responsible investing; (2) appropriateness and rigor of quantitative methods; and (3) novelty of results.

References

References marked with an asterisk indicate studies included in the meta-analysis.
*Abbott, W. F. & Monsen, J. R. (1979). On the measurement of corporate social responsibility: Self-reported disclosure as a method of measuring corporate social involvement. *Academy of Management Journal, 22*, 501–515.

Agle, B. R., Mitchell, R. K. & Sonnenfeld, J. A. (1999). Who matters to CEOs? An investigation of stakeholder attributes and salience, corporate performance, and CEO values. *Academy of Management Journal, 42,* 507–525.

*Alexander, G. J. & Buchholz, R. A. (1978). Corporate social performance and stock market performance. *Academy of Management Journal, 21,* 479–486.

Anderson, J. C. & Frankle, A. W. (1980). Voluntary social reporting: An iso-beta portfolio analysis. *Accounting Review, 55,* 467–479.

*Anderson, J. C. & Frankle, A. W. (1980). Voluntary social reporting: An iso-beta portfolio analysis. *Accounting Review, 55,* 467–479.

Anderson, R. C. (1998). *Mid-course correction: Toward a sustainable enterprise: The Interface model.* White River Junction, VT: Chelsea Green.

*Aupperle, K. E., Carroll, A. B. & Hatfield, J. D. (1985). An empirical investigation of the relationship between corporate social responsibility and profitability. *Academy of Management Journal, 28,* 446–463.

Barnes, B., Bloor, D. & Henry, J. (1996). *Scientific knowledge: A sociological analysis.* Chicago, IL: University of Chicago Press.

Baron, D. P. (2006). *Business and its environment* (5th ed.). Upper Saddle River, NJ: Prentice Hall.

Bazerman, M. H. (2005). Conducting influential research: The need for prescriptive implications. *Academy of Management Review, 30*(1), 25–31.

*Belkaoui, A. (1976). The impact of the disclosure of the environmental effects of organizational behavior on the market. *Financial Management, 5*(4), 26–31.

Beyer, J. M., Chanove, R. G. & Fox, W. B. (1995). The review process and the fates of manuscripts submitted to AMJ. *Academy of Management Journal, 38*(5), 1219–1260.

*Blackburn, V. L., Doran, M. & Shrader, C. B. (1994). Investigating the dimensions of social responsibility and the consequences for corporate financial performance. *Journal of Managerial Issues, 6*(2), 195–212.

*Bowman, E. H. & Haire, M. (1975). A strategic posture toward corporate social responsibility. *California Management Review, 18*(2), 49–58.

*Bowman, E. H. (1976). Strategy and the weather. *Sloan Management Review, 17,* 49–58.

*Bowman, E. H. (1978). Strategy, annual reports, and alchemy. *California Management Review, 20*(3), 64–71.

*Bragdon, J. H., Jr. & Marlin, J. A. T. (1972). Is pollution profitable? *Risk Management, 19,* 9–18.

*Brown, B. & Perry, S. (1994). Removing the financial performance halo from Fortune's "Most Admired Companies". *Academy of Management Journal, 37,* 1346–1359.

*Brown, B. & Perry, S. (1995). Halo-removed residuals of Fortune's "responsibility to the community and environment": A decade of data. *Business & Society, 34*(2), 199–215.

Burrell, G. & Morgan, G. (1979). *Sociological paradigms and organisational analysis.* London: Heinemann.

Burrell, G. (1996). Normal science, paradigms, metaphors, discourses and genealogies of analysis. In S. R. Clegg, C. Hardy & W. R. Nord (eds), *Handbook of organization studies* (pp. 642–658). London: Sage.

Carr, A. Z. (1968). Is business bluffing ethical? *Harvard Business Review, 46,* 145–153.

Chatterji, A. K. & Levine, D. (2006). Breaking down the wall of codes: Evaluating non-financial performance measurement. *California Management Review, 48*(2), 29–51.

*Chen, K. H. & Metcalf, R. W. (1980). The relationship between pollution control record and financial indicators revisited. *Accounting Review, 55*(1), 168–177.

*Cochran, P. L. & Wood, R. A. (1984). Corporate social responsibility and financial performance. *Academy of Management Journal, 27*, 42–56.

Cohen, J. (1994). The Earth is round (*p* *bl.05). *American Psychologist, 49*, 997–1003.

*Conine, T. F. & Madden, G. P. (1987). Corporate social responsibility and investment value: The expectational relationship. In W. D. Guth (ed.), *Handbook of business strategy 1986/1987 yearbook* (pp. 181–189). Boston: Warren, Gorham & Lamont.

Cook, T. D. & Campbell, D. T. (1979). *Quasi-experimentation: Design & analysis issues for field settings*. Boston, MA: Houghton Mifflin.

Cooper, H. M. & Hedges, L. V. (1994). *The handbook of research synthesis*. New York: Russell Sage Foundation.

Cooper, H. M. (1989). *Integrating research: A guide for literature reviews* (2nd ed.). Newbury Park, CA: Sage.

*Cowen, S. S., Ferreri, L. B. & Parker, L. D. (1987). The impact of corporate characteristics on social responsibility disclosure: A typology and frequency-based analysis. *Accounting, Organizations and Society, 12*(2), 111–122.

Dalai Lama, H. H. (1999). *Ethics for the new millennium*. New York: Riverhead Books.

*Davidson, W. N. I. & Worrell, D. L. (1992). Research notes and communications: The effect of product recall announcements on shareholder wealth. *Strategic Management Journal, 13*, 467–473.

Davis, K. (1973). The case for and against business assumptions of social responsibilities. *Academy of Management Journal, 16*, 312–317.

Donaldson, L. (1990). The ethereal hand: Organizational economics and management theory. *Academy of Management Review, 15*(3), 369–381.

*Dooley, R. S. & Lerner, L. D. (1994). Pollution, profits, and stakeholders: The constraining effect of economic performance on CEO concern with stakeholder expectations. *Journal of Business Ethics, 13*, 701–711.

Entine, J. (2003). The myth of social investing: A critique of its practices and consequences for corporate social performance research. *Organization & Environment, 16*, 352–368.

Ferraro, F., Pfeffer, J. & Sutton, R. I. (2005). Economics language and assumptions: How theories can become self-fulfilling. *Academy of Management Review, 30*(1), 8–24.

Feyerabend, P. K. (1978). *Science in a free society*. London: NLB.

Fisher, R. A. (1932). *Statistical methods for research workers* (4th ed.). Edinburgh, Scotland: Oliver & Boyd.

*Fogler, H. R. & Nutt, F. (1975). A note on social responsibility and stock valuation. *Academy of Management Journal, 18*, 155–160.

*Fombrun, C. & Shanley, M. (1990). What's in a name? Reputation building and corporate strategy. *Academy of Management Journal, 33*, 233–258.

*Freedman, M. & Jaggi, B. (1982). Pollution disclosures, pollution performance and economic performance. *Omega: The International Journal of Management Science, 10*(3), 167–176.

*Freedman, M. & Jaggi, B. (1986). An analysis of the impact of corporate pollution disclosures included in annual financial statements on investors' decisions. *Advances in Public Interest Accounting, 1,* 192–212.

Friedman, B. M. (2005). *The moral consequences of economic growth.* New York: Knopf.

Friedman, M. (1962). *Capitalism and freedom.* Chicago: University of Chicago Press.

Friedman, M. (1970, September 13). The social responsibility of business is to increase its profits. *New York Times Magazine,* 33+.

Friedman, M. (2005). Making philanthropy out of obscenity. *Reason, 37*(5), 32–33.

Frooman, J. (1997). Socially irresponsible and illegal behavior and shareholder wealth: A meta-analysis of event studies. *Business & Society, 36*(3), 221–249.

Gans, J. S. & Shepherd, G. B. (1994). How are the mighty fallen: Rejected classic articles by leading economists. *Journal of Economic Perspectives, 8,* 165–179.

Ghoshal, S. (2005). Bad management theories are destroying good management practices. *Academy of Management Learning & Education, 4*(1), 75–91.

Godfrey, P. C. (2005). The relationship between corporate philanthropy and shareholder wealth: A risk management perspective. *Academy of Management Review, 30*(4), 777–798.

*Graves, S. B. & Waddock, S. A. (1994). Institutional owners and corporate social performance. *Academy of Management Journal, 37,* 1034–1046.

*Greening, D. W. (1995). Conservation strategies, firm performance, and corporate reputation in the U.S. electric utility industry. In *Research in Corporate Social Performance and Policy* (Vol. Supplement 1, pp. 345–368). Greenwich, CT: JAI Press.

*Griffin, J. J. & Mahon, J. F. (1997). The corporate social performance and corporate financial performance debate: Twenty-five years of incomparable research. *Business & Society, 36,* 5–31.

*Hansen, G. S. & Wernerfelt, B. (1989). Determinants of firm performance: The relative importance of economic and organizational factors. *Strategic Management Journal, 10,* 399–411.

Hedges, L. V. & Olkin, I. (1985). *Statistical methods for meta-analysis.* Orlando, FL: Academic Press.

*Heinze, D. C. (1976). Financial correlates of a social involvement measure. *Akron Business and Economic Review, 7*(1), 48–51.

*Herremans, I. M., Akathaporn, P. & McInnes, M. (1993). An investigation of corporate social responsibility reputation and economic performance. *Accounting, Organizations and Society, 18,* 587–604.

Holliday, C. O., Schmidheiny, S. & Watts, P. (2002). *Walking the talk: The business case for sustainable development.* San Francisco: Greenleaf.

Hosmer, L. T. (1999). Somebody out there doesn't like us: A study of the position and respect of Business Ethics at Schools of Business Administration. *Journal of Business Ethics, 22,* 91–106.

Hunt, M. (1997). *How science takes stock: The story of meta-analysis.* New York: Russell Sage Foundation.

Hunter, J. E. & Schmidt, F. L. (2004). *Methods of meta-analysis: Correcting error and bias in research findings* (2nd ed.). Thousand Oaks, CA: Sage.

Huselid, M. A. (1995). The impact of human resource management practices on turnover, productivity, and corporate financial performance. *Academy of Management Journal, 38*, 635–672.

*Ingram, R. W. & Frazier, K. B. (1980). Environmental performance and corporate disclosure. *Journal of Accounting Research, 18*, 614–622.

*Ingram, R. W. (1978). An investigation of the information content of (certain) social responsibility disclosures. *Journal of Accounting Research, 16*, 270–285.

*Jacobson, R. (1987). The validity of ROI as a measure of business performance. *American Economic Review, 77*(3), 470–478.

Jones, T. M. (1995). Instrumental stakeholder theory: A synthesis of ethics and economics. *Academy of Management Review, 20*(2), 404–437.

Kahneman, D., Slovic, P. & Tversky, A. (1982). *Judgment under uncertainty: Heuristics and biases.* New York: Cambridge University Press.

*Kedia, B. L. & Kuntz, E. C. (1981). The context of social performance: An empirical study of Texas banks. In L. E. Preston (ed.), *Research in corporate social performance and policy* (Vol. 3, pp. 133–154). Greenwich, CT: JAI Press.

Kuhn, T. S. (1996). *The structure of scientific revolutions* (3rd ed.). Chicago: The University of Chicago Press.

Latour, B. & Woolgar, S. (1986). *Laboratory life: The construction of scientific facts* (2nd ed.). Princeton, NJ: Princeton University Press.

Levitt, T. (1958). The dangers of social responsibility. *Harvard Business Review, 36*(5), 38–44.

*Levy, F. K. & Shatto, G. M. (1980). Social responsibility in large electric utility firms: The case for philanthropy. In L. E. Preston (ed.), *Research in corporate social performance and policy* (Vol. 2, pp. 237–249). Greenwich, CT: JAI Press.

Locke, E. A. (2006). Business ethics: A way out of the morass. *Academy of Management Learning & Education, 5*(3), 324–332.

Lodahl, J. B. & Gordon, G. (1972). The structure of scientific fields and the functioning of university graduate departments. *American Sociological Review, 37*, 57–72.

Logsdon, J. M. & Wood, D. J. (2002). Reputation as an emerging construct in the Business and Society field: An introduction. *Business & Society, 41*(4), 365–370.

*Long, W. F. & Ravenscraft, D. J. (1984). The misuse of accounting rates of return: comment. *American Economic Review, 74*, 494–501.

Mahon, J. F. (2002). Corporate reputation: A research agenda using strategy and stakeholder literature. *Business & Society, 41*(4), 415–445.

*Marcus, A. A. & Goodman, R. S. (1986). Compliance and performance: Toward a contingency theory. In L. E. Preston (ed.), *Research in corporate social performance and policy* (Vol. 8, pp. 193–221). Greenwich, CT: JAI Press.

McCloskey, D. N. (1998). *The rhetoric of economics* (2nd ed.). Madison, WI: University of Wisconsin Press.

McCloskey, D. N. (2006). *The bourgeois virtues: Ethics for an age of commerce.* Chicago: The University of Chicago Press.

*McGuire, J. B., Sundgren, A. & Schneeweis, T. (1988). Corporate social responsibility and firm financial performance. *Academy of Management Journal, 31*, 854–872.

McWilliams, A. & Siegel, D. (1997). Event studies in management research: Theoretical and empirical issues. *Academy of Management Journal, 40*(3), 626–657.

McWilliams, A. & Siegel, D. (2000). Corporate social responsibility and financial performance: Correlation or misspecification? *Strategic Management Journal, 21*, 603–609.

McWilliams, A. & Siegel, D. (2001). Corporate social responsibility: A theory of the firm perspective. *Academy of Management Review, 26*, 117–127.

McWilliams, A., Siegel, D. & Teoh, S. H. (1999). Issues in the use of event study methodology: A critical analysis of corporate social responsibility studies. *Organizational Research Methods, 2*(4), 340–365.

Morgan, G. (1997). *Images of organization* (2nd ed.). Thousand Oaks, CA: Sage.

Moustakas, C. (1994). *Phenomenological research methods*. Thousand Oaks, CA: Sage.

*Newgren, K. E., Rasher, A. A., LaRoe, M. E. & Szabo, M. R. (1985). Environmental assessment and corporate performance: A longitudinal analysis using a market-determined performance measure. In L. E. Preston (ed.), *Research in corporate social performance and policy* (Vol. 7, pp. 153–164). Greenwich, CT: JAI Press.

Nola, R. (2003). *Rescuing reason: A critique of anti-rationalist views of science and knowledge*. Boston, MA: Kluwer Academic.

Nozick, R. (1974). *Anarchy, state, and utopia*. New York: Basic Books.

*O'Neill, H. M., Saunders, C. B. & McCarthy, A. D. (1989). Board members, corporate social responsiveness and profitability: Are tradeoffs necessary? *Journal of Business Ethics, 8*, 353–357.

Orlitzky, M. & Benjamin, J. D. (2001). Corporate social performance and firm risk: A meta-analytic review. *Business & Society, 40*(4), 369–396.

Orlitzky, M. & Swanson, D. L. (2002). Value attunement: Toward a theory of socially responsible executive decision making. *Australian Journal of Management, 27*(Special Issue), 119–128.

Orlitzky, M. (2001). Does organizational size confound the relationship between corporate social performance and firm financial performance? *Journal of Business Ethics, 33*(2), 167–180.

Orlitzky, M., Schmidt, F. L. & Rynes, S. L. (2003). Corporate social and financial performance: A meta-analysis. *Organization Studies, 24*(3), 403–441.

Orlitzky, M., Swanson, D. L. & Quartermaine, L.-K. (2006). Normative myopia, executives' personality, and preference for pay dispersion: Toward implications for corporate social performance. *Business & Society, 45*(2), 149–177.

Orum, A. M. (1990). Sociology's self-imposed moral dilemma. *American Sociologist, 25*, 72–75.

Paine, L. S. (2003). *Value shift: Why companies must merge social and financial imperatives to achieve superior performance*. New York: McGraw-Hill.

*Parket, I. R. & Eilbirt, H. (1975). Social responsibility: The underlying factors. *Business Horizons, 18*(3), 5–10.

*Patten, D. M. (1990). The market reaction to social responsibility disclosures: The case of the Sullivan Principles signings. *Accounting, Organizations and Society, 15*(6), 575–587.

*Pava, M. L. & Krausz, J. (1995). *Corporate responsibility and financial performance: The paradox of social cost*. Westport, CT: Quorum.

Peters, D. P. & Ceci, S. (1982). Peer-review practices of psychological journals: The fate of published articles, submitted again. *The Behavioral and Brain Sciences, 5*, 187–195.

Pfeffer, J. (1993). Barriers to the advance of organizational science: Paradigm development as a dependent variable. *Academy of Management Review, 18*(4), 599–620.

Pfeffer, J. (1998). *The human equation: Building profits by putting people first.* Boston, MA: Harvard Business School Press.

Pfeffer, J., Leong, A. & Strehl, K. (1977). Paradigm development and particularism: Journal publication in three scientific disciplines. *Social Forces, 55*, 938–951.

Porter, M. E. & Kramer, M. R. (2006). Strategy & society: The link between competitive advantage and corporate social responsibility. *Harvard Business Review, 84*(12), 78–92.

Post, J. E. (ed.). (1991). *Research in corporate social performance and policy* (Vol. 12). Greenwich, CT: JAI Press.

*Preston, L. E. (1978). Analyzing corporate social performance: Methods and results. *Journal of Contemporary Business, 7*, 135–150.

Rahman, S., Waddock, S. A., Andriof, J. & Husted, B. (eds). (2002). *Unfolding stakeholder thinking: Theory, responsibility and engagement.* Sheffield, UK: Greenleaf Publishing.

*Reimann, B. C. (1975). Organizational effectiveness and management's public values: A canonical analysis. *Academy of Management Journal, 18*, 224–241.

*Riahi-Belkaoui, A. (1991). Organizational effectiveness, social performance and economic performance. In J. E. Post (ed.), *Research in corporate social performance and policy* (Vol. 12, pp. 143–153). Greenwich, CT: JAI Press.

*Roberts, R. W. (1992). Determinants of corporate social responsibility disclosure: An application of stakeholder theory. *Accounting, Organizations and Society, 17*, 595–612.

Rorty, R. (1997). *Truth, politics, and 'post-modernism'.* Assen, Netherlands: Van Gorcum.

Rothbard, M. N. (1998). *The ethics of liberty.* New York: New York University Press.

*Russo, M. V. & Fouts, P. A. (1997). A resource-based perspective on corporate environmental performance and profitability. *Academy of Management Journal, 40*, 534–559.

Sackett, P. R., Harris, M. M. & Orr, J. M. (1986). On seeking moderator variables in the meta-analysis of correlational data: A Monte Carlo investigation of statistical power and resistance to Type I error. *Journal of Applied Psychology, 71*, 302–310.

Salancik, G. R. & Pfeffer, J. (1974). The bases and use of power in organizational decisions: The case of a university. *Administrative Science Quarterly, 19*, 453–473.

Schmidt, F. L. (1996). Statistical significance testing and cumulative knowledge in psychology: Implications for training and researchers. *Psychological Methods, 1*, 115–129.

*Shane, P. B. & Spicer, B. H. (1983). Market response to environmental information produced outside the firm. *Accounting Review, 58*, 521–538.

Shapin, S. & Schaffer, S. (1985). *Leviathan and the air-pump: Hobbes, Boyle and the experimental life.* Princeton, NJ: Princeton University Press.

Sharfman, M. (1996). The construct validity of the Kinder, Lydenberg & Domini social performance ratings data. *Journal of Business Ethics, 15*(3), 287–296.

*Sharfman, M. (1996). The construct validity of the Kinder, Lydenberg & Domini social performance ratings data. *Journal of Business Ethics, 15*(3), 287–296.

*Simerly, R. L. (1994). Corporate social performance and firms' financial performance: An alternative perspective. *Psychological Reports, 75*, 1091–1103.

*Simerly, R. L. (1995). Institutional ownership, corporate social performance, and firms' financial performance. *Psychological Reports, 77*, 515–525.

Simon, J. G., Powers, C. W. & Gunnemann, J. P. (1972). *The ethical investor: Universities and corporate responsibility*. New Haven, CT: Yale University Press.

Solomon, R. C. (1985). *It's good business*. New York: Atheneum.

Solomon, R. C. (1992). *Ethics and excellence: Cooperation and integrity in business*. New York: Oxford University Press.

Solomon, R. C. (1999). *A better way to think about business: How personal integrity leads to corporate success*. New York: Oxford University Press.

*Spencer, B. A. & Taylor, S. G. (1987). A within and between analysis of the relationship between corporate social responsibility and financial performance. *Akron Business and Economic Review, 18*, 7–18.

*Spicer, B. H. (1978). Investors, corporate social performance and information disclosure: An empirical study. *Accounting Review, 53*, 94–111.

*Starik, M. (1990). Stakeholder management and firm performance: Reputation and financial relationships to U.S. electric utility consumer-related strategies. University of Georgia, Athens.

Starik, M. (1995). Should trees have managerial standing? Toward stakeholder status for non-human nature. *Journal of Business Ethics., 14*, 207–217.

Staw, B. M. (1985). Repairs on the road to relevance and rigor: Some unexplained issues in publishing organizational research. In L. L. Cummings & P. J. Frost (eds), *Publishing in the organizational sciences* (pp. 96–107). Homewood, IL: Irwin.

*Sturdivant, F. D. & Ginter, J. L. (1977). Corporate social responsiveness: Management attitudes and economic performance. *California Management Review, 19*(3), 30–39.

Suchman, M. C. (1995). Managing legitimacy: Strategic and institutional approaches. *Academy of Management Review, 20*, 571–610.

Swanson, D. L. (1996). Neoclassical economic theory, executive control, and organizational outcomes. *Human Relations, 49*, 735–756.

Traub, R. E. (1994). *Reliability for the social sciences: Theory and applications* (Vol. 3). Thousand Oaks, CA: Sage.

*Turban, D. B. & Greening, D. W. (1996). Corporate social performance and organizational attractiveness to prospective employees. *Academy of Management Journal, 40*(3), 658–672.

Ullmann, A. (1985). Data in search of a theory: A critical examination of the relationship among social performance, social disclosure, and economic performance. *Academy of Management Review, 10*, 540–577.

Van Maanen, J. (1995). Style as theory. *Organization Science, 6*(1), 133–143.

*Vance, S. (1975). Are socially responsible firms good investment risks? *Management Review, 64*(8), 18–24.

*Venkatraman, N. & Ramanujam, V. (1987). Measurement of business economic performance: An examination of method convergence. *Journal of Management, 13*, 109–122.

*Waddock, S. A. & Graves, S. B. (1997). The corporate social performance-financial performance link. *Strategic Management Journal, 18*, 303–319.

Waddock, S. A. & Graves, S. B. (1997a). The corporate social performance-financial performance link. *Strategic Management Journal, 18*, 303–319.

Waddock, S. A. & Graves, S. B. (1997b). Quality of management and quality of stakeholder relations: Are they synonymous? *Business & Society, 36*(3), 250–279.

Waddock, S. A. (2003). Myths and realities of social investing. *Organization & Environment, 16*(3), 369–380.

*Wartick, S. L. (1988). How issues management contributes to corporate performance. *Business Forum, 13*(2), 16–22.

Webb, E. J., Campbell, D., Schwartz, R., Sechrest, L. & Grove, J. (1981). *Nonreactive measures in the social sciences*. Boston: Houghton Mifflin.

Willums, J.-O. (1999, May 3). Social responsibility and shareholder value. *Business Week*, 85.

Windsor, D. (2001). "Corporate social responsibility: A theory of the firm perspective" – some comments. *Academy of Management Review, 26*(4), 502–504.

*Wiseman, J. (1982). An evaluation of environmental disclosures made in corporate annual reports. *Accounting, Organizations and Society, 7*, 53–63.

*Wokutch, R. E. & Spencer, B. A. (1987). Corporate sinners and saints: The effects of philanthropic and illegal activity on organizational performance. *California Management Review, 29*, 62–77.

*Wolfe, R. (1991). The use of content analysis to assess corporate social responsibility. In J. E. Post (ed.), *Research in corporate social performance and policy* (Vol. 12, pp. 281–307). Greenwich, CT: JAI Press.

Wood, D. J. & Jones, R. E. (1995). Stakeholder mismatching: A theoretical problem in empirical research on corporate social performance. *International Journal of Organizational Analysis, 3*, 229–267.

Wood, D. J. (1991). Corporate social performance revisited. *Academy of Management Review, 16*, 691–718.

Wood, D. J. (1995). The Fortune database as a CSP measure. *Business & Society, 34*, 197–198.

Zuckerman, H. (1988). The sociology of science. In N. J. Smelser (ed.), *Handbook of sociology* (pp. 511–571). Newbury Park, CA: Sage.

Part III

Implications for Measurement and Implementation: Toward an Integrative Perspective on Corporate Citizenship

Introduction to Part III

Part III builds on the theoretical foundation of Part I and the empirical results of Part II. In this last section of the book, we will focus on the measurement and implementation of corporate social performance (CSP) and discuss issues of application in practice, while pointing to some broader strategic implications for integrative corporate citizenship (CC).

More specifically, Chapter 8 points out how the measurement of CSP could be improved in the future. It starts off with the argument, akin to MacIntyre's (1984) view, that 'doing good' has no self-evident, objective meaning, even though many empirical studies presume this quality. To illustrate this point, this chapter briefly reviews the different meanings and operationalizations of CSP, which is often used to convey a company's 'good deeds' in trying to create a better society. It is argued that a deliberate shift in focus from motives and processes to outcomes and performance will allow future researchers to use statistical generalizability theory (G theory) to improve quantitative measures of CSP in surveying stakeholder groups directly. A hypothetical data set illustrates the usefulness of G theory for assessing the psychometric quality of CSP decision making factors, the number of raters, and the number of questionnaire items needed in stakeholder group surveying. This is not to say that processes are not integral to CSP. After all, the value processes laid out in Chapter 2 point to the importance of executive decision making in determining a firm's CSP posture, which is the focus of Chapter 9. However, at this point in time, a focus on outcomes is needed to improve the validity of CSP measures.

In contrast to the applied measurement focus of Chapter 8, Chapter 9 extends prior theorizing by utilizing Swanson's concept of *normative myopia* (defined as the propensity of executives to downplay or ignore the values at stake in their decision making) as a point of reference for studying executives' preference for high pay dispersion. As part of this study, we designed a survey to examine hypothesized relationships between myopia, personality, and executives' preference for highly stratified organizational pay structures. Data from 133 executive respondents suggest that myopic executives tend to prefer top-heavy compensation systems. In addition, our findings point to an inverse relationship between the personality factor agreeableness and normative myopia, with the former offsetting the latter. We reject the alternative hypothesis that gender influences both agreeableness and myopia and conclude with some implications for business and society, including Swanson's proposition that normative myopia at the top contributes to a neglectful form of corporate social performance. In other words, we extend the theoretical models laid out in Chapters 1 and 2 by empirically examining a certain type of executive decision making in terms of its implications for firm-level CSP.

Chapter 10 leverages the first nine chapters of the book to explore how the following areas are relevant to the successful implementation of integrative corporate citizenship: (1) a strategic orientation (2) social and environmental accounting, and (3) fit and flexibility in strategic human resource management. We conclude this chapter and the book with suggestions for future research aimed at integrative corporate citizenship.

References

MacIntyre, A. (1984). *After virtue: A study in moral theory* (2nd ed.). Notre Dame, IN: University of Notre Dame Press.

8
Corporate Social Performance, Stakeholder Satisfaction, and Generalizability Theory

Corporate social performance research implies that, ideally, organizational researchers can measure fairly accurately when a company 'does good' and strives for a better society. However, in a post-Enlightenment world in which moral language seems to have lost much of its substance (MacIntyre, 1984), we cannot, in fact, presume that 'good' corporate behavior is self-evident. Instead, researchers must continuously keep a critical attitude toward many so-called 'good' organizational policies, such as those related to affirmative action and work/life balance, for instance. Organizational activities or values are rarely absolutely or generally 'good', but instead the virtue of particular actions can only be evaluated in particular contexts by particular stakeholder groups (MacIntyre, 1988). This goes to the importance of an organization's ability to incorporate feedback from stakeholders, as stressed in Chapter 3.

MacIntyre (1984) argued that different communities usually draw on incommensurable moral ideologies; yet many researchers presume that, at organizational or even societal levels, they can generally and validly identify and know 'good' behavior when they see it. For example, in a book on *The Moral Consequences of Economic Growth*, Friedman (2005: ix) identified 'openness of opportunity, tolerance, economic and social mobility, fairness, and democracy' as 'crucial elements' of social and moral progress. In the abstract, these values seem sensible enough, but their *implementation* also raises a number of moral questions. For example, does a company operating abroad have an obligation or right to second-guess

This chapter is a revision of the paper *The Meaning and Measurement of 'Doing Good' at the Company Level of Analysis*, presented at the Academy of Management conference, Philadelphia, PA in August 2007.

– or passively resist – autocratic government policies inconsistent with democratic principles (e.g., China's one-child policy), even though limiting population growth may be crucial from an ecological perspective? Or, as another example, organic, local produce may be marketed as 'ethical food', but upon closer examination may actually result in greater environmental costs than benefits (Economist, 2006). Thus, in pluralistic societies and on the international stage, evaluations of 'the good' typically differ from one community to another, which goes to the dilemma of cultural relativism broached in Chapter 2. However, empirical investigations of corporate ethics often take as a given certain characteristics of 'good' organizational behavior without examining further '*why* these characteristics of a society are desirable, much less moral' (Friedman, 2005, p. ix, italics in original).

As summarized in Chapters 1, 2, 3, and 4, research spanning several decades has attempted to study 'doing good' at the company level of analysis. The concept of *corporate social performance* (CSP) has been of central interest in this research program (Orlitzky, Schmidt & Rynes, 2003; Swanson, 1995, 1999; Ullmann, 1985; Wartick & Cochran, 1985; Wood, 1991a). As noted in the Introduction, *corporate citizenship* might now be a more descriptive term for this concept insofar as it calls attention to those discretionary organizational activities that are designed to meet broad community needs, such as those aimed at enhancing ecological sustainability (Anderson, 1998; Holliday, Schmidheiny & Watts, 2002; Matten & Crane, 2005; Orlitzky, 2008; Willums, 1999). At any rate, this research has historically raised basic questions about the validity and reliability of particular measures of CSP (Brown & Perry, 1994; Entine, 2003; Wood, 1995). Unfortunately, among many observers, the impression persists that 'the existing cacophony of scorekeepers [of CSP] does little more than add to the confusion' and the perception that there is a 'jumble of largely meaningless' measures (Porter & Kramer, 2006, p. 81).

This chapter makes the case for approaching CSP measurement from an outcomes-oriented perspective so that the concept can become more meaningful to scholarship and useful in practice. As part of this project, generalizability theory is advanced as a statistical technique for measuring diverse stakeholders' levels of satisfaction. More specifically, this chapter proposes a measurement framework that is centered on stakeholder satisfaction and focused on organization-level assessments of CSP. However, it is important to note that, from a broader theoretical perspective (as explicated in Chapter 2), an attuned business and society relationship should ultimately be informed by a normative understanding of the values that underpin stakeholder satisfaction (see Frederick,

1995, for an example of such a theory), so that not just anything counts as socially responsible performance. The importance of normative inquiry to integrative corporate citizenship will be revisited in Chapter 10.

CSP, outcomes, and stakeholder satisfaction

As argued in Chapters 2 and 3, no consensus has yet emerged about the appropriate values, motivations, or principles underpinning social, ecological, and moral progress. Therefore, in a pluralist society that acknowledges various definitions of 'the good', CSP cannot be conceptualized as an additive or multiplicative function of moral motivation and outcomes (i.e., Motivation added to Outcomes or Motivation multiplied by Outcomes). Such a conceptualization would raise fundamental questions about the validity and appropriateness of the measurement of moral motivation. Even if there were agreement that the best measure of moral motivation was, for example, Kohlberg's measure of cognitive moral development (e.g., Colby & Kohlberg, 1987), this would raise an immediate follow-up question about the appropriate level of analysis for assigning motivation or social responsibility. Should we assign it to executives? Or to all employees of the firm? To the firm's owners or shareholders? Or to the Board of Directors? In terms of moral agency, business ethicists do not agree on which unit or level of analysis to use. Moreover, they vigorously debate the relative advantages of applying different moral frameworks (e.g., deontology, utilitarianism, Rawlsian theory of justice, Libertarianism) to organizational decision making. Often, differences in these and other views of moral goodness lead to fundamental disagreements about which actions should be sanctioned (MacIntyre, 1984), a dilemma that presents a host of problems for assessing concrete situations. For example, the utilitarian optimal solution (derived from cost-benefit analysis) of companies' carbon credits trading to minimize overall pollution may be questionable from Kantian (duty) or Rawlsian (justice) perspectives (Baron, 2006).[1] Generally speaking, these two moral frameworks, as well as others, pose fundamental problems for assessment (Hartman, 1996; Locke, 2006). This chapter does not delve into such philosophical matters. The point is that such problems can thwart the development of measurable CSP standards for organizational use.

From a measurement perspective, CSP assessment could benefit from a deliberate shift from predictors to actual measurable outcomes such as stakeholder satisfaction. Because of the aforementioned incommensurability of different views of 'the good' (MacIntyre, 1984), tapping actual stakeholder perceptions could represent an operational advance in assessing CSP outcomes. As researchers strive to assess the extent to which a firm has effectively met various stakeholders' demands, stakeholder satisfaction can become a central measurable aspect of CSP (Clarkson, 1995). Consistent with this idea, Husted (2000, p. 27) regards CSP as 'the ability of the firm to meet or exceed stakeholder expectations regarding social issues'. More broadly, Wartick and Cochran (1985) and Wood (1991b) stress the advantages of a clear focus on performance and concrete outcomes. Even Swanson's (1995) CSP model, the most inclusive to date in terms of processes and normative content, ultimately stresses social impacts in terms of economic and ecological outcomes (see Chapter 1). Clarkson (1995) succinctly summarizes the advantages of focusing on an outcome orientation to CSP as follows:

> [...] performance is what counts. Performance can be measured and evaluated. Whether a corporation and its management are motivated by enlightened self-interest, common sense, or high standards of ethical behavior cannot be determined by the empirical methodologies available today. [...] They are interesting questions, but they are not relevant when it comes to evaluating a company's performance in managing its relationships with its stakeholder groups. (p. 105)

From such a stakeholder-oriented perspective, organizational values and processes may be *predictors* of, or antecedents to, CSP, but they are not necessarily integral elements of CSP defined as the *outcome* of organizational decision processes. A point of comparison is that while individual motivation, personality, ability, and effort may be seen as predictors of individual job performance, they are not integral elements of this outcome. In the same way that these three predictors of job performance are studied in their own right, the theorized predictors of CSP are also deserving of empirical investigation – and to some extent this has already happened (e.g., Agle, Mitchell & Sonnenfeld, 1999; Deckop, Merriman & Gupta, 2006; Orlitzky, Swanson & Quartermaine, 2006). Apart from these empirical studies of possible predictors of CSP, a more outcomes-oriented definition of CSP may be useful for evaluating to what extent organizations have accomplished socially responsible outcomes.

Including *effort* as one dimension of social *performance* may be counterproductive because it may allow the firm (and/or industry and/or managers) to distort the meaning of CSP. A firm may claim to be socially responsible by virtue of certain espoused values or unquantifiable processes of stakeholder dialogue. This could degenerate into the same meaningless window-dressing that Enron practiced when in its rhetoric the firm emphasized four core values (communication, respect, integrity, excellence), even though many of the firm's outcomes were contrary to them (Sims & Brinkmann, 2003). In fact, such gaps between corporate rhetoric and actions might be fairly common (Beder, 2000). In short, what observers of 'good' company actions need is a valid and reliable measure of CSP in which they can have confidence (Chatterji & Levine, 2006) – independent of the philosophical disputes about 'good' values and moral agency.

Traditional measures of CSP

As shown before (especially in Chapters 4 and 5), the CSP measurement literature already reflects a preference for a relatively narrow, stake-holder-based, and outcome-oriented definition of CSP. One measure that has been used in many CSP studies is the *Fortune* data base, which ranks 'Most Admired' companies on a number of dimensions, including 'community and environmental responsibility'. Each year, *Fortune* magazine calculates and publishes a single, composite indicator of CSP reputation by surveying financial analysts and business executives for their evaluations of this and other aspects of company performance. However, researchers have started to point out the weaknesses of the *Fortune* measure. For example, it has been shown to be affected by prior financial performance (Brown & Perry, 1994). In addition, fundamental questions were raised about the sampling, reliability, and validity of the *Fortune* ratings (Baucus, 1995). Although some CSP researchers have argued for the usefulness of the corrected (i.e., halo-removed) *Fortune* data in certain rigorously delimited research contexts (Brown & Perry, 1995; Logsdon & Wartick, 1995; Sodeman, 1995), others have been more pess-imistic in their *de facto* rejection of the *Fortune* data (Baucus, 1995; Wood, 1995).

Scholarly concerns about the *Fortune* perceptual data have led to the increasing use of the KLD ratings in academic studies of CSP. KLD Research & Analytics, Inc. (previously referred to as 'Kinder, Lydenberg, Domini & Co.') collects social and environmental data from five sources: (1) company directors (2) media reports (3) government and nongovern-ment organizations (4) company public documents (Securities and Exchange Commission filings), and (5) other Socially Responsible Invest-ment funds' reports on non-US companies. Although KLD's reporting on separate dimensions of CSP represents an advance in measurement, two main concerns remain. One, some dimensions of KLD seem to be so idiosyncratic that they are inconsistent with particular definitions of 'doing good' (Entine, 2003). The problem of political bias (e.g., nuclear technology considered 'bad' for society) raises some basic questions about construct validity, which is addressed in greater depth in the next paragraph. Two, KLD methodology does not directly survey (or, at least, privilege in its measurement of CSP) the stakeholders that are the actual beneficiaries of these organizational activities. In this way, KLD research might rely too much on (likely biased) company reports and prioritize organizational stakeholder management processes over actual outcomes. According to many definitions of CSP (see Clarkson, 1995 and Husted, 2000 above), CSP represents an assessment of the extent to which a company is able to live up to stakeholder expectations. Ignoring these (necessarily subjective) stakeholder expectations or guessing about them by asking third parties or 'self-appointed human rights vigilantes' (Elliott & Freeman, 2001) may be rhetorically compelling but conceptually unpersuasive because it does not reflect the field's definitions of CSP – not even the narrow ones.

To clarify the psychometric properties of the KLD measures, Sharfman (1996) investigated their construct validity. He correlated six different KLD measures with the *Fortune* data to establish the KLD data's criterion-related validity. In general, the KLD-*Fortune* correlations (r) varied between .25 and .40. With other socially responsible investment (SRI) fund holdings, the KLD ratings were associated at r between .17 and .31, depending on the specific time period and KLD measure. Although all these correlations generally reached statistical significance, the effect sizes were of only moderate magnitude (as defined by Cohen, 1992). In the context of construct validation, the magnitude of effect sizes such as r is more important than statistical significance (Nunnally & Bernstein, 1994). Also, reliance on the *Fortune* data as a criterion to validate KLD may be problematic because of the aforementioned debate about the suitability of the *Fortune* data set. In addition, Sharfman acknowledged that three dimensions of the KLD data may be irrelevant or inappropriate (nuclear power, apartheid, and military contracting), an empirical finding which anticipated Entine's (2003) conceptual concerns.

Moreover, a more comprehensive construct validation study may require broader statistical analysis in the five areas outlined by Schwab (1999) as: (1) convergent validity (2) content validity (3) reliability, and (4) discriminant validity. Sharfman's study accomplished the first element to some extent, with the proviso that more appropriate criterion variables than the *Fortune* CSP data should be used in future evaluations of KLD convergent validity. Recent studies have extended Sharfman's research by including a broader set of criterion variables (Chatterji & Levine, 2007; Chatterji, Levine & Toffel, in press). In terms of the second element of construct validation, experts could review the data collection procedures used by KLD and pass an overall judgment on the content validity of the dimensions. To a large extent, this has happened (Entine, 2003; Sharfman, 1996; Waddock, 2003). In consideration of the third element of construct validity, KLD generally does not provide sufficient data to assess the reliability of each dimension (i.e., reliability *within* each dimension), although researchers can calculate the *cross*-dimensional correlations as evidence of such. Finally, discriminant validity differentiates CSP from similar constructs (e.g., organizational sustainability, reputation) and examines whether the correlations with other measures of CSP are larger than correlations with similar but different constructs (in line with Campbell & Fiske, 1959; Lim & Ployhart, 2006). Taken together, these procedures suggest that more empirical work is needed before the KLD data can be accepted as the single best measure of CSP.

A CSP measure that comes closer to the meaning of CSP as developed in previous sections is Clarkson's (1991) RDAP scale. The RDAP scale assesses the firm's *r*eactive, *d*efensive, *a*ccommodative, or *p*roactive posture toward stakeholder issues – as opposed to social issues more broadly. Based on this RDAP scale, Clarkson (1995) proposed the development of a survey measure of primary stakeholder satisfaction as a good proxy measure of CSP. This method, with its emphasis on posture toward stakeholders, may have the advantage of tapping corporate social responsiveness in specific contexts, which could be seen as a refinement to the CSP modeling discussed in Chapters 1 and 2. Although there was no psychometric follow-up on this suggestion of stakeholder surveying, the first steps showed that at least one academic refused to leave the measurement of CSP to practitioners (e.g., SRI fund analysts), who may not be as knowledgeable about quantitative measurement and research design as trained Ph.D.s are.

Given this brief review of the measurement literature on CSP, a pluralist definition of CSP seems unavoidable, particularly given the cultural relativism that marks global business environments. As there is (still) no one single best measure of CSP (Carroll, 1991; Wolfe & Aupperle, 1991), it is no surprise that arriving at 'objective' or 'actual' CSP has been an elusive goal. This elusiveness is implicit in the observation that 'stakeholders define the norms for corporate behavior [...] and they make judgments about these expectations' (Wood & Jones, 1995, p. 231). Thus, if researchers are not cognizant of the social construction of reality by a diverse set of organizational constituents, CSP is bound to remain elusive. CSP is invariably a subjective construct (Husted, 2000), depending on stakeholders' subjective assessments of a given firm's actions toward them. To pay tribute to the subjective nature of CSP, stakeholders rather than *a priori* principles ought to be privileged in its measurement of CSP (Burton & Dunn, 1996; Clarkson, 1995). In other words, a company's CSP can only be evaluated with reference to its ability to meet or exceed particular stakeholder claims by particular individuals (constituting, perhaps, identifiable overlapping stakeholder groups). Yet, as noted in the Introduction to this chapter, these claims must ultimately be analyzed with normative standards in mind so that not just anything counts as socially responsible performance.

The role for such standards notwithstanding, a practical consideration for companies is whether a broad range of stakeholder groups' beliefs converge around a particular assessment of the firm's social responsibility outcomes.[2] Toward this end, Davenport's (2000) Delphi study, which surveyed consumers, employees, investors, and suppliers as stakeholder groups, indicates that even reasonably high reliability within *one* stakeholder group may be difficult to obtain. This study found greater within-group variance than between-group variance. From a measurement perspective, we would expect higher levels of agreement from the same group of raters on the same dimension of CSP than between different stakeholders evaluating different CSP dimensions. Confronted by these measurement problems, we face the need for a pluralist index of CSP that is reliable, valid, and generalizable within each stakeholder group. To ensure comparability of studies, we may also desire a stakeholder satisfaction measure that could be generalizable across firms and industries. Given the multitude of stakeholder groups typically affected by organizational activities, these goals might strike many researchers as unrealistic. To them, reliance on other indirect measures of CSP (such as KLD) may seem like an attractive compromise. After all, isn't measurement of stakeholder satisfactions unrealistic because the data collection costs are prohibitive? Some observers might take up this argument, proposing that, in order to be reliable, stakeholder surveys would have to include too many items or be based on too many raters. This chapter argues that stakeholder surveying as the proposed alternative is not only practically desirable but also viable at this stage in the evolution of CSP measurement.

Efficient measurement solution: generalizability theory

To measure diverse stakeholders' levels of satisfaction with a company's CSP, an efficient solution draws on statistical generalizability theory

(Cronbach, Gleser, Nanda & Rajaratnam, 1972; Cronbach, Gleser & Rajaratnam, 1963; Finn & Kayande, 1997; Nunnally & Bernstein, 1994; Shavelson & Webb, 1991; Shavelson, Webb & Rowley, 1989). Without the statistical insights of generalizability theory (G theory), reliable measurement of stakeholder attitudes would indeed be very costly, inefficient, and thus suboptimal. At the same time, reliability of measurement must remain a central concern whenever a construct is measured, or, even more importantly, correlated with other constructs (Nunnally & Bernstein, 1994; Price & Mueller, 1986; Schwab, 1980, 2005). Most CSP studies published since the 1980s have relied on classical reliability theory, in which the reliability coefficient is the ratio of true-score variance to observed-score variance of the measurement items forming the construct of CSP. In mathematical notation, reliability is defined as $r_{XX} = \frac{\sigma_t^2}{\sigma_X^2}$ or, for dependent variables, $r_{YY} = \frac{\sigma_t^2}{\sigma_Y^2}$ (Nunnally & Bernstein, 1994; Traub, 1994). The most commonly calculated estimates of (classical) reliability are coefficient alpha and inter-rater reliability.

Yet, reliance on classical reliability theory ignores the fact that the *purpose* of measuring a particular stakeholder's satisfaction with CSP (in a specific context) will lead to particular *objects of measurement* and particular *facets of generalization*. An object of measurement is a factor whose levels must be scaled by the measurement instrument. A facet of generalization is a factor over which the researcher requires the findings to generalize. In other words, classical reliability theory does not reflect advances in statisticians' thinking about quantitative measurement of variables because it fails to disaggregate overall variance into the different facets of generalization, analogous to factorial designs in ANOVA used in substantive research. The following paragraphs point out the usefulness of these advances for cost-efficient measurement of stakeholder perceptions of CSP.

The *object of measurement* is a function of the purpose of measurement. Typically, when we try to assess CSP, organizations are our object of measurement because we either want to know organizations' relative accomplishments with respect to CSP or absolute, criterion-based CSP. Thus, CSP research is usually concerned with benchmarking one firm's CSP against the CSP of other forms in the industry (objects of measurement = organizations within an industry). In such a study design, CSP measures would constitute rankings of organizations relative to each other. Insofar as organizations' CSP outcomes can be ranked across industries, all organizations in a cross-industry sample may constitute the study's objects of measurement. Although the organization is more often than not the object of measurement, this need not be the case. For example, some researchers may want to evaluate the CSP of a particular strategic business unit (SBU) over a particular time period (objects of measurement = SBU over that time period). Or a firm may want to evaluate how a particular CSP initiative has increased the goodwill among a particular stakeholder, whether it be customers, government officials, or environmental activists (objects of measurement = members of these particular stakeholder groups). As can be seen from these examples, psychometric considerations like these become important, especially for a multilevel construct like CSP (e.g., Clarkson, 1995, p. 104).

The choice of *facets* we want to *generalize* is a question separate from the objects of measurement. These facets of generalization may be the different questionnaire items asking for assessments of different aspects of CSP, different time periods, different raters of CSP, etc. The facets of generalization and the objects of measurement depend on the *purpose* of CSP measurement. Table 8.1 illustrates how the purpose of measurement may influence decisions about the objects of measurement and facets of generalization.

The coefficient of reliability in classical reliability theory provides an answer to the following question: How accurately do observed scores reflect true scores? The higher the value of r_{XX}, the lower the measurement error and the more precise the measure under consideration. Generalizability theory answers a slightly different question: How accurately do observed scores permit us to generalize about organizations' (CSP) outcomes across different facets of generalization? Like classical coefficients of reliability, the coefficient of generalization is a measure of the psychometric quality of a given measurement instrument. Furthermore, experts in measurement theory consider G theory to be pertinent to questions of the reliability *and* validity of variables (Cronbach *et al.*, 1972; Marcoulides, 1998).

The analogous formula for estimating a measure's reliability in the context of G theory reflects the conceptual adjustments described above:

$E\hat{\rho}^2 = \dfrac{\sigma^2_{us}}{\sigma^2_{us} + \sigma^2_{rel}}$, where $E\hat{\rho}^2$ = estimated coefficient of generalization (this

estimate of the expected value of ρ^2 is analogous to the reliability coefficient in classical reliability theory); σ^2_{us} = variance component associated with the objects of measurement ('*us*' stands for 'universe score' and is equivalent to true score variance (σ^2_t) in classical reliability theory); and σ^2_{rel} = the sum of only those variance components that

Table 8.1   Illustration of Generalizability Theory (Examples)

Purpose of Measurement	Measurement Need	Objects of Measurement (Scaling of)	Facets of Generalization (Generalize over)
CSP rankings	Identify how the focal firm fares with respect to its CSP relative to other firms	Firms within an industry (possibly all organizations in the sample)	Raters (stakeholder respondents), questions in CSP measurement instrument, possibly time periods (if longitudinal design)
r between group-level characteristics of the firm and stakeholder satisfaction	CSP quality provided by each department within the firm	Departments within the firm	Raters (stakeholder respondents), questions in CSP measurement instrument, possibly time periods (if longitudinal design)
What aspect of CSP is most in need of improvement within one organization?	Identify areas in need of improvement	Aspects of CSP	Different departments or SBUs, raters (stakeholder respondents), questions in CSP measurement instrument, possibly time periods (if longitudinal design)

affect the scaling of levels of the object of measurement (*'rel'* stands for 'relative error'). The last column in Table 8.1 (facets of generalization) suggests the particular elements of σ_{rel}^2. So, let's assume that in a CSP study all sources of variation are random. In an organizations-by-items-by-raters design (o*i*r), the estimated relative error variance is given by the sum of all variance components representing interactions with the object of measurement, i.e., in mathematical notation, $\sigma_{rel}^2 = \dfrac{\sigma_{or}^2}{n_r} + \dfrac{\sigma_{oi}^2}{n_i} + \dfrac{\sigma_{ori,e}^2}{n_r n_i}$,

where σ_{or}^2 = variance due to organization-by-rater interaction effects, n_r = number of raters, σ_{oi}^2 = variance due to organization-by-item interaction effects, n_i = number of items, and $\sigma_{ori,\,e}^2$ = residual error variance, or the mean square for the residual. Study designs that differ from this random, fully crossed, two-facet design, such as nested designs or designs with fixed facets, require adjustments in these formulas (Shavelson & Webb, 1991).

For example, let's assume that we conducted a pilot study in which 15 organizations (o) were rated by two raters (r), who evaluated three CSP questions (i) each. This is a two-facet (r and i), crossed, random design (o*r*i). Based on the hypothetical data presented in Table 8.2, Table 8.3 reports the degrees of freedom (*df*), mean sums of squares (*MS*), and estimated variance components. The largest variance component, that for organizations (1.342), accounts for about 69% of the total variance in CSP ratings. This indicates that organizations, the objects of measurement, differed systematically in the CSP ratings they received. The variance of items and of the interaction of items and raters was negative. In G studies, small negative estimates of variance components may be due to sampling error (or other causes) and should be substituted by estimates of zero. With a sample size of 15 organizations, sampling error is the most likely culprit responsible for the small negative variances in Table 8.3. Applying the error variance formula introduced above leads to $\sigma_{rel}^2 = .138$, and the estimated coefficient of generalizability $E\hat{\rho}^2 = .92$. These calculations suggest that, given this particular data set, there is no need to include more items or more raters to generate high-reliability, high-validity estimates of CSP.

Table 8.2   Hypothetical Data

org	rater1 item1	rater1 item2	rater1 item3	rater2 item1	rater2 item2	rater2 item3
1	1.00	2.00	1.00	2.00	1.00	1.00
2	1.00	1.00	1.00	1.00	1.00	1.00
3	1.00	1.00	2.00	1.00	2.00	2.00
4	2.00	3.00	2.00	3.00	3.00	3.00
5	2.00	1.00	1.00	2.00	2.00	3.00
6	2.00	2.00	2.00	2.00	2.00	3.00
7	3.00	2.00	3.00	3.00	3.00	3.00
8	3.00	3.00	3.00	3.00	3.00	3.00
9	3.00	3.00	3.00	4.00	3.00	4.00
10	4.00	4.00	3.00	5.00	5.00	4.00
11	4.00	3.00	5.00	4.00	4.00	4.00
12	4.00	4.00	4.00	4.00	4.00	3.00
13	4.00	5.00	4.00	5.00	4.00	5.00
14	4.00	5.00	5.00	5.00	4.00	4.00
15	5.00	5.00	5.00	5.00	5.00	5.00

Note: CSP ratings range from 1 (low) to 5 (high).

Table 8.3 Estimated Variance Components for a Hypothetical CSP Rating Example: Crossed, Two-Facet, Random Design

Source of Variation	*df*	*MS*	Estimated Variance Component	Percentage of Total Variance[a]
Organizations (o)	14	6.977	1.342	69%
Items (i)	2	.141	–0.005 (0)	0
Raters (r)	1	.576	.010	1
o*i	28	.543	.126	6
o*r	14	.519	.084	4
i*r	1	.043	–.016 (0)	0
o*i*r,e	29	.324	.324	17

[a] The percentages do not sum exactly to 100 due to rounding.

In fact, we can use the aforementioned $E\hat{\rho}^2$ formula to determine whether we actually need two raters or three items in this case. The estimate of $E\hat{\rho}^2$ with only one rater of CSP and three items would be .85 (satisfactory), and the estimate of $E\hat{\rho}^2$ with only one CSP question and two raters would be .80 (still satisfactory). Generally, we would use the calculations from such a G study to determine empirically how many survey respondents and questions we need in future assessments of CSP.

If we assume that, conceptually, we can derive three distinct questions about CSP that exhaust *all* aspects of CSP, similar to Davenport's (2000) dimensions mentioned in a previous section, then the items facet becomes a fixed factor. This change in assumptions changed our G-study procedure as follows. First, we performed a random design ANOVA as shown in Table 8.3, assuming that all facets (including items) are random. Second, we identified the random portion of the mixed design and the associated, new variance components to be calculated. In this case, the random variance components would be σ_{o*}^2, σ_{r*}^2, and $\sigma_{or,e*}^2$. Finally, we calculated the new variance components for the random portion of the mixed design:

$$\sigma_{o*}^2 = \sigma_o^2 + \frac{1}{n_i}\,\sigma_{oi}^2$$

$$\sigma_{r*}^2 = \sigma_r^2 + \frac{1}{n_i}\,\sigma_{ri}^2$$

$$\sigma_{or,e*}^2 = \sigma_{or}^2 + \frac{1}{n_i}\,\sigma_{ori,\,e*}^2.$$

Averaging over three CSP items, we concluded from Table 8.4 that most of the variation is due to universe-score variation (92%). In short,

Table 8.4   Estimated Variance Components for a Hypothetical CSP Rating Example: Mixed Design with Items as Fixed Facet

Source of Variation	df	Estimated Variance Component	Percentage of Total Variance[a]
Organizations (o*)	14	1.384	92%
Raters (r*)	1	.010	1
or,e*	14	.118	8

[a] The percentages do not sum exactly to 100 due to rounding.

if we assume the CSP items represent a fixed facet, the estimate of the generalizability coefficient would even be larger ($E\hat{\rho}^2 = .96$) than under the two-facet, crossed, random design. (Alternatively, if theory suggests the necessity of separate analyses for each of the measurement items or if the estimated variance components associated with the fixed facet are large, we could perform three separate random design G studies – one for each item/dimension of CSP.)

More complex designs such as nested facets are possible but beyond the scope of this chapter. The designs presented in this chapter are optimal for a G-study (i.e., fully crossed designs), but sometimes different raters must be used to assess different CSP dimensions, which produces nested-facet designs. If not all raters evaluate all dimensions of CSP or raters change during certain time periods, nested-facet calculations become necessary (Shavelson & Webb, 1991).

In short, the G-theory approach allows us to identify the optimal balance between two contradictory goals: (1) maximize the reliability of CSP measurement (i.e., minimize CSP measurement error) and (2) minimize the cost of CSP data collection. As is generally known, researchers can improve measurement by including more items in the measurement instrument or more raters. However, at some point, the marginal benefit of improving measurement is exceeded by its marginal cost (e.g., dropping response rate and missing values with excessively long surveys). Because the G-theory approach consists of two parts, we can arrive at the optimal balance between the aforementioned two goals. First, a generalizability study (G study) develops a measurement procedure as described in earlier sections. Second, a decision study (D study) applies the procedure, so that generalizability within a prespecified set of limited resources is maximized. What firms and researchers are striving for with any measure of CSP is good measurement (i.e., reliable and valid measures) at lowest cost. As was illustrated previously, in many instances the G study findings suggest that we can make do with fewer raters and/or fewer questionnaire items in stakeholder surveys. Expressed more formally, this measurement optimization problem translates into the following analytical problem in a D study:

Minimize: $C = f(c_0, \tilde{C}, \tilde{N}, n_{obj})$,

where
C = total cost of measurement,
c_0 = the fixed cost of the survey instrument,
$\tilde{C}$ = vector with elements representing the cost of an observation on each facet,
$\tilde{N}$ = vector with elements $n_1, n_2, ..., n_F$ representing the number of F facets of generalization,
and n_{obj} = number of objects of measurement (Finn & Kayande, 1997).

This analytical problem can be solved via integer programming in EXCEL, for example, with the branch-and-bound algorithm (Finn & Kayande, 1997; Salkin, 1975). As a rule of thumb, stakeholder 'raters' and items will be added until the coefficient of generalization ($E\hat{\rho}^2$) reaches satisfactory levels (e.g., .75 or .80). Sometimes we may even conclude, as in the hypothetical example above, that CSP can be measured reliably even with *fewer* raters and/or *fewer* items. D studies may show that, for certain objects of CSP measurement, one or two questions and a handful of stakeholder respondents may be sufficient for the purpose of our CSP study. In fact, the G and D study calculations may lead to the conclusion that as few as one rater and one item may be sufficient.

The application of a G-theory framework to the area of CSP requires a researcher's expertise in quantitative measurement and variance component analysis (in the G study). Although the estimation of reliability becomes more complex with this approach, organizations and CSP researchers could benefit from the statistical technique advocated in this chapter in several ways. If stakeholder measurement of CSP is taken over a span of many years (which ought to happen for comparison purposes or trend analysis anyway), then the long-term cost savings could be substantial. As mentioned before, cost consists of the fixed costs of the stakeholder satisfaction measurement instrument, the cost of an observation on each facet, the number of facets of generalization, and the number of objects of measurement. In classical reliability theory, high reliability is achieved through the inclusion of many measurement items for each construct, the inclusion of many raters, or both. In short, generalizability theory provides a solution to measuring CSP not only reliably and validly but also cost-effectively. Specifically, the intra-organizational standardization of stakeholder satisfaction scales can help justify the costs incurred by generalizability and decision studies (such as the set-up costs of such a measurement system) in the context of CSP measurement.

Conclusion

This chapter began with the observation that 'doing good' has no self-evident, objective meaning in a post-Enlightenment climate of thought marked by cultural relativism. It was argued that, from an organization science perspective, a deliberate shift in focus from measuring motives and processes to measuring outcomes and performance is required for enhancing the reliability and validity of CSP as a construct. Notably, this empirical shift may allow future researchers to use statistical generalizability theory to improve quantitative measures of CSP by surveying stakeholder groups directly. The caveat is that ultimately, stakeholder expectations should also be subjected to normative inquiry, just as we examine executive decision making as a vehicle for value-based considerations. This recalls the proposed unification of 'the normative' and 'the descriptive', discussed in Chapter 2, as a necessary step toward an integrative understanding of corporate citizenship. Specifically, we take up part of this project in Chapter 9 where we circle back to examining executives' values, attitudes, and personality traits as factors that can affect corporate social performance, particularly in terms of a firm's ability to respond to stakeholder expectations. Finally, we offer some suggestions for the implementation of integrative corporate citizenship in the last chapter.

Notes

1. Baron (2006) shows how, from a utilitarian perspective, emissions trading is morally good and should not be compromised. In contrast, a Rawlsian perspective points to the possibly unfair consequences of such a pollution credits trading system because it can lead to 'hot spots' of extremely high pollution. Thus, the latter, justice perspective would advocate sacrificing overall efficiency of such a trading system to considerations of environmental justice. Similarly, many Kantians would stipulate pollution reduction as a duty and would, thus, question the morality of creating markets for environmental emissions.

2. One exception to this stakeholder evaluation of CSP may be the relatively objective measures of corporate environmental performance (CEP). Insofar as CEP cannot be measured objectively for comparisons across industries, environmental groups could be surveyed about their evaluations of a firm's CEP. Objective measures of CEP may frequently, but not always, be preferable to stakeholder assessments of CEP.

References

Agle, B. R., Mitchell, R. K. & Sonnenfeld, J. A. (1999). Who matters to CEOs? An investigation of stakeholder attributes and salience, corporate performance, and CEO values. *Academy of Management Journal, 42*, 507–525.

Anderson, R. C. (1998). *Mid-course correction: Toward a sustainable enterprise: The Interface model*. White River Junction, VT: Chelsea Green.

Baron, D. P. (2006). *Business and its environment* (5th ed.). Upper Saddle River, NJ: Prentice Hall.

Baucus, M. S. (1995). Commentary: Halo-adjusted residuals – prolonging the life of a terminally ill measure of corporate social performance. *Business & Society, 34*, 227–235.

Beder, S. (2000). *Global spin: The corporate assault on environmentalism* (rev. ed.). Melbourne: Scribe.

Brown, B. & Perry, S. (1994). Removing the financial performance halo from Fortune's 'Most Admired Companies'. *Academy of Management Journal, 37*, 1346–1359.

Brown, B. & Perry, S. (1995). Halo-removed residuals of Fortune's 'responsibility to the community and environment': A decade of data. *Business & Society, 34*(2), 199–215.

Burton, B. K. & Dunn, C. P. (1996). Feminist ethics as moral grounding for stakeholder theory. *Business Ethics Quarterly, 6*(2), 133–147.

Campbell, D. T. & Fiske, D. W. (1959). Convergent and discriminant validation by the multitrait-multimethod matrix. *Psychological Bulletin, 56*, 81–105.

Carroll, A. B. (1991). Corporate social performance measurement: A commentary on methods for evaluating an elusive construct. In J. E. Post (ed.), *Research in corporate social performance and policy* (Vol. 12, pp. 385–401). Greenwich, CT: JAI Press.

Chatterji, A. K. & Levine, D. (2006). Breaking down the wall of codes: Evaluating non-financial performance measurement. *California Management Review, 48*(2), 29–51.

Chatterji, A. K. & Levine, D. (2007). *Imitate or differentiate? Evaluating the validity of corporate social responsibility ratings?* Unpublished manuscript, Durham, NC.

Chatterji, A. K., Levine, D. & Toffel, M. W. (in press). How well do social ratings actually measure corporate social responsibility? *Journal of Economics and Management Strategy*.

Clarkson, M. B. E. (1991). Defining, evaluating, and managing corporate social performance: The stakeholder management model. In J. E. Post (ed.), *Research in corporate social performance and policy* (Vol. 12, pp. 331–358). Greenwich, CT: JAI Press.

Clarkson, M. B. E. (1995). A stakeholder framework for analyzing and evaluating corporate social performance. *Academy of Management Review, 20*(1), 92–117.

Cohen, J. (1992). A power primer. *Psychological Bulletin, 112*(1), 155–159.

Colby, A. & Kohlberg, L. (1987). *The measurement of moral judgment: Vol. 1. Theoretical foundations and research validations.* Cambridge, MA: Cambridge University Press.

Cronbach, L. J., Gleser, G. C., Nanda, H. & Rajaratnam, N. (1972). *The dependability of behavioral measurements: Theory of generalizability for scores and profiles.* New York: John Wiley.

Cronbach, L. J., Gleser, G. C. & Rajaratnam, N. (1963). Theory of generalizability: A liberalization of reliability theory. *British Journal of Mathematical and Statistical Psychology, 16*, 137–173.

Davenport, K. (2000). Corporate citizenship: A stakeholder approach for defining corporate social performance and identifying measures for assessing it (Dissertation Abstract). *Business & Society, 39*(2), 210–219.

Deckop, J. R., Merriman, K. K. & Gupta, S. (2006). The effects of CEO pay structure on corporate social performance. *Journal of Management, 32*(3), 329–342.

Economist. (2006, Dec. 9). Good food? *Economist, 381,* 12.

Elliott, K. A. & Freeman, R. B. (2001). *White hats or Don Quixotes? Human rights vigilantes in the global economy.* Unpublished manuscript, Cambridge, MA.

Entine, J. (2003). The myth of social investing: A critique of its practices and consequences for corporate social performance research. *Organization & Environment, 16*, 352–368.

Finn, A. & Kayande, U. (1997). Reliability assessment and optimization of marketing research. *Journal of Marketing Research, 34*, 262–275.

Frederick, W. C. (1995). *Values, nature, and culture in the American corporation.* New York: Oxford University Press.

Friedman, B. M. (2005). *The moral consequences of economic growth.* New York: Knopf.

Hartman, E. M. (1996). *Organizational ethics and the good life.* New York: Oxford University Press.

Holliday, C. O., Schmidheiny, S. & Watts, P. (2002). *Walking the talk: The business case for sustainable development.* San Francisco: Greenleaf.

Husted, B. W. (2000). A contingency theory of corporate social performance. *Business & Society, 39*, 24–48.

Lim, B.-C. & Ployhart, R. E. (2006). Assessing the convergent and discriminant validity of Goldberg's International Personality Item Pool: A multitrait-multimethod examination. *Organizational Research Methods, 9*(1), 29–54.

Locke, E. A. (2006). Business ethics: A way out of the morass. *Academy of Management Learning & Education, 5*(3), 324–332.

Logsdon, J. M. & Wartick, S. L. (1995). Commentary: Theoretically based applications and implications for using the Brown and Perry database. *Business & Society, 34*, 222–226.

MacIntyre, A. (1984). *After virtue: A study in moral theory* (2nd ed.). Notre Dame, IN: University of Notre Dame Press.

MacIntyre, A. (1988). *Whose justice? Which rationality?* London: Duckworth.

Marcoulides, G. A. (1998). *Modern methods for business research.* Mahwah, NJ: Lawrence Erlbaum.

Matten, D. & Crane, A. (2005). Corporate citizenship: Toward an extended theoretical conceptualization. *Academy of Management Review, 30*(1), 166–179.

Nunnally, J. C. & Bernstein, I. H. (1994). *Psychometric theory* (3rd ed.). New York: McGraw-Hill.

Orlitzky, M. (2008). Corporate social performance and financial performance: A research synthesis. In A. Crane, A. McWilliams, D. Matten, J. Moon & D. Siegel (eds), *The Oxford Handbook of CSR* (pp. 113–134). Oxford, UK: Oxford University Press.

Orlitzky, M., Schmidt, F. L. & Rynes, S. L. (2003). Corporate social and financial performance: A meta-analysis. *Organization Studies, 24*(3), 403–441.

Orlitzky, M., Swanson, D. L. & Quartermaine, L.-K. (2006). Normative myopia, executives' personality, and preference for pay dispersion: Toward implications for corporate social performance. *Business & Society, 45*(2), 149–177.

Porter, M. E. & Kramer, M. R. (2006). Strategy & society: The link between competitive advantage and corporate social responsibility. *Harvard Business Review, 84*(12), 78–92.

Price, J. L. & Mueller, C. W. (1986). *Handbook of organizational measurement* (2nd ed.). Marshfield, MA: Pitman.

Salkin, H. M. (1975). *Integer programming*. Reading, MA: Addison-Wesley.

Schwab, D. P. (1980). Construct validity in organizational behavior. In B. M. Staw & L. L. Cummings (eds), *Research in Organizational Behavior* (Vol. 2, pp. 3–43). Greenwich, CT: JAI Press.

Schwab, D. P. (1999). *Research methods for organizational studies*. Mahwah, NJ: Lawrence Erlbaum.

Schwab, D. P. (2005). *Research methods for organizational studies* (2nd ed.). Mahwah, NJ: Erlbaum.

Sharfman, M. (1996). The construct validity of the Kinder, Lydenberg & Domini social performance ratings data. *Journal of Business Ethics, 15*(3), 287–296.

Shavelson, R. J. & Webb, N. M. (1991). *Generalizability theory: A primer*. Newbury Park, CA: Sage.

Shavelson, R. J., Webb, N. M. & Rowley, G. L. (1989). Generalizability theory. *American Psychologist, 44*, 922–932.

Sims, R. R. & Brinkmann, J. (2003). Enron ethics (or: Culture matters more than codes). *Journal of Business Ethics, 45*(3), 243–256.

Sodeman, W. A. (1995). Commentary: Advantages and disadvantages of using the Brown and Perry database. *Business & Society, 34*(2), 216–221.

Swanson, D. L. (1995). Addressing a theoretical problem by reorienting the corporate social performance model. *Academy of Management Review, 20*, 43–64.

Swanson, D. L. (1999). Toward an integrative theory of business and society: A research strategy for corporate social performance. *Academy of Management Review, 24*, 506–521.

Traub, R. E. (1994). *Reliability for the social sciences: Theory and applications* (Vol. 3). Thousand Oaks, CA: Sage.

Ullmann, A. (1985). Data in search of a theory: A critical examination of the relationship among social performance, social disclosure, and economic performance. *Academy of Management Review, 10*, 540–577.

Waddock, S. A. (2003). Myths and realities of social investing. *Organization & Environment, 16*(3), 369–380.

Wartick, S. L. & Cochran, P. L. (1985). The evolution of the corporate social performance model. *Academy of Management Review, 10*, 758–769.

Willums, J.-O. (1999, May 3). Social responsibility and shareholder value. *Business Week*, 85.

Wolfe, R. & Aupperle, K. E. (1991). Introduction. In J. E. Post (ed.), *Research in corporate social performance and policy* (Vol. 12, pp. 265–268). Greenwich, CT: JAI Press.

Wood, D. J. (1991a). Corporate social performance revisited. *Academy of Management Review, 16*, 691–718.

Wood, D. J. (1991b). Toward improving corporate social performance. *Business Horizons, 34*(4), 66–73.

Wood, D. J. (1995). The Fortune database as a CSP measure. *Business & Society, 34*, 197–198.

Wood, D. J. & Jones, R. E. (1995). Stakeholder mismatching: A theoretical problem in empirical research on corporate social performance. *International Journal of Organizational Analysis, 3*, 229–267.

9

Normative Myopia, Executives' Personality, and Preference for Pay Dispersion: Implications for Corporate Social Performance

For a number of years, there has been a trend toward ever-increasing salary differentials in business organizations. While pay for the lowest-earning workers decreased between 1960 and 1990, compensation for top managers increased greatly (Feenstra & Hanson, 1996; Juhn, Murphy & Pierce, 1993; Mishel, Bernstein & Schmitt, 1996). However, these pay disparities may not be warranted by companies' performance records (Colvin, Harrington & Hjelt, 2001; Craig, 2003; Loomis, 2001; Useem & Florian, 2003). Moreover, some corporate governance structures have apparently allowed executives to receive extremely large pay packages in the form of stock options even while investors suffered losses (Fox, 2002). This has prompted *Fortune*, a pro-business magazine, to call current executive pay practices 'over-the-top CEO piggishness' (Fox, 2002, p. 70) and 'outrageous,' 'madness,' or 'grossly high – astronomical' (Colvin, Harrington & Hjelt, 2001, p. 64). Even Professor Michael Jensen, an advocate of high executive pay, has professed: 'I've generally worried these guys weren't getting paid enough [...]. But now even I'm troubled' (Colvin, Harrington & Hjelt, 2001, p. 64).

Despite such criticism, only a few companies have tried to rein in the income gaps between executives and nonexecutives (Morgenson,

This chapter was originally published in 2006 as Marc Orlitzky, Diane L. Swanson & Laura-Kate Quartermaine, 'Normative myopia, executives' personality, and preference for pay dispersion: Toward implications for corporate social performance', *Business & Society, 45*(2), 149–177. It was revised for publication in this book. The material of the original chapter was used with permission of SAGE Publications. From 2000 to 2003, this study was supported by a grant administered by the Center for Corporate Change at the Australian Graduate School of Management.

2005), a state of affairs that seems contrary to the view that socially responsible firms should try to reward their employees – one of their most important stakeholder groups – fairly for their contributions (Waddock, 2002; see also De George, 1986; Shaw & Barry, 2004; Van Buren, 2005). Besides the issue of employee fairness, there is also a concern that large disparities in pay may contribute to a variety of internal problems, such as discouraging cooperation and trust among workers (Bloom, 1999; Bloom & Michel, 2002; Cohen & Prusak, 2001; Pfeffer, 1998) while encouraging exaggerated egoism among executives that can cause them to be out of touch with organizational realities (Swanson, 1996). More broadly, excessive pay has been linked to top managers' failure to attend to their responsibilities to a variety of stakeholders (Nocera, 2002; Quinn, 2002; Sloan, 2003).

In this preliminary study we explore the relationship between *normative myopia* and executives' preference for high organizational pay dispersion and conclude with some implications for business and society, especially corporate social performance. Normative myopia, a concept introduced by Swanson (1999), as explicated in Chapters 2 and 3, refers to the propensity of executives to ignore, suppress, or deny the role of ethical values in their decisions. This definition encapsulates three closely related beliefs. The first is the assumption that normative issues (ethics and values) have no place in managerial life (see Jackall, 1988). The second is the fallacy that values and facts can be separated in decision making (see Frederick, 1994). Finally, a closely related myth is the opinion held by many practitioners that normative issues lie outside the realm of business and, therefore, should not be discussed publicly (Toffler, 1986). In contrast to this type of decision making, Swanson (1999, p. 515) described *normative receptivity* as the belief that values and facts are inseparable in executive policy formulation. Although normative myopia is consistent with the definition of amoral management as a failure to consider ethics in business (Carroll, 1987, 2001), its psychological aspects remain undeveloped. So far, there has been no empirical evidence – and little theorizing, we might add – on personality-based predictors of normative myopia.

This chapter represents a first step in addressing this gap. In our hypotheses, executive normative myopia assumes a key role as the mediating variable between the personality trait 'agreeableness' (defined later) and preference for pay dispersion. By using this approach, we hope to shed more light on the question of how business executives countenance the income inequalities that exist in today's corporations. Along these lines we ask whether a lack of agreeableness might explain the propensity of top managers to downplay or ignore ethical values and, if so, whether this disposition helps predict their preference for greater pay dispersion in organizations. Specifically, our survey is designed to examine some hypothesized relationships between executive normative myopia, agreeableness, and preference for highly stratified organizational pay. To preview, our data suggest that (normatively) *myopic* executives tend to prefer top-heavy compensation systems. In addition, our findings point to an inverse relationship between agreeableness and normative myopia, with the former offsetting the latter. We compare this result to an alternative hypothesis that gender influences myopia and conclude with some implications for business and society, including Swanson's proposition, expanded upon in Chapter 2, which is that normative myopia at the top of organizations contributes to a neglectful form of corporate social performance.

Hypothesis development

Consequences and predictors of normative myopia

Generally speaking, organizations have great discretion in designing their compensation systems (Rynes & Milkovich, 1986). Top executives can play a direct role in this policy formulation when they serve on boards of directors and sit on compensation committees. Their influence can be indirect as well because they often select the consultants and board members who help craft organizational pay structures (Crystal, 1991). This state of affairs suggests a need to understand executives' attitudes toward corporate salary distributions and the implications these preferences have for corporate social performance. In this section we focus on the former by exploring a role for normative myopia. Specifically, we propose that executives' preference for highly unequal pay structures may be a consequence of normative myopia or the propensity to downplay or ignore the ethical values at stake in their decisions. Our reasoning is straightforward. Pay equity involves normative considerations of fairness and distributive justice for all employees (Blockson, 1998; May & Pauli, 2002; Van Buren, 2005). Executives who score high on normative myopia are unlikely to factor these concerns into their preferences for organizational pay systems because myopic decision makers are, by definition, insensitive to the value interests of others and, therefore, inclined to prefer top-heavy compensation systems that benefit their own vested interests.

Hypothesis 1: Normative myopia is positively related to executives' preference for high pay dispersion in organizations.

Exploring whether executives' preference for high pay dispersion might be consequential to normative myopia is only part of our research agenda. We are also interested in what drives or helps predict normative myopia, especially since Swanson (1999) did not broach this subject in her conceptualization of the term. Personality is a likely candidate, since it generally accounts for a lot of variance in individuals' values, perceptions, motivations, and behaviors (Buss, 1989; Barrick & Mount, 1991; Kreitler & Kreitler, 1990). With this in mind we empirically tested *agreeableness* – which denotes an individual's inclination to be cooperative, friendly, altruistic, tender-minded, and trusting – drawn from the widely respected *five-factor model of personality* as a possible influence on normative myopia. The remaining factors are *conscientiousness, extraversion, emotional stability,* and *openness to experience* (for discussions of these factors, see Digman, 1990; Hogan, Hogan & Roberts, 1996; McCrae & Costa, 1997). While we do not expect any relationships between myopia and the other personality factors, we propose that executives who are more agreeable are less likely to profess normative myopia.

This proposition requires further discussion because Swanson (1999) did not explore the distinctions between self- and other-orientations in terms of value-free (*myopic*) and value-inclusive (*receptive*) decision making. With the addition of a personality factor, however, we can postulate an affinity between narrowly focused self-interest and normative myopia on the one hand and agreeableness as an indicator of normative receptivity and the propensity to include the interests of others on the other. As depicted in Figure 9.1, these relationships can be arrayed according to decision-making orientations in a two-by-two matrix that depicts our expectation of a negative relationship between agreeableness and normative myopia.

Specifically, Quadrant II indicates a correspondence between decision making professed to be value-free and a narrow focus on self. (We use the term 'professed' because our survey of executives, described later, is designed to tap executives' self-reported attitudes toward values in their decision making.) Conversely, Quadrant IV shows that attention to values goes hand in hand with a willingness to include others in decision making (Etzioni, 1988; see also psychological research on adolescents reported in Nelson & Buchholz, 2004). That other- and value-inclusive dimensions converge in Quadrant IV is consistent with the idea that individuals classified as agreeable demonstrate a greater sensitivity to the needs and expectations of others and are more other-regarding and caring (Digman, 1990; Peabody & Goldberg, 1989). They are also more likely to conform to social norms (Fiske, 1949) and more

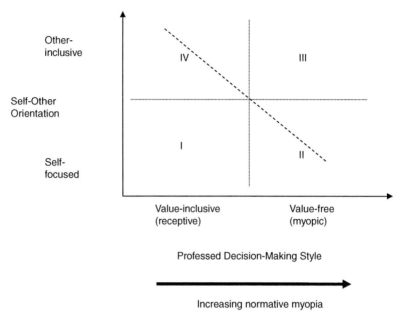

Figure 9.1 Values-Oriented Management

sensitive to maintaining a positive social identity than disagreeable individuals (see Greening & Turban, 2000, on social identity in related Business and Society literature; see also Tajfel & Turner, 1985, more generally). Since such sensitivity implies the ability to recognize beliefs held by others, it is logically problematic to talk of other-inclusive decision making that is value-free (Benhabib, 1987), which is what Quadrant III represents.

Our expectation of a negative relationship between agreeableness and normative myopia is denoted by the dashed line sloping downward from Quadrant IV to Quadrant II. It is important to point out that this line represents a continuum between the extreme poles of self-focused (myopic) and other-inclusive (receptive) decision making, based on the understanding that individuals differ in the degrees to which they balance self-interest with value commitments to others (Etzioni, 1988). Given what has been said so far, we expect that most of our observations will fall in Quadrants IV and II because Quadrants I and III are logically problematic in combining value-inclusive, self-focused and value-free, other-inclusive dimensions, respectively. In other words, Quadrants I and III appear to involve more complex psychological dynamics in need of further explanation. Briefly, Quadrant I might include tyrants, terrorists, and others who justify selfish actions through manipulative appeals to other-regarding values in order to maintain a positive self-image and favorable role identity while not openly professing egotism, manipulation, and abuse of power. On the other hand, Quadrant III could represent individuals who deny the other-regarding values that influence their decisions, thereby succumbing to 'moral muteness' intentionally or unintentionally (see Bird & Waters, 1989; Jackall, 1989; Toffler, 1986; Weaver & Treviño, 1999). In other words, managers may score high in other-regarding values, but education or other factors may train them to deny these values in their professed decision-making style. Given the nature of these dynamics, which include self-deception, future studies regarding Quadrants I and III would probably have to rely on a variety of data collection strategies, not only self-reports.

Besides the arguments presented so far, the proposed inverse relationship between agreeableness and normative myopia depicted in Figure 9.1 is consistent with two ethics perspectives. One, because agreeableness is a personality trait that captures sensitivity to the needs of others, it harkens to the ethics-of-care moral reasoning that emphasizes the values that support relationship-building (Gilligan, 1982; Noddings, 1984), alluded to in Chapter 3. Two, the hypothesized relationship between agreeableness and normative myopia recalls Kohlberg's (1981) third and fourth stages of cognitive moral development, which encapsulate an ability to refer to interpersonal and social relations as norms for moral reasoning instead of the focus on self that mark lower stages (see Weber & Wasieleski, 2001).

Hypothesis 2: Agreeableness is inversely related to normative myopia.

To correctly specify the relationships proposed so far, it is important to control for gender, which could provide an alternative explanation for Hypothesis 2. That is, gender might be the real cause of the inverse relationship between agreeableness and normative myopia if female gender predicts both agreeableness and myopia. This possibility is worth considering, since some studies suggest that women generally (1) exhibit more ethical attitudes and behaviors than men (Borkowski & Ugras, 1998; Jones & Gautschi, 1988; Ruegger & King, 1992) (2) demonstrate greater concern for ethical issues (Beltramini, Peterson & Kozmetsky, 1984) (3) are more caring (Beutel & Marini, 1995), and (4) reach higher stages of moral reasoning (Eynon, Hill & Stevens, 1997). Two meta-analyses have substantiated these findings, one by providing evidence that women have higher ethical standards (Franke, Crown & Spake, 1997) and the other by revealing their greater care orientation (Jaffee & Hyde, 2000). Other studies, especially older ones (e.g., Derry, 1989; Lifton, 1985; Rest, 1986; Snarey, 1985), found few or no such differences between the sexes (for a review, see Weber & Wasieleski, 2001). However, given the more recent meta-analyses, it is important to consider that gender could conceivably be the real cause of high scores in agreeableness, low scores in myopia, and thus be a confounding variable. If so, the relationships found in support of Hypothesis 2 may be spurious. To examine this possibility, we will statistically control for gender effects in our study.

Agreeableness and executives' preference for pay dispersion

Research indicates that individuals who are more agreeable tend to prefer team-oriented, collectivist cultures in which trust, support, and cooperation are valued more than individualism (Bretz & Judge, 1994; Cable & Judge, 1994; Judge & Cable, 1997; O'Reilly *et al.*, 1991). We expect agreeable executives to exhibit this same tendency. In their case, however, it might be based on other considerations as well. That is, given their span of authority, agreeable executives may take into account the turnover among managers, decreased teamwork, and lower organizational performance associated with high pay dispersion (Bloom, 1999; Bloom & Michel, 2002; Judge & Cable, 1997; Leana & Van Buren, 1999; Shaw, Gupta & Delery, 2002). At any rate, since greater levels of agreeableness suggest more concern for the needs and interests of others, we propose that executives who score high in agreeableness will favor more egalitarian pay systems. This expectation is buttressed by evidence that narcissism and greed are indicators of extremely low agreeableness (Costa & McCrae, 1992; Goldberg, 1992), which simply reinforces the possibility of a positive correlation between agreeableness and a regard for others' interests, including their stakes in fair pay distributions. Or, as Hypothesis 3 conveys, agreeable executives are less likely to prefer highly stratified systems of organizational pay.

Hypothesis 3: Agreeableness is inversely related to an executive's preference for high pay dispersion in organizations.

Normative myopia as a mediator of agreeableness-pay dispersion preference

Putting our theoretical model together, we have proposed in Hypotheses 1 through 3 that normative myopia mediates the aforementioned relationship between agreeableness and executives' preference for highly stratified pay structures. Our last hypothesis combines the previous ones by depicting the three variables as antecedent, mediator, and consequence. That is, we expect agreeableness (antecedent) to be inversely related to normative myopia (mediator), which, in turn, positively predicts an executive's preference for high organizational pay dispersion (consequence). Hypothesis 4 summarizes these proposed relationships.

Hypothesis 4: The relationship between executives' agreeableness and preference for high organizational pay dispersion is mediated by normative myopia.

Method

Sample

To test our hypotheses, we sampled 195 executives enrolled in the Executive MBA (EMBA) program of an Australian business school in a metropolitan city. Although our study was confined to Australia, it can be argued that our findings are highly relevant to executives in the United States (Swanson & Orlitzky, 2006). According to Hofstede's (2001) well-known cultural comparisons, Australia is the country most similar to the United States in individualism and power distance. In fact, no other countries score as closely on these two dimensions. The shared emphasis on individualism equates to a preference for personal initiative rather than an emotional dependence on a community of others that marks collectivism. The similar scores on power distance mean that both cultures tend to justify power distance or inequities in prestige, wealth, and status by expertise legitimised through reward systems. The two countries are also very close in masculinity and uncertainty avoidance, the former denoting a predominant socialisation pattern for men to appear autonomous, aggressive, and dominant and for females to appear nurturing, helpful, humble, and affiliating. That both cultures score similarly in uncertainty avoidance translates into a relatively high tolerance for ambiguity and informal work arrangements. In the final analysis, a preference for individualism (versus collectivism) is believed to have the greatest impact on management practice (Hoppe, 2004; Triandis, 2004). Given the cultural affinity between Australia and the United States in this area, as well as the other similarities, we can generalize our findings to a United States population of executives with a high degree of confidence, keeping in mind that we are in the preliminary stages of research.

Of the surveys distributed in an Organization Structure class, 133 were returned, for a response rate of 68%. All respondents were full-time employed managers or executives and part-time graduate students in their final year of the EMBA program. Respondents' age ranged from 26 to 52 years, with an average age of 36 years (and a median age of 35 years). Seventy-one percent of the respondents were male. On average, respondents had 11 years of industry experience and had been working for their organization for 6 years. The average respondent had taken three Economics, four Finance, and two Corporate Strategy courses at the university level. Most executives surveyed worked in financial services and banking (24%), manufacturing (16%), and information technology (10%). Five percent of the respondents were employed in public service, government, or nonprofit organizations.

Procedure

Surveys were distributed to the EMBA students before the final-year module on Organizational Design. The survey stated that the present study was about managerial beliefs, decision-making styles, and human resource practices. Students were assured that their responses would be confidential and anonymous. In order to deliver on this promise, we numbered the questionnaires so that they could be matched with anonymity in a lagged collection of independent and dependent variables. Opportunities for demand characteristics or individual biases were minimized because all respondents had completed similar EMBA coursework, which did not include business ethics. After analyzing the results, we sent an executive summary to those respondents who had requested an overview of our findings.

Measures

To measure *agreeableness* we relied on an existing measure from Goldberg's (2001) inventory of 50 Likert-scale items, which captures the five factors of personality. In our analyses, the coefficient alpha reliability for the ten items of agreeableness was .82. The four remaining personality measures of extraversion, emotional stability, conscientiousness, and openness to experience had coefficient alpha reliabilities of .89, .84, .77, and .75, respectively. Goldberg's (2001) web site presents further evidence of the reliability and construct validity of these personality factors (http://ipip.ori.org/new_home.htm).

We devised 19 Likert-scale items to measure *normative myopia* in terms of three dimensions, presented earlier as the beliefs that (1) ethical values have no place in managerial life (2) values and facts can be separated, and

(3) normative issues fall outside the realm of business. For the purpose of construct validation, we followed Nunnally and Bernstein's (1994, pp. 101–104) suggestion to pretest items. We did so with a sample of MBA students, doctoral students, and the first author's academic colleagues, who recommended a number of revisions and clarifications. As part of the construct validation in the pilot-study sample of MBA students, the scree plot of the exploratory factor analysis suggested three principal components. In the final EMBA sample, we eliminated seven items with relatively small or ambiguous factor loadings after varimax rotation. Illustrated in Table 9.1, the first and second dimensions are captured by two items each and the third dimension by eight. In the final EMBA sample, the 12 remaining items that constituted our exploratory measure of normative myopia had a coefficient alpha reliability of .73. Moreover, the construct validity of the scale was tested with the final EMBA sample,

Table 9.1   Rotated Factor Matrix of Final 12 Items Measuring Normative Myopia

Items	Factor 1	Factor 2	Factor 3
To be effective, managers must separate their personal lives from their professional responsibilities.	.55		
Good managers are able to apply their personal values in corporate life. (reverse-coded).	.53		
Facts are usually more important than values in any decision I make in my company.		.58	
The main difference between facts and values is that facts can be analyzed objectively whereas values cannot.		.58	
If managers factored values into their decisions, chaos would result.			.67
Social values have a place in corporate life. (reverse-coded).			.61
Business ethics is irrelevant to good decisions.			.60
Ethics officers provide helpful information for management decisions. (reverse-coded).			.60
I factor values into my decisions. (reverse-coded).			.57
Corporations should foster a climate where individual values are discussed freely. (reverse-coded).			.56
Business ethics is a contradiction in terms.			.54
Ethical training programs are a waste of time.			.53

as part of the confirmatory factor analysis implied by Figure 9.2 and discussed later in the Results section.

Because normative myopia is an aggregate multidimensional construct (as is job satisfaction, for example), the dimensions can be algebraically combined to form an overall representation of the construct (Law, Wong & Mobley, 1998). That is, our conceptualization of normative myopia is not as a latent construct that exists at a higher, more abstract level than its dimensions. These dimensions do not represent different manifestations of the construct, nor does the construct *lead to* these dimensions. Instead, normative myopia is *formed from* them (see Law *et al.*, 1998). Because of these construct characteristics, it is proper to aggregate the item scores and, for reasons of comparability, divide this aggregate by the number of items to calculate a normative myopia score for each respondent.

Preference for pay dispersion was measured in three ways. First, we aggregated and averaged the responses to three Likert-scale items (PD1) about executives' preferences for relatively equal or unequal pay systems. Second, the respondents indicated in a dichotomous item whether they preferred a 'more egalitarian' compensation system or a compensation system that 'has greater pay differentiation' (PD2). Third, after being provided with current highest-to-lowest pay ratios, the respondents were asked for their own preferred highest-to-lowest pay ratios in their organizations. As is evident from Table 9.2, the three Likert-scale items (PD1) had a coefficient alpha of .79. In addition, Table 9.2 shows that the three different measures of pay structure preference were highly correlated. The third measure was used only to validate the other two measures of preference for compensation distributions and, thus, was discarded from further statistical analysis. We were reluctant to use the third measure because, although the means were significantly different (at $p < .05$) between those respondents with egalitarian preferences (average highest-to-lowest pay ratio of 42:1) and those respondents with preferences for pay dispersion (73:1), the difference was relatively small.

Control variables

Several demographic measures, such as respondent gender, age, organizational tenure (in years), industry experience (in years), and amount of business education (operationalized as the aggregate of three Likert-scale items measuring the amount of semester-long courses in Economics, Finance, and Corporate Strategy) were added as controls. It was important to include the latter control variable, given assertions that economics and similar coursework can negatively affect individuals' ability to consider ethics, values, and concerns of organizational stake-holders (Ferraro, Pfeffer & Sutton, 2005; Frank, Gilovich & Regan, 1993; Ghoshal, 2005).

Data analysis

To test Hypotheses 1 through 3, we performed ordinary least-squares (OLS) and logistic regression analyses. For the test of mediation (Hypothesis 4), we applied two different data analysis techniques (1) structural equation modeling and (2) Baron and Kenny's (1986) regression tests of mediation. Summarized briefly, structural equation modeling simultaneously and parsimoniously tests all variables included in the theoretical specification of a model by using statistical assumptions more stringent than those required for the Baron and Kenny technique, which relies on straightforward correlation and regression analysis (Byrne, 2001; Sharma, 1996). Since both methods are subject to their own strengths and weaknesses, we conservatively tested Hypothesis 4 by considering whether their results point in the same direction. We can have greater confidence in the results if they do. In the measurement model of the structural analysis, we included the conventional correction for measurement error $(1 - r_{ii})$. Across items measuring the same latent construct, r_{ii} may, for example, be defined as Cronbach's coefficient alpha, an estimate of reliability (Byrne, 2001; Nunnally & Bernstein, 1994).

Results

Descriptive statistics

Table 9.2 shows descriptive statistics (means, standard deviations, and correlations) of all measures included in the analyses. Our findings are consistent with most previous empirical evidence that women generally receive higher scores on agreeableness (Costa, Terracciano & McCrae, 2001; Du, Bakish & Hrdina, 2000; Feingold, 1994), lower scores on emotional stability, and higher scores on openness to experience than men (Feingold, 1994). Emotional stability refers to an individual's tendency to adjust confidently to psychologically challenging situations (and in particular, react well to stress), while openness to experience indicates an individual's tendency to be imaginative, original, and intellectually curious. These gender-specific tendencies are evident from the positive correlations between gender and agreeableness and openness to experience, respectively, as well as the negative correlation between gender and emotional stability in Table 9.2. These correlations

Table 9.2 Descriptive Statistics: Means, Standard Deviations, and Correlations

Variable	M	SD	1	2	3	4	5	6	7	8	9	10	11	12	13	14
1. Amount of Business Education	6.54	2.83	(.74)													
2. Gender[a]	.29	.45	-.03													
3. Age	35.56	5.35	-.01	-.13												
4. Industry Experience	10.51	6.89	-.07	-.02	.61											
5. Org. Tenure	5.64	5.51	-.09	-.11	.35	.52										
6. Preference for pay dispersion (PD1)	2.75	.78	.24	-.10	.02	.00	-.01	(.79)								
7. Preferred pay ratio	56.57	74.00	.23	.00	-.12	-.07	.00	.29								
8. Preferred pay system (PD2)[b]	.50	.50	.21	-.15	-.06	-.14	-.05	.51	.21							
9. Extraversion	3.39	.72	.09	-.02	-.22	-.06	-.16	.15	-.01	.09	(.89)					
10. Agreeableness	3.68	.40	-.09	.19	.00	.14	-.07	-.28	-.15	-.25	.21	(.82)				
11. Conscientiousness	3.60	.55	.12	-.02	.07	.01	.06	.05	.00	.13	-.09	-.01	(.77)			
12. Emotional Stability	3.57	.64	.14	-.26	.17	.17	.13	.10	-.01	.08	.20	.13	.05	(.84)		
13. Openness to Experience	3.86	.44	-.12	.21	.03	.14	-.05	.00	.08	.00	.16	.17	-.18	.09	(.75)	
14. Normative Myopia	2.22	.38	.06	.01	-.17	-.13	-.01	.23	.13	.22	-.03	-.25	.02	-.08	-.13	(.73)

Note. $N = 133$. Figures in parentheses on diagonal represent coefficient alpha reliability coefficients.
[a] 1= female, 0 = male.
[b] 0 = egalitarian, 1 = large pay differentials.

can also be regarded as evidence of construct validity in that they confirm the operationalization of Big Five personality traits proposed by Goldberg (2001). Interestingly, amount of business education in Strategy, Economics, and Finance was positively related to preference for pay dispersion in the bivariate correlation matrix (the average r was .23 across the three different operationalizations of preferred pay dispersion) as well as the baseline model (column a) in Table 9.3 (*beta* = .25, $p < .01$). Tables 9.3 and 9.4 provide regression analysis results related to Hypotheses 1 through 3.

Hypothesis 1: Normative Myopia and Preference for High Pay Dispersion

Hypothesis 1 predicted a positive relationship between normative myopia and preference for more unequal pay structures. According to Table 9.3, the data support Hypothesis 1 in that normative myopia is shown to be positively related to executives' preferences for relatively high pay dispersion (*beta* = .23, $p < .05$; column b of Table 9.3). This relationship remained significant (*beta* = .17, $p < .05$, one-tailed) even when agreeableness was added (see column c of Table 9.3). Patterns similar to the results

Table 9.3   Predictors of Preference for Compensation Systems with Relatively High Levels of Pay Differentiation (PD1)

Independent Variables	Standardized Regression Coefficients (*Beta*)				
Controls:	(a)	(b)	(c)	(d)	(e)
Gender	–.11	–.09	–.06	–.06	–.06
Respondent Age	.00	.04	.00	–.02	.01
Industry Experience	–.01	.03	.09	.06	.09
Org. Tenure	.05	–.03	–.06	.00	–.06
Amount of Business Education	.25**	.22*	.20*	.22*	.20*
Theoretical Predictors:					
Normative Myopia		.23*	.17[t]		.17[t]
Agreeableness			–.22*	–.27**	–.22*
Multiple R	.27	.34	.39	.38	.39
R^2	.08	.11	.15	.14	.15
Adjusted R^2	.04	.07	.10	.10	.10
F associated with change in R^2	7.38**	6.59**	5.44*	8.71**	3.57[t]
		(b vs. a)	(c vs. b)	(d vs. a)	(e vs. d)

[t] Results significant at $p < .10$ (two-tailed).
* Results significant at $p < .05$ (two-tailed).
** Results significant at $p < .01$ (two-tailed).

depicted in Table 9.3 were found in a set of logistic regressions with the dichotomous measure of preferred compensation system (PD2) used as the dependent variable.[1]

Hypothesis 2: Agreeableness and Normative Myopia

Table 9.4 gives the results of our regression analysis of the relationships expressed in Hypothesis 2 (that agreeableness is inversely related to normative myopia). In support of this hypothesis, Table 9.4 shows that agreeableness is negatively related to our measure of normative myopia (*beta* of $-.27$, $p = .007$), suggesting that more agreeable executives may be less myopic and, thus, more likely to include the value interests of others in their decision making. Based on the unstandardized measures of association (regression weight B of $-.35$ with standard error of .13), we would expect an average 1-point increase in agreeableness (equivalent to 2.5 standard deviations) to correspond to an average 0.35-point decrease in normative myopia, when other personality factors are held constant. In addition, Table 9.4 also indicates that the addition of the other four personality factors (extraversion, conscientiousness, emotional stability, and

Table 9.4 **Agreeableness as a Predictor of Normative Myopia**

Independent Variables	Standardized Regression Coefficients *Beta*		
	(a)	(b)	(c)
Controls:			
Gender	.00	.01	.05
Respondent Age	$-.16$	$-.17$	$-.19$
Industry Experience	$-.07$	.03	.02
Org. Tenure	.09	.07	.03
Amount of Business Education	.06	.06	.03
Personality Variables:			
Extraversion		$-.05$	$-.01$
Conscientiousness		.00	.01
Emotional Stability		$-.04$	$-.01$
Openness to Experience		$-.10$	$-.09$
Agreeableness			$-.27$**
Multiple R	.20	.23	.37
R^2	.04	.06	.14
Adjusted R^2	.00	.00	.06
F associated with change in R^2	.93	.46	7.06**

* Results significant at $p < .05$ (two-tailed).
** Results significant at $p < .01$ (two-tailed).

openness to experience) did not contribute to a better explanation of normative myopia. When the other four personality traits were excluded from the multiple regression equation, agreeableness remained highly negatively correlated with normative myopia (*beta* = –.29, *p* = .003). In short, agreeableness was found to be a statistically significant predictor of normative myopia.

In sum, these findings confirm our expectation of a negative relationship between agreeableness and normative myopia, conveyed in Figure 9.1 by the dashed line sloping downward from Quadrant IV to Quadrant II. A cross tabulation of data further supports this expectation. Specifically, we observed the largest number of cases in Quadrant IV (34.6%), followed by the second-largest number in Quadrant II (26.2%). (20.0% of observations fell in Quadrant I, and 19.2% in Quadrant III.) The overall *chi-square* test was statistically significant (χ^2 = 5.72, *p* = .017), with an *eta* of .21, indicating that the two dimensions in Figure 9.1 (self/other-orientation and professed style of decision making) are *not* independent, providing further support for the reasoning used to derive Hypothesis 2. In fact, a scatter plot of the continuous observations arrayed as Figure 1 was consistent with the logic presented to introduce Hypothesis 2.

Rejecting gender as an alternative explanation for Hypothesis 2

As previously discussed, it is necessary to rule out gender as an alternative to explanations that support Hypothesis 2. As such, we reexamined our data with the alternative explanation of gender in mind. Specifically, the women in our sample (*n* = 38) did score higher on agreeableness than the men (*n* = 95). The respective average scores were 3.80 and 3.63, with the difference being statistically significant at *p* = .03. *Eta,* a bivariate measure of association, was .19 (see correlation reported in Table 9.2). Thus, sex did make a difference with respect to agreeableness. However, the sexes scored similarly on normative myopia. (Indeed, the female executives who were surveyed received slightly higher scores on normative myopia – 2.25 for women and 2.20 for men. But the difference was statistically nonsignificant). This finding runs contrary to the alternative explanation of gender. A further test of the effect of gender on the association between agreeableness and normative myopia is provided by the partial correlation coefficient between those two variables, controlling for gender. This partial correlation was –.27 (*p* = .002) and, thus, actually slightly larger in magnitude than the zero-order correlation between agreeableness and normative myopia shown in Table 9.2 (*r* = –.25). Given this evidence, we concluded that, in our sample, the within-gender variance of agreeableness explained differences in normative myopia better than gender. (Also note that gender was included as a control variable in Tables 9.3 and 9.4.)

Hypothesis 3: Agreeableness and Preference for Pay Dispersion

Consistent with Hypothesis 3, more agreeable executives tended to prefer more egalitarian compensation systems (see column d of Table 9.3). More specifically, the *beta* regression weight of agreeableness predicting preference for pay dispersion was $-.27$ ($p < .01$) without normative myopia in the model, and $-.22$ ($p < .05$) with normative myopia included (column e in Table 9.3). These results suggest, in support of Hypothesis 3, that agreeableness is negatively related to preference for high pay dispersion.

Hypothesis 4: Mediation Effects

Finally, we tested for mediation effects. According to Hypothesis 4, agreeableness is expected to be inversely related to normative myopia which, in turn, positively predicts a preference for high pay dispersion. Hypothesis 4 implies the path model shown in Figure 9.2, which can be tested in structural equation analyses. To compare Figure 9.2 (fully mediated path model) to a simple unmediated model (i.e., agreeableness directly influences pay structure preference), we used the *chi-square* (χ^2) statistic to test the difference between these two nested path models. According to this comparison ($\chi^2 = 42.94$, $p < .05$), the fit of the mediated model was better. The various fit statistics (e.g., the comparative fit index or the Tucker-Lewis Index) reported at the bottom of Figure 9.2 generally suggest the same conclusion. Also, the fit indices of other mediation models (i.e., other causal orders) were inferior to those of the hypothesized model shown in Figure 9.2. That is, our empirical analyses indicate that agreeableness affects normative myopia, which in turn influences preference for organizational pay structures. Furthermore, the test statistics at the bottom of Figure 9.2 indicate a good fit of the measurement model underpinning Figure 9.2 as well.

As pointed out in the Method section, structural equation modeling often requires fairly stringent assumptions. One is the requirement of relatively large sample sizes. Therefore, to be more confident in our results we performed Baron and Kenny's (1986) test for mediation. According to this test, three inferential conditions must be met. First, agreeableness must be negatively correlated with preference for high pay differentiation. Second, normative myopia must be positively related to preference for high pay differentiation. Third, the regression co-efficient between

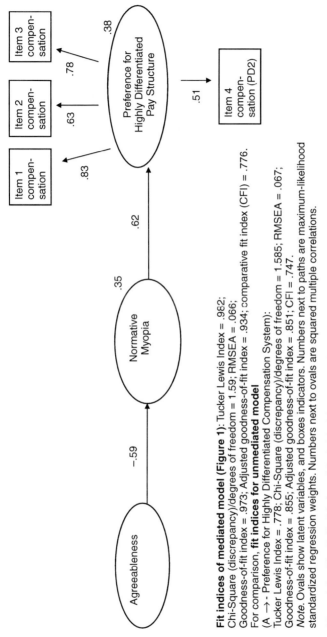

Fit indices of mediated model (Figure 1): Tucker Lewis Index = .982; Chi-Square (discrepancy)/degrees of freedom = 1.59; RMSEA = .066; Goodness-of-fit index = .973; Adjusted goodness-of-fit index = .934; comparative fit index (CFI) = .776. For comparison, **fit indices for unmediated model** (A → - Preference for Highly Differentiated Compensation System): Tucker Lewis Index = .778; Chi-Square (discrepancy)/degrees of freedom = 1.585; RMSEA = .067; Goodness-of-fit index = .855; Adjusted goodness-of-fit index = .851; CFI = .747.

Note. Ovals show latent variables, and boxes indicators. Numbers next to paths are maximum-likelihood standardized regression weights. Numbers next to ovals are squared multiple correlations.

Figure 9.2   The Fully Mediated Path Model (Empirical Results)

agreeableness and preference for pay differentiation must decrease to statistical nonsignificance after normative myopia is added to the regression equation. The bivariate results in Table 9.2, previously mentioned, indicate that the first two conditions are satisfied. After comparing columns d and e in Table 9.3 (as well as the results in the table of logistic regressions, not shown in this chapter), we concluded that while the regression weight of agreeableness becomes smaller with the addition of normative myopia, it retains some statistical significance. That is, even when the model includes normative myopia, agreeableness still exerts a significant direct influence on pay structure preference. This suggests partial rather than full mediation.

In other words, our statistical analyses do not fully support Hypothesis 4 that agreeableness is inversely related to normative myopia which, in turn, positively predicts a preference for high pay dispersion. Instead, we found that normative myopia only partially mediates the negative relationship between agreeableness and preference for highly differentiated pay systems. It may be one of the causal mechanisms through which agreeableness affects preference for pay dispersion, but it is not the only one.

Discussion

To recap, we found evidence to support our expectation that agreeable executives are less likely to exhibit normative myopia and preference for highly stratified organizational pay. Moreover, our findings suggest that agreeableness partially mediates this relationship and that gender does not seem to be causal to it.

Implications for business and society research and education

We will confine our concluding remarks mostly to implications for corporate social performance models. Discussed in Chapters 1 and 2, these models encompass corporate responsibilities to society, ways by which corporations can respond to their environments (corporate social responsiveness), and resulting social impacts (Wood, 1991; see also Carroll, 1979, 2000; Epstein, 1987; Frederick, 1987; Jones, 1983; Sethi, 1979; Swanson, 1995; Wartick & Cochran, 1985; Wood, 2000). Although these models have advanced research by classifying linkages among many business and society topics, normative issues – including the role of executive decision making and value preferences – have not been adequately included (Frederick, 1998; Swanson, 1995). Swanson (1999) addressed this state of affairs by proposing that if executive managers exhibit normative myopia and encourage this type of decision making as the standard for other employees, then whole organizations can eventually lose touch with stakeholder expectations of responsibility. The resulting tendency is a neglectful or sluggish form of corporate social responsiveness, which she refers to as 'value neglect'. In contrast, Swanson proffers normative receptivity as representational of executive decision making that consciously strives to incorporate the value-based expectations of stakeholders while encouraging other employees to do the same. In other words, normative receptivity at the top can be thought of as necessary (but not sufficient) to a firm's ability to respond constructively to the social environment, which Swanson dubs the possibility of 'value attunement'.[2] According to Swanson, a fuller understanding of value attunement awaits a specification of the values that contribute to corporate social responsibility as well as a better understanding of what that responsibility entails. In this way, attunement theorizing is more tentative than value neglect. Even so, the value processes proposed by Frederick (1995) and outlined in Chapter 1 might be avenues for further attunement theorizing.

Although Swanson proposes that normative myopia at the top can contribute to an organization's neglectful posture toward society, she did not speculate on the role of executive personality. Nor did she consider executives' preference for compensation structures. These may be important concepts to consider because if myopia mediates the relationship between agreeableness and preference for highly differentiated pay systems, then these types of pay structures may in and of themselves be symptomatic of some level of value neglect or an organizational tendency to ignore or downplay stakeholder expectations of responsibility (see also Nocera, 2002; Quinn, 2002; Sloan, 2003). In contrast, if executive normative receptivity and sensitivity to a fair pay distribution go hand in hand, then this correspondence may signify some capacity for attunement, especially since highly competitive compensation systems can undermine the cooperation, trust, and social capital among employees needed for constructive responses to external constituents and interactive and dialogue-based relationships with them (see Baron & Kreps, 1999; Cohen & Prusak, 2001; Donaldson & Preston, 1995; Leana & Van Buren, 1999; Schein, 1992; Szwajkowski, 2000; Waddock & Graves, 1997). In other words, large pay disparities may be counterproductive to value-attuned corporate social performance. If so, it is important to understand the role executives play.

Future research aimed at understanding this role should clarify the relationships between executive agreeableness, normative myopia, and preference for pay structures. Recall that the former may exert either a direct influence on pay structure preference or an indirect influence through a mediator other than normative myopia. This suggests the need for other studies designed to examine associations between preference for pay dispersion and other variables that could be implicated in these dynamics. One candidate for exploration is the role of organizational structure (see also Gerde, 2001), since large bureaucratic organizations with tall chain-of-command structures tend to produce hierarchical decision making that is slow to react to novel information (Frederick, 1995; Jackall, 1988; Perrow, 1986; Schein, 1992). The corollary is that responsiveness to stakeholders would be more likely in organizations with flatter structures (Swanson, 1999). By extension, we would expect greater responsiveness if flatter structures co-vary with lower executive-worker pay ratios, since such covariance suggests less myopia in executive decision making. That said, we do not claim that organizational pay scales exhibiting large differentials between the top and bottom strata signify a lack of social responsibility *per se*. Surely there are many contingencies to consider, such as firm size, type of industry, and scarcity of executive expertise. In general, though, our study implies that organizational pay distributions deserve further scrutiny in terms of corporate social performance, especially since highly stratified compensation systems may have the aforementioned counterproductive effects on organizational behavior.

The role of business education is another area ripe for inquiry. Although not hypothesized, our findings indicate that executives with more business education tended to prefer organizational compensation systems with relatively greater pay inequalities (r = .24 and .21, respectively) and larger highest-to-lowest pay ratios (r = .23). Respondents' qualitative comments suggest that this preference might be due to a self-interested expectation that their business education will pay off. A complementary explanation is that business education itself may encourage an exaggerated self-interest that ignores or downplays the needs of others (Feldman, 2002; Ferraro *et al.*, 2005; Ghoshal, 2005; Krishnan, 2006; Swanson & Frederick, 2005; Swanson & Orlitzky, 2006; Waddock, 2003). Investigating this possibility would require sampling a larger population of business students from different countries with more diverse educational backgrounds. It would be particularly interesting to know whether the response patterns of students who have business backgrounds differ from those who do not.

Study limitations

Like any study, ours has weaknesses that could be addressed in future research. One major weakness is that associational measures based on self-reports of several variables can overstate the real relationships. Yet, this methodological problem of common method bias might not be grave.[3] For one thing, we can safely assume that most respondents know their decision-making preferences better than any observer. At any rate, self-reports are difficult to avoid in many studies. Even so, future researchers could try to come up with valid measures collected from different sources over time. Such observational, longitudinal data could circumvent this potential threat to internal validity and help clarify the implications of normative myopia for organizations. Future studies that examine *actual* organizational consequences of normative myopia (e.g., actual organizational pay structures, human resource and compensation systems) in a longitudinal design might provide further confirmation of our results.

Potential response distortion might also cast doubt on our conclusions. Along those lines, it could be argued that, because of social desirability, respondents would be more likely to inflate their scores on agreeableness and artificially deflate their scores on normative myopia and preference for relatively high pay dispersion. For various reasons, we do not believe that this alternative explanation accounts for our findings, primarily because we put heavy emphasis on assuring the anonymity, confidentiality, and desired descriptive accuracy of responses. Additionally, there is some evidence that response distortion tends to be low for personality measures, especially if little or nothing is at stake for the respondent (Barrick & Mount, 1996; McClelland & Rhodes, 1969; Schwab & Packard, 1973). It should also be noted that, because the mean score of normative myopia was close to the midpoint of the scale, most of the items, some reverse-coded, did not elicit socially desirable responses (see Tables 9.1 and 9.2). Finally, social desirability might have had no impact on the dependent variable, preference for pay dispersion, because Australia, the location for the study, is a highly individualistic country, much like the United States (Hofstede, 2001). Egalitarianism does not register as an important social norm in either country (Hofstede, 2001). Hence, response distortion of the dependent variable due to social desirability is unlikely.

Even so, we double-checked the data for response distortion. First, some of the respondents' comments to open-ended qualitative questions clearly invoked self-interest, which indicates relatively honest responses. We have no reason to think that respondents would be candid in their qualitative responses, but dishonest in quantitative indicators. Second, we did not see any evidence of range restriction in our measures. The standard deviations (SD) were relatively large, especially if divided by the means (see Table 9.2). If *all* respondents gave socially desirable responses, range restriction (i.e., a small standard deviation) would occur around a relatively high mean. Furthermore, if *all* responses were distorted to the same extent, a constant would *de facto* be added to each true score $_{NM}$ of normative myopia. As can be shown mathematically, an addition of a constant does not affect correlation or standardized regression coefficients. In fact, prior empirical evidence shows that response distortion does not attenuate the predictive validity of personality measures (Barrick & Mount, 1996). Finally, an argument that social desirability bias accounts for our findings begs an explanation of why other personality measures that are more likely to be associated with social desirability in work settings (conscientiousness, emotional stability, and openness to experience) were not found to be correlated with normative myopia (see Table 9.4).

Put differently, to argue that social desirability accounts for our findings is equivalent to arguing that only *certain* respondents are prone to response distortion on *certain* items. This issue probably warrants future empirical examination in a research design similar to Barrick and Mount's (1996). Such a study would specifically control for the effects of impression management and self-deception, the two elements of response distortion.

Our exploratory measurement of normative myopia is another area in need of improvement. As shown in Table 9.1, the factor loadings hover in the 50s and 60s. Consistent with this suboptimal factor structure, internal reliability for normative myopia was satisfactory, but relatively low (Cronbach alpha of .73) – especially given the relatively high number of scale items (12). This low reliability may attenuate our findings. Orlitzky, Schmidt, and Rynes (2003) and Orlitzky and Benjamin (2001) explain how and why unreliable measures attenuate statistical associations in a related research domain. (These two studies, presented as Chapters 4 and 5, were updated and revised for this book.) Applied to this area, the real relationships between normative myopia and its predictor and consequence may, in fact, be higher than they appear in this study, at least as far as the multiple regressions are concerned (as pointed out above, we corrected for measurement error in the structural equation models). Unreliability not only attenuates mean associations, but it makes statistical relationships less certain due to large confidence intervals around mean values. An improved scale of normative myopia, which would ideally be shorter yet exhibit higher reliability, would reduce such empirical uncertainty.

Overall, the limitations of our study should be considered in light of the fact that, as far as we know, we are the first researchers to develop a survey instrument to operationalize normative myopia. Moreover, we sampled an executive population notoriously difficult to access. Because our sample response rate was quite high (68%), we can have greater confidence in the generalizability of our findings compared to more typical response rates of 10 to 30%.

Conclusion

In this study we have investigated personality as a predictor of executives' normative myopia and preference for highly stratified systems of organizational pay. Our findings suggest that more agreeable executives are less prone to normative myopia and less apt to prefer disproportionately top-heavy compensation systems. In terms of corporate social performance, these types of executives might also be more adept at guiding organizations to respond constructively to stakeholder expectations of social responsibility. This prospect is highly relevant to future business and society inquiry, especially given increased interest in corporate malfeasance and escalating levels of executive salaries. It is also relevant to practice in terms of recruiting aimed at hiring executives and other employees for normative receptivity, a point to which we shall return in our final chapter on the implementation of corporate citizenship in domestic and international environments.

Notes

1. These logistic regression results were omitted from this chapter, but are available from the first author.
2. As covered in Chapter 2, Swanson extended previous corporate social performance models, including those mentioned in this chapter, by conceptualizing normative myopia and value neglect on the one hand and normative receptivity and value attunement on the other as *ideal types* or systems of logical implications drawn from extant research that can be used as contrasting points of reference for inquiry into the relationship between executive decision making and corporate social performance. By using this method, Swanson relied on Max Weber's (1922/1947) construction of an ideal type as a simplified model that focuses attention on a subject's distinctive features in order to highlight logical implications systematically. In keeping with ideal-type modeling, we would expect executives to exhibit degrees of normative myopia and receptivity instead of pure forms of these decision processes. In fact our survey, described in the Method section, is designed to measure normative myopia on a scale from one to five. The same is true on the organizational level in that Swanson conceptualized value neglect and value attunement as contrasting points of reference for corporate social performance influenced by executive normative myopia and receptivity, respectively. Because

Swanson's theoretical perspective is based on ideal types or systems of logical implications across the individual, organizational, and societal domains, it lends itself to research that seeks to understand the antecedents and moderators of specified relationships, which is what our study is intended to do, although limited in scope.

3. Methodological research shows that common method variance does not result in as much inflation of correlations as was typically assumed (Crampton & Wagner, 1994; Spector, 1987). A survey of business research published in top-tier journals also reveals that structural equation models and confirmatory factor analyses are often based on cross-sectional data from the same source. We collected lagged data from the same source.

References

Baron, J. N. & Kreps, D. M. (1999). *Strategic human resources: Frameworks for general managers*. New York: Wiley.

Baron, R. & Kenny, D. (1986). The moderator-mediator variable distinction in social psychological research: Conceptual, strategic, and statistical considerations. *Journal of Personality and Social Psychology, 51*, 1173–1182.

Barrick, M. R. & Mount, M. K. (1991). The Big Five personality dimensions and job performance: A meta-analysis. *Personnel Psychology, 44*, 1–26.

Barrick, M. R. & Mount, M. K. (1996). Effects of impression management and self-deception on the predictive validity of personality constructs. *Journal of Applied Psychology, 81*, 261–272.

Beltramini, R. F., Peterson, R. & Kozmetsky, G. (1984). Concerns of college students regarding business ethics. *Journal of Business Ethics, 3*, 195–200.

Benhabib, S. (1987). The generalized and the concrete other: The Kohlberg-Gilligan controversy and feminist theory. In S. Benhabib & D. Cornell (eds), *Feminism as critique* (pp. 77–95). Minneapolis, MN: University of Minnesota Press.

Beutel, A. M. & Marini, M. M. (1995). Gender and values. *American Sociological Review, 60*, 436–448.

Bird, F. & Waters, F. (1989). The moral muteness of managers. *California Management Review, 32*, 73–88.

Blockson, L. C. (1998). "E for effort" or distributive justice? *Business & Society, 37*, 111–112.

Bloom, M. (1999). The performance effects of pay dispersion on individuals and organizations. *Academy of Management Journal, 42*, 25–40.

Bloom, M. & Michel, J. G. (2002). The relationships among organizational context, pay dispersion, and managerial turnover. *Academy of Management Journal, 45*, 33–42.

Borkowski, S. & Ugras, Y. J. (1998). Business students and ethics: A meta-analysis. *Journal of Business Ethics, 17*. 1117–1127.

Bretz, R. D. Jr. & Judge, T. A. (1994). The role of human resource systems in job applicant decision processes. *Journal of Management, 20*, 531–551.

Buss, A. H. (1989). Personality as traits. *American Psychologist, 44*, 1378–1388.

Byrne, B. M. (2001). *Structural equation modeling with AMOS: Basic concepts, applications, and programming*. Mahwah, NJ: Erlbaum.

Cable, D. M. & Judge, T. A. (1994). Pay preferences and job search decisions: A person-organization fit perspective. *Personnel Psychology, 47,* 317–348.

Carroll, A. B. (1979). A three-dimensional conceptual model of corporate social performance. *Academy of Management Review, 4,* 497–506.

Carroll, A. B. (1987, March/April). In search of the moral manager. *Business Horizons,* 7–15.

Carroll, A. B. (2000). A commentary and an overview of key questions on corporate social performance measurement. *Business & Society, 39,* 466–478.

Carroll, A. B. (2001). Models of management morality for the new millennium. *Business Ethics Quarterly, 11,* 365–371.

Cohen, D. & Prusak, L. (2001). *How social capital makes organizations work.* Boston, MA: Harvard Business School Press.

Colvin, G., Harrington, A. & Hjelt, P. (2001, June 25). The great CEO pay heist. *Fortune, 143,* pp. 64–70.

Costa, P. T. Jr. & McCrae, R. R. (1992). *Revised NEO personality inventory (NEO-PI-R) and NEO five-factor (NEO-FFI) inventory professional manual.* Odessa, FL: PAR.

Costa, P. Jr., Terracciano, A. & McCrae, R. R. (2001). Gender differences in personality traits across cultures: Robust and surprising findings. *Journal of Personality & Social Psychology, 8,* 322–331.

Craig, S. (2003, March 4). Wall Street pain stops at the top – CEOs of big financial firms still pull down fat paychecks despite a dismal environment. *Wall Street Journal,* p. C1.

Crampton, S.M. & Wagner, J.S. (1994). Percept-percept inflation in micro-organizational research: An investigation of prevalence and effect. *Journal of Applied Psychology, 79,* 67–76.

Crystal, G. S. (1991). *In search of excess: The overcompensation of American executives.* New York: Norton.

De George, R. T. (1986). *Business ethics* (2nd ed.). New York: Macmillan.

Derry, R. 1989. An empirical study of moral reasoning among managers. *Journal of Business Ethics, 8,* 855–862.

Digman, J. M. (1990). Personality structure: Emergence of the five-factor model. *Annual Review of Psychology, 41,* 417–440.

Donaldson, T. & Preston, L. E. (1995). The stakeholder theory of the corporation: Concepts, evidence, and implications. *Academy of Management Review, 20,* 65–91.

Du, L., Bakish, D. & Hrdina, P. D. (2000). Gender differences in association between serotonin transporter gene polymorphism and personality traits. *Psychiatric Genetics, 10,* 159–164.

Epstein, E. M. (1987). The corporate social policy process: Beyond business ethics, corporate social responsibility, and corporate social responsiveness. *California Management Review, 29*(3), 99–114.

Etzioni, A. (1988). *The moral dimension: A new economics.* New York: The Free Press.

Eynon, G., Hill, N. T. & Stevens, K. (1997). Factors that influence the moral reasoning abilities of accountants: Implications for universities and the profession. *Journal of Business Ethics, 16,* 1297–1309.

Feingold, A. (1994). Gender differences in personality: A meta-analysis. *Psychological Bulletin, 116,* 429–456.

Feenstra, R. C. & Hanson, G. (1996). Globalization, outsourcing, and wage inequality. *American Economic Review, 86,* 240–245.

Feldman, S. P. (2002). *Memory as a moral decision: The role of ethics in organizational culture*. New Brunswick, NJ: Transaction Publishing.

Ferraro, F., Pfeffer, J. & Sutton, R. I. (2005). Economics language and assumptions: How theories can become self-fulfilling. *Academy of Management Review, 30*, 8–24.

Fiske, D. W. (1949). Consistency of the factorial structures of personality ratings from different sources. *Journal of Abnormal Social Psychology, 44*, 329–344.

Fox, J. (2002, June 24). Pay CEOs, yeah-but not so much. *Fortune, 145*, pp. 54–56.

Frank, R. H., Gilovich, T. & Regan, D. T. (1993). Does studying economics inhibit cooperation? *Journal of Economic Perspectives, 7*, 159–171.

Franke, G. R., Crown, D. F. & Spake, D. F. (1997). Gender differences in ethical perceptions of business practices: A social role theory perspective. *Journal of Applied Psychology, 82*, 920–934.

Frederick, W. C. (1987). Theories of corporate social performance. In S. P. Sethi & C. Falbe (eds), *Business and society: Dimensions of conflict and cooperation* (pp. 142–161). New York: Lexington Books.

Frederick, W. C. (1994). The virtual reality of fact vs. value: A symposium commentary. *Business Ethics Quarterly, 4*, 171–174.

Frederick, W. C. (1995). *Values, nature, and culture in the American corporation*. New York: Oxford University Press.

Frederick, W. C. (1998). Moving to CSR4: What to pack for the trip. *Business & Society, 37*, 40–59.

Gerde, V. W. (2001). The design dimensions of the just organization: An empirical test of the relation between organization design and corporate social performance. *Business & Society, 40*, 472–477.

Ghoshal, S. (2005). Bad management theories are destroying good management practices. *Academy of Management Learning & Education, 4*, 75–91.

Gilligan, C. (1982). *In a different voice*. Cambridge, MA: Harvard University Press.

Goldberg, L. R. (1992). The development of markers for the Big-Five factor structure. *Psychological Assessment, 4*, 26–42.

Goldberg, L. R. (2001). Web site: International Personality Item Pool. Retrieved from the World Wide Web on March 29, 2004: http://ipip.ori.org/new_home.htm

Greening, D. W. & Turban, D. B. (2000). Corporate social performance as a competitive advantage in attracting a quality workforce. *Business & Society, 39*, 254–280.

Hofstede, G. (2001). *Culture's consequences* (2nd ed.). Thousand Oaks, CA: Sage.

Hogan, R., Hogan, J. & Roberts, B. W. (1996). Personality measurement and employment decisions: Questions and answers. *American Psychologist, 51*, 469–477.

Hoppe, M. H. (2004). An interview with Geert Hofstede. *Academy of Management Executive, 18*(1), 75–79.

Jackall, R. (1988). *Moral mazes: The world of corporate managers*. New York: Oxford University Press.

Jaffee, S. & Hyde, J. S. (2000). Gender differences in moral orientation: A meta-analysis. *Psychological Bulletin, 126*, 703–726.

Jones, T. M. (1983). An integrating framework for research in business and society: A step toward the elusive paradigm. *Academy of Management Review, 8*, 559–564.

Jones, T. M. & Gautschi, F. H., II. (1988). Will the ethics of business change? A survey of future executives. *Journal of Business Ethics, 7*, 231–248.

Judge, T. A. & Cable, D. M. (1997). Applicant personality, organizational culture, and organization attraction. *Personnel Psychology, 50,* 359–394.

Juhn, C., Murphy, K. M. & Pierce, B. (1993). Wage inequality and the rise in returns to skill. *Journal of Political Economy, 10,* 410–442.

Kohlberg, L. (1981). *Essays in moral development: The philosophy of moral development.* New York: Harper & Row.

Kreitler, S. & Kreitler, H. (1990). *The cognitive foundations of personality traits.* New York: Plenum Press.

Krishnan, V. R. (2006, June). Does management education make students better actors? A longitudinal study of change in values and self-monitoring. *Proceedings of the Annual Conference of the Administrative Sciences Association of Canada,* Banff (Alberta).

Law, K., Wong, C. S. & Mobley, W. H. (1998). Toward a taxonomy of multi-dimensional constructs. *Academy of Management Review, 23,* 741–755.

Leana, C. R. & Van Buren, H. J. (1999). Organizational social capital and employment practices. *Academy of Management Review, 24,* 538–555.

Lifton, P. D. (1985). Individual differences in moral development: The relation of sex, gender, and personality to morality. *Journal of Personality, 53,* 306–334.

Loomis, C. J. (2001, June 25). This stuff is wrong. *Fortune, 143*(14), 72–84.

May, D. R. & Pauli, K. P. (2002). The role of moral intensity in ethical decision making. *Business & Society, 41,* 84–117.

McClelland, J. N. & Rhodes, F. (1969). Prediction of job success for hospital aides and orderlies from MMPI scores and personal history data. *Journal of Applied Psychology, 53,* 49–54.

McCrae, R. R. & Costa, P. T., Jr. (1997). Personality trait structure as a human universal. *American Psychologist, 52,* 509–516.

Mishel, L., Bernstein, J. & Schmitt, J. (1996, November/December). The state of American workers. *Challenge, 39*(6), 33–42.

Morgenson, G. (2005, October 9). Companies not behaving badly, *New York Times,* online ed. Retrieved from the World Wide Web on October 14, 2005: http://www.nytimes.com

Nelson, A. K. & Buchholz, E. S. (2004). Adolescent girls' perceptions of goodness and badness and the role of will in their behavioral decisions. *Adolescence, 38*(151), 421–440.

Nocera, J. (2002, June 24). System failure. *Fortune, 145*(13), 62–65.

Noddings, N. (1984). *Caring: A feminine approach to ethics and moral education.* Berkeley, CA: University of California Press.

Nunnally, J. C. & Bernstein, I. H. (1994). *Psychometric theory* (3rd ed.). New York: McGraw-Hill.

O'Reilly, C. A., Chatman, J. A. & Caldwell, D. (1991). People of organizational culture: A profile comparison approach to assessing person-organization fit. *Academy of Management Journal, 34,* 487–516.

Orlitzky, M. & Benjamin, J. D. (2001). Corporate social performance and firm risk: A meta-analytic review. *Business & Society, 40,* 369–396.

Orlitzky, M., Schmidt, F. L. & Rynes, S. L. (2003). Corporate social and financial performance: A meta-analysis. *Organization Studies, 24*(3), 403–441.

Peabody, D. & Goldberg, L. R. (1989). Some determinants of factor structures from personality-trait descriptors. *Journal of Personality & Social Psychology, 57,* 552–567.

Perrow, C. (1986). *Complex organizations: A critical essay* (3rd ed.). New York: Random House.

Pfeffer, J. (1998). *The human equation: Building profits by putting people first.* Boston, MA: Harvard Business School Press.

Quinn, J. B. (2002, June 10). In search of 'clean' stocks. *Newsweek, 139*(23), p. 43.

Rest, J. R. (1986). *Moral development: Advances in theory and research.* New York: Praeger.

Ruegger, D. & King, E. W. (1992). A study of the effect of age and gender upon student business ethics. *Journal of Business Ethics, 11,* 179–186.

Rynes, S. L. & Milkovich, G. T. (1986). Wage surveys: Dispelling some myths about the 'market wage'. *Personnel Psychology, 39,* 71–90.

Schein, E. H. (1992). *Organizational culture and leadership* (2nd ed.). San Francisco, CA: Jossey-Bass.

Schwab, D. P. & Packard, G. L. (1973). Response distortion on the Gordon Personal Inventory and the Gordon Personal Profile in a selection context: Some implications for predicting employee tenure. *Journal of Applied Psychology, 58,* 372–374.

Sethi, S. P. (1979). A conceptual framework for environmental analysis of social issues and evaluation of business response patterns. *Academy of Management Review, 4,* 63–74.

Sharma, S. (1996). *Applied multivariate techniques.* New York: John Wiley & Sons.

Shaw, J. D., Gupta, N. & Delery, J. E. (2002). Pay dispersion and workforce performance: Moderating effects of incentives and interdependence. *Strategic Management Journal, 23,* 491–512.

Shaw, W. H. & Barry, V. (2004). *Moral issues in business.* Belmont, CA: Wadsworth.

Sloan, A. (2003, September 22). A case of big greed at the big board. *Newsweek, 142(12),* p. 33.

Snarey, J. R. (1985). Cross-cultural universality of social-moral development: A critical review of Kohlbergian research. *Psychological Bulletin, 97,* 202–232.

Spector, P. E. (1987). Method variance as an artifact in self-reported affect and perceptions at work: Myth or significant problem? *Journal of Applied Psychology, 72,* 438–443.

Swanson, D. L. (1995). Addressing a theoretical problem by reorienting the corporate social performance model. *Academy of Management Review, 20,* 43–64.

Swanson, D. L. (1996). Neoclassical economic theory, executive control, and organizational outcomes. *Human Relations, 49,* 735–756.

Swanson, D. L. (1999). Toward an integrative strategy of business and society: A research strategy for corporate social performance. *Academy of Management Review, 24,* 506–521.

Swanson, D. L. & Frederick, W. C. (2005). Denial and leadership in business ethics education. In O. C. Ferrell & R. A. Peterson (eds), *Business ethics: The new challenge for business schools and corporate leaders* (pp. 222–240). New York: M. E. Sharpe.

Swanson, D. L. & Orlitzky, M. (2006). Executive preference for compensation structure and normative myopia: A business and society research project. In R. W. Kolb (ed.), *The ethics of executive compensation* (pp. 13–31). Malden, MA: Blackwell Publishing.

Szwajkowski, E. 2000. Simplifying the principles of stakeholder management: The three most important principles. *Business & Society, 39,* 379–396.

Tajfel, H. & Turner, J. C. (1985). The social identity theory of intergroup behavior. In S. Worchel & W. G. Austin (eds), *Psychology of intergroup relations* (pp. 7–24). Chicago: Nelson-Hall.

Toffler, B. (1986). *Tough choices*. New York: Wiley.

Triandis, H. C. (2004). The many dimensions of culture. *Academy of Management Executive, 18*(1), 88–93.

Useem, J. & Florian, E. (2003, April 28). Have they no shame? *Fortune, 147*(8), 38–43.

Van Buren, H. J. (2005). An employee-centered model of corporate social performance. *Business Ethics Quarterly, 15,* 687–709.

Waddock, S. (2002). *Leading corporate citizens: Vision, values, value added*. Boston, MA: McGraw-Hill.

Waddock, S. A. (2003, August). A radical agenda for business in society education. Paper presented at the Academy of Management, Social Issues in Management Division, Seattle.

Waddock, S. A. & Graves, S. B. (1997). Quality of management and quality of stakeholder relations: Are they synonymous? *Business & Society, 36,* 250–279.

Wartick, S. L. & Cochran, P. L. (1985). The evolution of the corporate social performance model. *Academy of Management Review, 10,* 758–769.

Weaver, G. R. & Treviño, L. K. (1999). Compliance and values orientated ethics programs: Influences on employees' attitudes and behavior. *Business Ethics Quarterly, 9,* 315–335.

Weber, M. (1922/1947). *The theory of social and economic organization.* (Translated and edited by A. H. Henderson & T. Parsons.) New York: Oxford University Press.

Weber, J. & Wasieleski, D. (2001). Investigating influences on managers' moral reasoning: The impact of context and personal and organizational factors. *Business & Society, 40,* 79–111.

Wood, D. J. (1991). Corporate social performance revisited. *Academy of Management Review, 16,* 691–718.

Wood, D. J. (2000). Theory and integrity in Business and Society. *Business & Society, 39,* 359–378.

10
Prospects for Integrative Citizenship in Research and Practice

The previous chapters presented theoretical and empirical advances in corporate social performance research. Part I addressed theory building problems, arguing for a better understanding of organizational dynamics instead of defaulting to the assumption of a strict dichotomy between economic performance and other important social goals. Certain organizational processes were identified, particularly the receptivity to values in executive decision making, that may mitigate perceived tradeoffs between these goals, theoretically aligning them to a greater extent than previously modeled. This emphasis on value-inclusive decision processes is important, given the findings presented in Part II that attending to economic, social, and ecological goals simultaneously can pay off while reducing financial risk for a firm. As a practical matter, it is also important to be able to point to a valid measure of socially responsible outcomes, such as that advanced in Chapter 8. We proposed the phrase 'integrative corporate citizenship' to convey this comprehensive approach to corporate social performance.

In this final chapter, consistent with the accent on integrating theory and practice in Part III, we offer some thoughts on implementing socially responsible goals as an agenda for future research. In doing so, we rely on Swanson's (1995, 1999) frameworks, set out in Chapters 1 and 2 and elaborated upon elsewhere, that suggest some theoretical moderators in this area. Specifically, Swanson proposed that organizational decision processes – directed by executives and manifest as formal programs, policies, and procedures shaped by informal culture – set the stage for an organization's posture toward the stakeholder environment. With this emphasis on internal mechanisms in mind, we propose some elements integral to implementing corporate citizenship in practice and conclude with some implications for further research.

Some elements integral to implementing corporate citizenship

We propose that three elements integral to implementing corporate citizenship are (1) a strategic orientation to corporate social performance (2) a high-quality social and environmental accounting system, and (3) an employee-centered orientation that maximizes fit with these elements and, at the same time, exhibits high flexibility. Again, the executive's role is critical to directing these efforts.

Adopting a strategic orientation to corporate citizenship

As argued in Part II, social and environmental management can be an important strategic tool for enhancing the financial sustainability of both large and small organizations (Chapter 6). Because risk (Chapter 5) and reputation (Chapter 4) are the main levers for such orientation, business executives and public affairs managers must continuously monitor social and environmental issues (Chapters 1 and 2). That said, addressing mainstream, highly institutionalized issues, such as global warming, may hold greater strategic promise than attending to issues of which the public is largely unaware (Orlitzky, 2005). A focus on unfamiliar areas, such as lobbying for changes in water access rights, may only show positive financial pay-offs in the long run when the organization's leaders can argue that they were the first to deal with them. Even then, there is no guarantee that a first mover in a little-understood social area will reap rewards. Therefore, from a firm-centered perspective, visible, tangible, and well-understood actions related to corporate social responsibility are preferable to those that do not generate a lot of publicity. However, because the public increasingly dismisses such publicity as 'window-dressing' or 'green-washing' exercises (Forbes & Jermier, 2002; see also Chapter 3), it may backfire for managers to call attention to these initiatives indiscriminately. Astute engagement with the media may help executives increase the credibility of their efforts and build reputational advantages (Orlitzky, 2005), especially if such efforts are based on ongoing, trustful dialogue with stakeholders and transparency in reporting the results (Fombrun, Gardberg & Barnett, 2000; Palazzo & Scherer, 2006; see also Chapter 3). Moreover, such firm-centered pursuit of economic benefits through voluntary citizenship efforts may enhance social welfare (Husted & Allen, 2000; Husted & Salazar, 2006; Locke, 2006), which goes to our point that a dichotomy between economic and other social goals cannot be assumed. However, when such tradeoffs do exist (and firms strategically avoid addressing issues for which no apparent gain accrues) and important community needs are at stake, then government oversight may be called for, as conveyed in our concluding remarks.

In keeping with a strategic orientation, there is a growing consensus that citizenship cannot be relegated to *ad hoc* efforts with little or no connection to an organization's mission, systems, and structures (Hart, 1997, 2007; Hawken, Lovins & Lovins, 1999; Martin, 2002; Orlitzky, 2005; Porter & Kramer, 2002, 2006; Porter & van der Linde, 1995; Reinhardt, 1999). Pursuing mission-related targeted initiatives implies that a better understanding of accounting for social and environmental outcomes is needed.

Implementing social and environmental accounting

Accounting for social and environmental outcomes can help managers make informed choices about allocating resources to citizenship efforts. It can also help external stakeholders assess a firm's citizenship efforts. Along these lines, if verifiable disclosures of social and environmental outcomes are made available, then stakeholders might be more inclined to trust citizenship signals as a basis for their decisions (Orlitzky & Whelan, in press), just as markets function more efficiently when there is information symmetry and high trust between buyers and sellers (Akerlof, 1970). According to Chapter 8, reliable and valid measurement of outcomes in terms of stakeholder satisfaction is an important step in authenticating such signals. It follows that best practices would include tracking the optimal mix of social and environmental outcomes so that the difference between their benefits and costs for a firm can be maximized (Orlitzky & Whelan, in press). Expressed differently, social/environmental performance should be expanded up to the point where the firm-specific marginal benefits equal the marginal costs. We refer to such tracking as 'social and environmental accounting'.

Undoubtedly, this utilitarian calculus is no easy task for managers. The specification of all benefits and costs associated with socially responsible outcomes is daunting (Epstein, 2008; Orlitzky & Whelan, in press). However, this task can be made be easier if the choice of outcomes to pursue is focused on the firm's stakeholders rather than society at large (Clarkson, 1995; see also Chapter 8). Stakeholder-centered deliberation means calculating to whom the benefits and costs of a firm's activities will accrue. In contrast, reasoning based on broader societal needs is somewhat amorphous and would likely confound managers' estimation of the most efficient use of corporate resources for citizenship efforts. A role for public policy in meeting broader citizenship needs will be broached in our concluding remarks.

In terms of Chapter 2, a focus on stakeholders portends continuous improvements in a firm's ability to become attuned to their preferences. For example, what at one point in time is perceived as 'business as usual' (e.g., disposal of oil rigs in the North Sea) might shift – almost overnight – to a deeply moral issue in the minds of key stakeholders. Maintaining institutional flexibility in light of such developments can allow for innovative solutions and responses that are optimal for the firm and good for society as well (Husted & Salazar, 2006). Our point is that without rigorous and well-designed measurement and reporting systems, integrative citizenship will fall short of its promise. In business, what gets measured tends to get managed. For this and the other reasons given, we recommend social and environment accounting as an integral element of corporate citizenship.[1]

Aiming for fit and flexibility in human resource management

A strategic orientation to corporate citizenship requires that employee skills and behaviors lend themselves to implementing espoused social and environmental strategies. Elsewhere we have described this fit in terms of how the human resource management functions of staffing (recruitment and selection), performance appraisal, compensation, and training and development can be configured for socially responsible performance (Orlitzky & Swanson, 2006). Our main conclusions regarding this fit are summarized as follows:

1. *Recruitment and selection:* Hire executives and other employees who exhibit relatively high levels of cognitive moral development (Colby & Kohlberg, 1987; Weber, 1990, 1991) and to some extent the personality trait of agreeableness, which refers to an individual's predisposition to be caring, trusting, altruistic, friendly, and cooperative (Orlitzky & Swanson, 2006; Orlitzky, Swanson & Quartermaine, 2006; see also Chapter 9 and the comments that follow in this chapter). In doing so, it is also important to try to enlarge workforce diversity so that a variety of viewpoints can be brought to decision making (see Chapter 2 and the comments on training and development below).

2. *Performance appraisal*: Formulate criteria based on economic, social, and ecological performance objectives. Many companies have been moving in the direction of this kind of comprehensive perspective on performance evaluation. For example, Eastman Kodak tracks managers' records in the areas of health, safety, and environmental performance. By implementing such integrative standards for its managers, Kodak was able to achieve its health, safety, and environmental goals three years ahead of schedule (Epstein, 2008).

3. *Compensation:* Design pay systems that reward economic and social performance objectives while reducing potentially counterproductive pay dispersions viewed as unfair or arbitrary. In the case of top salaries, companies could link managers' bonuses to building staff diversity (as Wal-Mart has done) and/or to reducing greenhouse gas emissions (as British Petroleum, Shell, and Alcoa have done) (Epstein, 2008).
4. *Training & Development:* Train employees to be skilled in stakeholder engagement and communication (see Chapter 3). Along these lines, Hart and Sharma (2004) argue that it is important for employees to be able to integrate diverse viewpoints into decision making so that firms can respond knowledgeably to complex stakeholder environments. These authors point to DuPont and Excel as examples of firms with policies of stakeholder engagement.

While aiming for fit in the above areas is important, an integrative approach to citizenship also requires flexibility in human resource management (Wright & Snell, 1998). It is particularly important (and consistent with point 4 above) that employees be prepared to help their firms adapt quickly and effectively to changes in nonmarket environments, which are often more turbulent than market environments, especially in international domains (Baron, 2006). Broadly, this flexibility can be understood in terms of resources and coordination (Sanchez, 1995). In the first case, resource flexibility is defined as the extent to which a resource can be applied to a larger range of alternative uses, minimizing the costs and difficulties of switching from one alternative use to another, and the time required to do so. Coordination flexibility, in turn, refers to the extent to which a firm can resynthesize strategy and reconfigure and redeploy the chain of resources (Wright & Snell, 1998).

Fortunately, some of the mechanisms for enhancing the fit between human resource practices and citizenship also lend themselves to organizational flexibility. For example, hiring for heterogeneity or diversity among managers can result in a wider variety of behavioral scripts (Ginsberg, 1994) for their choices (Weick, 1979). In terms of the attunement model presented in Chapter 2, this practice can potentially improve an organization's range of responses to the social environment, especially if managers engage stakeholders in trustful dialogue to determine their preferences (Chapter 3). Such receptivity to stakeholder engagement may improve coordination flexibility. However, at the same time a diversity of viewpoints may increase the likelihood of interpersonal conflict, which in some cases might hamper decision-making effectiveness (see Amason, 1996; Wright & Snell, 1998). The challenge is to strike a balance, keeping in mind that homogeneous mindsets easily lead to a type of 'group-think' fatal to innovative decision making (Janis, 1982). Hence, an undue emphasis on hiring for one personality profile, such as highly agreeable individuals, may be counterproductive. A better alternative may be to seek an optimal mix of personality types (see Boudreau & Ramstad, 1997). However, hiring for relatively high levels of moral development (see #1 above) may be viewed as a best citizenship practice, since such cognitive development enhances the ability of managers and employees to factor normative considerations related to others in society into their decision making (Rest & Narvaez, 1994; Weber, 1990).

For the sake of flexibility, adjustments might be needed in the area of pay and performance, listed above. Pay structures perhaps should be differentiated enough so that employees in boundary-spanning roles are especially motivated to attend to changes in the stakeholder environment. So, while pay compression or reductions in salary dispersions may decrease the kind of politicking and power plays that detract from the tasks at hand (see Jackall, 1988; Oliver, 1997), adopting this approach whole cloth may not necessarily encourage the kind of flexibility needed for citizenship efforts. It can be seen that designing and implementing human resource practices that incorporate fit and flexibility in the service of citizenship is a balancing act, deserving of more research.

Some further implications for research

To this point, we have examined some areas that constitute a research agenda for integrating citizenship in practice. We now conclude with a few implications for public policy and international management.

Formulating a complementary role for public policy

While the chapters in this book have taken a firm-centered perspective on business citizenship, a few comments on a role for public policy are in order. Earlier, we argued that a firm's pursuit of socially responsible outcomes should be expanded to the point where the firm-specific marginal benefits equal the marginal costs and where only firm-specific benefits and costs are included in the formal, profit-maximizing calculus. Obviously, this approach will not reflect all social benefits and costs (see Baron, 2006 on social efficiency in general). Nor can it be expected to. It is not our intention to assert that business can or should attend to all aspects of the public good. Indeed, one important role for government is to ameliorate those adverse spillover effects that business has no incentive to address or fails to do so in a timely way. For instance, when life-threatening consumer products are imported from countries with lower product safety standards, it is reasonable for a domestic government agency to provide safety checks. While these products may eventually be pulled from the shelves by firms concerned about adverse reputational impacts, people can die or be injured in the interim. Hence, the need for providential government oversight and intervention.

In some instances, firms may resist a quest for citizenship out of habit or myopia, as described in Chapter 2. Alternatively, there may be hesitation because the first firm in an industry to address an area may not be the one to reap financial rewards, as in the case of issues unfamiliar to stakeholders, mentioned earlier. Another impediment is that the demand for social improvements from consumers may not seem to warrant changes, at least not in the short run. Consider the case of automobile emissions, one of the principal forms of air pollution. It appears unlikely that individual consumers *en masse* would request an emission control system if it were offered voluntarily as optional equipment. Lacking sufficient consumer demand, one alternative is for government to mandate improvements in this area of collective concern (Carroll & Buchholtz, 2006, p. 349). Suffice to say, there is a role for public policy that seeks to provide oversight and/or standards whenever important social needs are not being met. The point is to seek informed evenhandedness between the private and public sectors in devising policies attuned to social needs.

Given this goal, we advocate a cautionary, fine-grained approach to government regulation based on public policy that seeks to balance the desirability of continuous improvements in corporate social performance over time with the need to protect important human and environmental interests in the present. Such an approach would seek to understand the conditions under which the government should (1) leave social innovations to the business sector, removing existing regulations when appropriate; (2) devise incentives and disseminate educational material aimed at leveraging and encouraging virtuous cycles of corporate social responsibility (discussed in Chapters 4 and 5); or (3) impose command and control rules selectively (see Swanson, 2000). The ideal scenario is for public policy and regulation to be adaptive and flexible in light of changing circumstances. In other words, a contingency theory of regulation is called for that complements the attunement posture outlined in Chapter 2 in light of the empirical findings that corporate social responsibility can pay, presented in Chapter 4.